FOUR
VIEWS
ON

# THE SPECTRUM
OF **EVANGELICALISM**

# Books in the Counterpoints Series

### Church Life

*Exploring the Worship Spectrum: Six Views*

*Evaluating the Church Growth Movement: Five Views*

*Remarriage after Divorce in Today's Church: Three Views*

*Two Views on Women in Ministry*

*Understanding Four Views on Baptism*

*Understanding Four Views on the Lord's Supper*

*Who Runs the Church? Four Views on Church Government*

### Bible and Theology

*Are Miraculous Gifts for Today? Four Views*

*Five Views on Apologetics*

*Five Views on Law and Gospel*

*Five Views on Sanctification*

*Four Views on the Book of Revelation*

*Four Views on Divine Providence*

*Four Views on Eternal Security*

*Four Views on Hell*

*Four Views on Moving Beyond the Bible to Theology*

*Four Views on Salvation in a Pluralistic World*

*Four Views on the Spectrum of Evangelicalism*

*How Jewish Is Christianity? Two Views on the Messianic Movement*

*Show Them No Mercy: Four Views on God and Canaanite Genocide*

*Three Views on Creation and Evolution*

*Three Views on Eastern Orthodoxy and Evangelicalism*

*Three Views on the Millennium and Beyond*

*Three Views on the New Testament Use of the Old Testament*

*Three Views on the Rapture*

# FOUR VIEWS ON THE SPECTRUM OF EVANGELICALISM

Kevin T. Bauder

R. Albert Mohler Jr.

John G. Stackhouse Jr.

Roger E. Olson

Stanley N. Gundry, series editor
Andrew David Naselli and
Collin Hansen, general editors

ZONDERVAN

*Four Views on the Spectrum of Evangelicalism*
Copyright © 2011 by Andrew David Naselli, Collin Hansen, Kevin T. Bauder, R. Albert Mohler Jr., John G. Stackhouse Jr., and Roger E. Olson

This title is also available as a Zondervan ebook.

This title is also available in a Zondervan audio edition.

Requests for information should be addressed to:

Zondervan, 3900 Sparks Dr. SE, Grand Rapids, Michigan 49546

Library of Congress Cataloging-in-Publication Data

Four views on the spectrum of evangelicalism / Kevin Bauder ... [et al.]
contributors ; Andrew David Naselli and Collin Hansen, general editors.
        p. cm. — (Counterpoints)
    ISBN 978-0-310-29316-3 (softcover)
    1. Evangelicalism. I. Bauder, Kevin T. II. Naselli, Andrew David. III. Hansen,
Collin, 1981-
BR1640.F69 2011
    277.3'082 — dc22                                                    2011010573

*Cover design: Tammy Johnson*
*Cover photography: © Masterfile Corporation*
*Interior design: Matthew Van Zomeren*

*Printed in the United States of America*

HB 03.31.2021

# CONTENTS

# ABOUT THE AUTHORS

**Kevin T. Bauder** (DMin, Trinity Evangelical Divinity School; PhD, Dallas Theological Seminary) is past president of and current research professor of systematic and historical theology at Central Baptist Theological Seminary in Minneapolis. He is a general editor of *One Bible Only? Examining Exclusive Claims for the King James Bible.*

**R. Albert Mohler Jr.** (PhD, Southern Baptist Theological Seminary) is president and Joseph Emerson Brown Professor of Christian Theology at The Southern Baptist Theological Seminary. He is the author of several books, including *Words from the Fire: Hearing the Voice of God in the 10 Commandments,* and is a contributor to *Is Hell for Real: Or Does Everyone Go to Heaven?*

**John G. Stackhouse Jr.** (PhD, University of Chicago) is the Sangwoo Youtong Chee Professor of Theology and Culture at Regent College. He is the author or editor of eleven books, including *Making the Best of It: Following Christ in the Real World.* He is a former president of the Canadian Evangelical Theological Association.

**Roger E. Olson** (PhD, Rice University) is professor of theology at George W. Truett Theological Seminary of Baylor University. He is the author of many books, including *Questions to All Your Answers: The Journey from Folk Religion to Examined Faith; Reformed and Always Reforming: The Postconservative Approach to Evangelical Theology;* and *How to Be Evangelical without Being Conservative.*

**Andrew David Naselli** (PhD, Bob Jones University; PhD, Trinity Evangelical Divinity School) is research manager for D. A. Carson and administrator of the journal *Themelios.* He has taught New Testament Greek at the undergraduate and graduate levels, and he currently teaches exegesis and theology as adjunct faculty at several seminaries. He is the author of *Let Go and Let God? A Survey and Analysis of Keswick Theology.*

**Collin Hansen** (MDiv, Trinity Evangelical Divinity School) is editorial director for The Gospel Coalition. Formerly an associate editor for *Christianity Today*, he is the author of *Young, Restless, Reformed* and co-author with John Woodbridge of *A God-Sized Vision*. He has written for *Books & Culture*, *Tabletalk*, *Leadership*, and *Christian History & Biography*. He has appeared as a commentator on *Fox News*, and his work has been featured in *Time* magazine.

# INTRODUCTION

COLLIN HANSEN

Americans have little trouble identifying an evangelical: that would be someone who stayed loyal to George W. Bush before transferring allegiances to Sarah Palin. Expand your focus group to the rest of North America and Great Britain and the answer may grow somewhat more complicated. Still, evangelicals are most commonly known for advocating the gospel of free markets, strong defense, and traditional morals. Jesus might as well have been Ronald Reagan. To the watching public, evangelicals seem to share the same one view on any given issue. So who needs to publish a whole book trying to describe evangelicals by presenting four views?

We self-described evangelicals often lament such stunted descriptions. Evangelicalism predates the Religious Right and represents a variety of political views, even if many now vote Republican in America. Besides, evangelicals are not so much political activists as ambassadors for the kingdom of heaven, where Jesus Christ reigns and sustains the world. We will gladly explain that an evangelical testifies to the evangel, the good news that the one and only Son of God has come into the world to save sinners. We pass along a message of first importance: "that Christ died for our sins according to the Scriptures, that he was buried, that he was raised on the third day according to the Scriptures" (1 Cor. 15:3–4).

Yet all is not so clear within the evangelical camp either. Simply labeling ourselves evangelical no longer suffices. We are conservative, progressive, postconservative, and preprogressive evangelicals. We are traditional, creedal, biblical, pietistic, anticreedal, ecumenical, and fundamentalist. We are "followers of Christ" and "Red Letter Christians." We are everything, so we are nothing. If the descriptor *evangelical* cannot stand on its own, then it has little use. There is no coherent movement, only an endless collection of self-styled labels created by Christians for their Facebook profiles.[1]

---

1. Indeed, some theologians, including David Wells, have wondered whether evangelicalism matches the criteria for a movement. "Movements must exhibit three characteristics: (1)

Those of us who work for evangelical institutions often struggle to hold these factions together. Everyone has an opinion about where the movement should head. And everyone wants to offer his or her own special twist on defining evangelicalism. I have found myself simultaneously defending fellow evangelicals from skeptics, seeking to build consensus within the movement, offering my own perspective on key positions we must hold, and defending myself from evangelicals who do not regard me as sufficiently cooperative. Such is life in evangelicalism, which seems to be moving in several directions at once.

At the same time, the energy that threatens to pull evangelicalism apart supplies much-needed dynamism to Christianity in the West. In its history, evangelicalism has prodded the powers as a movement of renewal and revival. Evangelicals have called moribund ministers to theological renewal and called on God to send revival by the power of the Holy Spirit. Whatever their differences, evangelicals pledge allegiance to Christ alone, the only hope for self-absorbed sinners in any age or place, any stage or race. When tempted to leave behind the headaches of this eclectic movement with no leader and no membership, we pause and ask, "But where should we go?" So long as evangelicals testify to the words of eternal life, we count ourselves among their ranks. At its best, evangelicalism overcomes nonessential differences to unite likeminded Christians around the common cause of gospel proclamation and gospel living. If we lose evangelicalism to political captivity or rampant individualism, we lose a rare opportunity to demonstrate unity and mission outside the local church. We hope this book, then, will serve to shore up evangelicalism by highlighting common beliefs and fostering respectful disagreement where necessary.

## Biblical Testimony for the Evangel

Evangelicals take their name from the koine Greek word *euangelion*, translated into English as "good news." The word appears in Scripture with various nuances. But it frequently relates to the coming of Jesus Christ and his ministry to usher in the kingdom of God.

---

there must be a commonly owned direction, (2) there must be a common basis on which that direction is owned, and (3) there must be an *esprit* that informs and motivates those who are thus joined in their common cause." *No Place for Truth: or, Whatever Happened to Evangelical Theology?* (Grand Rapids: Eerdmans, 1993), 8.

An angel announced to shepherds outside Bethlehem the "good news" of great joy for all the people. In a message particularly rich in biblical significance for Jews, the angel explained that a Savior was born in the city of David who was Christ the Lord (Luke 2:10–11). At the beginning of his ministry in Galilee, Jesus proclaimed the "good news" of God. "The time has come," he said. "The kingdom of God has come near. Repent and believe the good news!" (Mark 1:15). Reading from Isaiah 61:1–2 in his hometown Nazareth synagogue, Jesus taught that he had fulfilled the prophet's words: "The Spirit of the Lord is on me, because he has anointed me to preach good news to the poor. He has sent me to proclaim freedom for the prisoners and recovery of sight for the blind, to set the oppressed free, to proclaim the year of the Lord's favor" (Luke 4:18–19). He reiterated this message to followers of John the Baptist who wanted to know if Jesus was "the one who is to come" (Luke 7:19). Indeed, Jesus testified that he is the Messiah who accords with prophecies proclaiming the coming of God's kingdom. He responded, "Go back and report to John what you have seen and heard: The blind receive sight, the lame walk, those who have leprosy are cleansed, the deaf hear, the dead are raised, and the good news is proclaimed to the poor" (v. 22; cf. Matt. 11:5).

Still today evangelicals bear this good news that Jesus Christ has fulfilled the messianic hopes of Israel, even if his followers did not expect him to submit to crucifixion and rise from the dead on the third day. Indeed, the first disciples eventually understood that these unexpected events only confirmed that the heavenly kingdom had dawned in Jesus. As the world awaits his second coming, we have the responsibility to repent of our sins and believe this good news. Amid much debate, the apostles began taking this good news that Jesus is the Christ to the nations (Acts 5:42). Philip evangelized an Ethiopian eunuch by explaining Isaiah 53:7–8, which gives particular attention to Jesus' crucifixion. "He was led like a sheep to the slaughter, and as a lamb before its shearer is silent, so he did not open his mouth" (Acts 8:32). The good news is that all who trust in this sacrifice for their sins have peace through Christ, who is Lord of all (Acts 10:36). No longer should we trust in the worthless idols made by human hands. Rather, we may trust in Jesus, who is the exact representation of the "living God, who made the heavens and the earth and the sea and everything in them" (Acts

14:15). Though unbelievers accuse us of mindless babbling, evangelicals understand that Jesus' resurrection is the only sure ground for hope (Acts 17:18). How beautiful are the feet of those who bear this good news, "who proclaim peace, who bring good tidings, who proclaim salvation, who say to Zion, 'Your God reigns!'" (Rom. 10:15; Isa. 52:7).

Evangelicals take criticism for adopting an essentially negative posture toward what the world regards as progress. It is true that evangelicals will side with Scripture when others bless moral behavior that God condemns. And the good news carries an initial bit of bad news that sin has broken the relationship between God and his creation. But evangelicals bear in their very name a message of the greatest joy imaginable. Though they sin, humans may be reconciled with their perfectly holy, perfectly powerful, perfectly loving Father. Through Jesus Christ, the Father adopts believers into his everlasting family, not based on anything they have done to earn his favor, but purely by his pleasure and will (Eph. 1:5). Wherever you may find them, whatever language they speak, evangelicals will gladly share this good news, the best news ever delivered.

## Agreement and Ambiguity

Jesus' first followers did not go by any one name in the New Testament. Those who were Jews did not necessarily feel compelled to adopt a new name, believing that Jesus Christ fulfilled the promises given to their forefathers. Persecutors, including the deadly Saul, pursued members of this group that became popularly known as "the Way" (Acts 9:2). Though ambiguous, the term was flexible enough to carry several meanings. Jesus had described himself as "the way and the truth and the life" (John 14:6). So it is possible that these followers of Jesus Christ were known for pointing the way to fellowship with the Father through his Son. Later, adopting the Greek term for the Hebrew Messiah, Jesus' disciples were first known as Christians at Antioch (Acts 11:26).

Even though the Bible has much to say about the gospel, Christians did not begin calling themselves evangelical until the Reformation of the sixteenth century. Martin Luther, a pious, earnest German monk, underwent what his biographer Roland Bainton described as an "evangelical experience" while teaching the Psalms and epistles to the Galatians and Romans between 1513 and 1517. "These studies proved to be for Luther the Damascus road," Bainton wrote, referring to Saul's unexpected conversion after encountering the risen Jesus (Acts 9).[2] While pouring over these biblical texts, Luther read good news that he believed contemporary Roman Catholic teaching had obscured. He previously resented a God he understood as just and angry. But while dwelling on Romans 1:17, Luther suddenly understood that "the justice of God is the righteousness by which through grace and sheer mercy God justifies us through faith." Luther felt as though he had been born again. The Scripture he had studied for so long took on a new meaning.

"If you have a true faith that Christ is your Savior, then at once you have a gracious God, for faith leads you in and opens up God's heart and will, that you should see pure grace and overflowing love," Luther wrote. "This is to behold God in faith that you should look upon his fatherly, friendly heart, in which there is no anger nor ungraciousness. He who sees God as angry does not see him rightly but looks only on a curtain, as if a dark cloud had been drawn across his face."[3]

Luther and other Reformers who criticized the Roman Catholic Church came to be known as evangelicals. To this day, Lutherans incorporate this term in their official titles, even if their usage more closely corresponds to the English term *Protestant*. But Luther protested Roman Catholic practice and theology out of concern for the biblical gospel. So *evangelical* captures the appeal of the Reformers' message and the beliefs that united them in a way that the negative *Protestant* does not.

Against the Reformation's historical backdrop, one can understand the benefit of resuscitating this descriptor during a time of crisis and eclipse in American Protestantism. Throughout the eighteenth and especially the nineteenth century, European skeptical biblical scholarship made inroads among American ministers and other church leaders. Scholars from Luther's native Germany in particular employed critical tools to cast doubt on the veracity of events recorded in Scripture. The so-called higher criticism changed the complexion of several American denominations. By the early twentieth century, many Protestants who defended the Bible felt besieged. Schools such as Princeton Seminary, once a bastion of conservative orthodoxy, was reorganized in 1929 to

2. Roland H. Bainton, *Here I Stand: A Life of Martin Luther* (New York: Meridian, 1955), 45–46.

3. Cited in ibid., 49–50.

include scholars who professed diverse beliefs about the Bible's authority and trustworthiness. Denominations such as the Methodist Episcopal Church, which had grown so rapidly in the nineteenth century through the tireless work of evangelists, now seemed more interested in advancing social causes such as prohibition.

Amid these changes, Christians united across denominational lines to reassert their belief in the fundamentals of the faith, including the veracity of biblical miracles such as the virgin birth and resurrection of Jesus. Some newer evangelical expressions, particularly Pentecostalism, thrived during the tumultuous years before World War II. But many evangelicals, now popularly known as fundamentalists, assumed a defensive posture that alienated them from the era's crucial debates over theology and social issues. By the time World War II ended in 1945, a younger generation including Harold John Ockenga agitated to reengage Western society on several fronts. Adapting an earlier term, Ockenga described this movement as neo-evangelicalism. These evangelicals would retain much fundamentalist theology and prioritize evangelism while building broader coalitions to apply the gospel to contemporary social concerns.

Carl F. H. Henry wrote in his 1947 call to arms, *The Uneasy Conscience of Modern Fundamentalism*:

> The evangelical task primarily is the preaching of the Gospel, in the interest of individual regeneration by the supernatural grace of God, in such a way that divine redemption can be recognized as the best solution of our problems, individual and social. This produces within history, through the regenerative work of the Holy Spirit, a divine society that transcends national and international lines. The corporate testimony of believers, in their purity of life, should provide for the world an example of the divine dynamic to overcome evils in every realm. The social problems of our day are much more complex than in apostolic times, but they do not on that account differ in principle. When the twentieth-century church begins to "out-live" its environment as the first-century church outreached its pagan neighbors, the modern mind, too, will stop casting about for other solutions.[4]

---

4. Carl F. H. Henry, *The Uneasy Conscience of Modern Fundamentalism* (Grand Rapids: Eerdmans, 1947), 88–89.

Henry and his allies had reason to believe the modern mind had indeed been intrigued by the gospel. Thousands turned out to hear evangelists such as Billy Graham during Youth for Christ rallies. Ockenga's native Boston hosted Graham in 1950 for an evangelistic crusade that recalled George Whitefield's visit at the dawn of the First Great Awakening in 1740. Yet by 1957, the nascent movement splintered, a divide that continues today as reflected in this book. Graham's relationship with self-described fundamentalists such as Bob Jones Sr., who once saw so much promise in the young evangelist's career, was already strained before he allied with the liberal Protestant Council of the City of New York for a 1957 crusade. But this decision led to a decisive break between the new evangelicals and fundamentalists.

It wasn't long before other cracks began showing in the evangelical ranks. Even as he continued to minister in Boston, Ockenga commuted to Pasadena, California, where he served as president for the flagship evangelical graduate school, Fuller Theological Seminary, founded in 1947. Daniel Fuller, son of the seminary's founder and who would become dean in 1963, argued to Ockenga in December 1962 that the Bible includes historical and scientific mistakes. His view carried the day as the seminary backed away from inerrancy, prompting several faculty members to leave. Despite the efforts of Ockenga, Graham, Henry, and others to forge unity through parachurch organizations, evangelicalism was tugged in sometimes competing directions. "Though it was not much recognized at the time," historian George Marsden writes, "American evangelicalism in the 1960s was a vast, largely disconnected conglomeration of widely diverse groups."[5]

While insiders foresaw looming problems, the watching public was just beginning to notice a resurgent evangelicalism. Graham continued to attract large crowds, but it took a peanut farmer from Georgia to convince mainstream media to recognize the broader evangelical movement. Jimmy Carter's candidacy sent journalists on a hunt to understand what he meant by saying he was "born again." As Carter marched on to victory over President Gerald Ford, *Newsweek* declared 1976 "The Year of the Evangelical." Despite the positive press, controversy continued to

---

5. George M. Marsden, *Reforming Fundamentalism: Fuller Seminary and the New Evangelicalism.* (Grand Rapids: Eerdmans, 1995), 230.

flare within the camp. Harold Lindsell, a former Fuller faculty member who succeeded Henry as editor of *Christianity Today*, scorched Fuller with his book *The Battle for the Bible*. But even some of his closest allies chided Lindsell for making inerrancy a litmus test for evangelicalism. Henry later recalled that the evangelical movement

> had emerged from obscurity to dramatic resurgence through a remarkable coalition of evangelical evangelism symbolized by Graham and of evangelical theology symbolized by *Christianity Today*, which had rallied an international, multi-denominational corps of scholars articulating conservative theology. But the sudden refocusing of all these issues on the criterion of biblical inerrancy—precisely at the peak of the movement's public impact—exposed the evangelical cause as itself deeply split over the issue of religious authority.[6]

## Retrospective on Our Roots

Looking back, we can see that evangelicalism has continued to shape public discourse, especially in the political realm, fulfilling Henry's call to cultural relevance. Evangelicals unite across theological lines for cooperative evangelism and social activism. Institutions founded during the postwar period, including Fuller Theological Seminary and *Christianity Today*, endure. But so do the disputes over authority. Evangelicals recognize that Scripture trumps every human authority, yet they do not agree on the extent and nature of biblical authority. They do not regard every theological issue as equally clear-cut or crucial, yet they do not agree on which doctrines should be of first importance. To many the doctrine of justification by faith alone, shaped by Romans and Galatians in particular as understood by Luther, makes cooperation with the Roman Catholic Church impossible as long as they continue to recognize the authority of the Council of Trent. To others the 1994 declaration "The Gift of Salvation", issued by Evangelicals and Catholics Together, signaled Catholic willingness to embrace the good news.

---

6. Carl F. H. Henry, *Confessions of a Theologian: An Autobiography* (Waco, Tex: Word, 1986), 384.

Other issues have likewise exposed evangelical division. That God knows, and even plans, the future is a matter of fundamental conviction to many evangelicals. Yet other theologians who have described themselves as evangelical, including John Sanders, Clark Pinnock, and Greg Boyd, have said that fidelity to Scripture compels them to believe that no one, including God, can know what has not yet happened. They argue that God is partly open to a future of possibilities contingent on our prayers and decisions. Likewise, many evangelicals believe that any gospel presentation that excludes the good news that Christ endured God's wrath as a substitute for sinners does not explain the gospel at all. Yet other theories propose to explain Christ's work on the cross, such as the belief that his primary triumph was to liberate sinners from evil. Is there any one privileged theory of the atonement? Or only many such theories? Do any of these theories fail to match the biblical evidence? Any gospel description depends on one's answers to these questions.

This book's four contributors offer their take on evangelicalism at its best and critique the movement at its worst. They present their own views on these matters before responding to one another. Division is evident, but we trust that open discussion will help us discern a way to navigate our differences and preserve the meaning and mission behind the name we each claim. Though assailed from many directions, evangelicals bear a name rich in biblical meaning and full of historical significance. It signifies unity around the core essentials of the Christian faith. May God bless us with conviction and courage and count us worthy of his calling (2 Thess. 1:11).

The four contributors are:

Kevin T. Bauder (fundamentalism)
R. Albert Mohler Jr. (confessional evangelicalism)
John G. Stackhouse Jr. (generic evangelicalism)
Roger E. Olson (postconservative evangelicalism)

Each seeks to define evangelicalism and locate his view in historical context. Since evangelicals describe themselves as people of the Book, each contributor discusses how he understands Scripture and its authority. For the purpose of clarity, we have asked each contributor to address three issues recently contested within evangelicalism. First, to explain their views on Christian cooperation, they will evaluate the

Evangelicals and Catholics Together movement led by Charles Colson and the late Richard John Neuhaus, which started in the 1990s. They may also address the more recent Manhattan Declaration to clarify any differences between cooperating on theological and social issues. Second, to illustrate their views on doctrinal boundaries, they will address debates over open theism that roiled denominations, schools, and the Evangelical Theological Society during the last two decades. Finally, to illustrate their views on a key doctrinal issue related to the gospel, they will explain their views on penal substitutionary atonement, the belief that Christ took on God's wrath meant for sinners. While many evangelicals regard this belief as the heart of the good news, others have described it as divine child abuse. And if there can be no agreement on the gospel among evangelicals, unity is a vain pursuit.

Coeditor Andy Naselli and I have not asked the contributors to write a full-orbed biblical defense of their views on any of these issues. Rather, we have asked them to use the limited space to ask what is good for evangelicalism. And what, if anything, is problematic about how evangelicals have discussed these issues? We trust that this approach will avoid merely abstract reflections in favor of dialogue and debate worked out in the crucible of real life with all the attendant consequences for evangelical unity and mission.

# FUNDAMENTALISM

### KEVIN T. BAUDER

Imagine the difficulty of explaining fundamentalism in a book about evangelicalism. Fundamentalism is generally treated like the cryptozoology of the theological world. It need not be argued against. It can simply be dismissed.[1]

Part of the fault lies with fundamentalists themselves. For a generation or more, they have produced few sustained expositions of their ideas. Perhaps a certain amount of stereotyping is excusable, and maybe even unavoidable. No fundamentalist has produced a critical history of fundamentalism.[2] Nor is any sustained, scholarly, theological explanation of core fundamentalist ideas available.[3] By virtue of its length, this essay can provide neither. Instead, it offers a very brief introduction to fundamentalism. No one can speak for all fundamentalists. Conse-

---

1. While fundamentalists generally consider themselves to be evangelicals, some self-identified evangelicals question whether an evangelical can be a fundamentalist. See Steve Wilkens and Don Thorsen, *Everything You Know about Evangelicals Is Wrong (Well, Almost Everything): An Insider's Look at Myths and Realities* (Grand Rapids: Baker, 2010), 139–40.

2. Fundamentalists have published two full-length histories. Each makes a modest contribution to fundamentalist historiography, but both are essentially popular works that were written to legitimate one particular version of fundamentalism. The two are George W. Dollar, *A History of Fundamentalism in America* (Greenville, S.C.: Bob Jones University Press, 1973); and David O. Beale, *In Pursuit of Purity: American Fundamentalism Since 1850* (Greenville, S.C.: Bob Jones University Press, 1986).

3. The best expositions of core fundamentalist ideas include Fred Moritz, *"Be Ye Holy": The Call to Christian Separation* (Greenville, S.C.: Bob Jones University Press, 1994); Mark Sidwell, *The Dividing Line: Understanding and Applying Biblical Separation* (Greenville, S.C.: Bob Jones University Press, 1998); Ernest Pickering, *Biblical Separation: The Struggle for a Pure Church*, 2nd ed. (Schaumburg, Ill.: Regular Baptist Press, 2008). Each of these discussions has value, but all are written for a popular readership, and none deals adequately with the larger orbit of ecclesiological issues that a thoughtful fundamentalism must face.

quently, this essay reflects my own vision of fundamentalism. I occasionally indicate areas in which I believe most fundamentalists would agree with me.

I am primarily addressing people who have had limited exposure to fundamentalism. I would like to introduce them to the movement. Therefore, my presentation takes the form of ecclesiastical show-and-tell. It is not so much a work of research as it is a personal perspective—perhaps even (in the best fundamentalist tradition) a personal testimony. This being the case, I must beg a measure of indulgence. I offer observations about fundamentalism that I cannot document statistically. Those observations, however, are informed by half a century of personal immersion in the fundamentalist movement and its idea. They are also tempered by education and conversation outside of fundamentalism.

In view of the foregoing, my stance toward fundamentalism is one of critical sympathy. I do not wish to excuse the blemishes of fundamentalists, but I see enough value in fundamentalism to attract me. Central to my discussion is a distinction between the idea of fundamentalism and the fundamentalist movement. Ideas are anterior to things, and words are signifiers, not merely of things, and much less of other words, but of ideas. This observation is particularly important in discussing intellectual movements.

Intellectual movements usually incarnate an idea. The incarnations, however, are rarely or never perfect. We often grasp the idea poorly. Sometimes we twist the idea to serve our own interests. We also tend to mix one idea with another, often unwittingly. The result is that the idea (in this case, fundamentalism) virtually never occurs in pristine form. These factors have resulted in a variety of fundamentalisms. Though I shall speak of "the fundamentalist movement," fundamentalism has never existed as a single, unified phenomenon. The idea of fundamentalism has been understood differently by different fundamentalists.

In the following pages, I offer a guided tour of the fundamentalist phenomenon. First, I explore a fundamentalist theory of minimal Christian fellowship. Second, I develop a fundamentalist theory of maximal Christian fellowship. These two sections together summarize the idea of fundamentalism. The third section explores two forms of fundamentalism that distort the idea, and in the final section, I evaluate the present status of fundamentalism. I conclude with observations about the possibility of rapprochement between fundamentalists and other evangelicals.

# The Idea of Fundamentalism and Minimal Christian Fellowship

Some analysts of fundamentalism believe that its primary motif is the purity of the church.[4] While purity is important to fundamentalists, I do not agree that it is their most central concern. Strange as it may sound, the primary motive of fundamentalism is the unity and fellowship of the church. I believe that fundamentalism is a serious attempt to wrestle with the nature of the church as the communion of the saints.

Unity and fellowship do not exist in themselves. They are byproducts of something else. Unity is always a function of something that unites. Fellowship (*koinônia*) means joint ownership. Properly speaking, fellowship involves something that two or more persons hold in common. These insights are the mainspring of fundamentalism. Fundamentalism is particularly concerned with *Christian* unity and fellowship. The question with which fundamentalism begins is, "What unites Christians? What do Christians hold in common?" Since Christian unity and fellowship may be greater or less, this question has both a minimal and a maximal answer.[5] At the minimal level, some criterion must exist for differentiating Christians from other people. Otherwise, all humans would be recognized as Christians. What is this criterion?

## The Gospel and the Church

In the New Testament, the locus of Christian unity is the church. The church is pictured as one flock (John 10:16), one new humanity (Eph. 2:15), and one body (Eph. 2:16; 1 Cor. 12:13). All Christians are united in this church. This unity is the work of the Spirit. The church has

---

4. This perspective is indicated by some of the titles in the literature, e.g., Beal, *In Pursuit of Purity: American Fundamentalism Since 1850*, and Pickering, *Biblical Separation: The Struggle for a Pure Church*.

5. I am suggesting that Christianity is both edge-bounded and center-bounded. It has a hard perimeter (an edge), outside of which Christian recognition is impossible. It also has a center. Those who are inside the boundary may be more or less close to the center.

access to the Father by one Spirit (Eph. 2:18). The baptism of this Spirit unites Christians with the body and, indeed, with Christ himself (1 Cor. 12:12–13). The unity that Christians are to maintain is the unity of the Spirit (Eph. 4:3). When Paul states that "we ... all" have been Spirit-baptized into one body (1 Cor. 12:13), he does not mean to include all humans. He includes himself, his readers, and all people everywhere who call on the name of the Lord Jesus Christ (1 Cor. 1:3). Evidently, the unity of which Paul speaks is related to the reception of the gospel.

In Ephesians 4:4–6, Paul names seven factors that unite Christians. The first two are the one body and the one Spirit. Paul then names one hope, one Lord, one faith, one baptism, and one God and Father. Clearly these uniting factors pertain only to people who have received the gospel. The gospel is pivotal to Christian unity.

Another way of viewing Christian unity is presented in Jesus' parable of the sheepfold (John 10:1–16). In the parable, the fold represents national Israel, which possessed a form of unity that was visible, external, and tangible. This form of unity, however, was not necessarily internal, for the nation (the fold) included some people who were Jesus' sheep and others who were not. In contrast to the external unity of the fold, Jesus says that he is going to lead his sheep "out." An example of this leading out had already occurred in John 9, where the man born blind was cast out of the synagogue because of his loyalty to Jesus. What was already true of the man born blind would become true of all Jesus' sheep. He would separate them from national Israel. Then he would bring his other sheep, sheep that had never been part of the fold, namely, Gentiles. These two groups of sheep would become "one flock" with "one shepherd" (John 10:16).

What would unite individual sheep into one flock? Jesus says that his sheep follow him because they know his voice. The flock is united by following the Shepherd. To follow the Shepherd can be understood as a metaphor for faith in the gospel. In contrast to the outward unity of Israel, the one flock would enjoy an inner, organic unity. Its unity would come through its trust in the Shepherd. Again, the gospel is pivotal to Christian unity.

As the foregoing shows, the church can be viewed in at least two ways. It can be seen as Christ's body, constituted by the baptizing work of the Spirit. The church can also be viewed as a flock, constituted as Jesus' sheep who hear his voice and follow him. From both of these perspectives, the essential unity of the church is invisible, inward, and organic. The church is created by, and the unity of the church consists in, the gospel itself.

What about Jesus' prayer for unity in John 17? Echoing the language of John 10, Jesus prays for those whom the Father has given him. He asks the Father to keep them in order that they might be one, just as Jesus and the Father are one (John 17:11).

Jesus specifies that his request includes both the circle of the disciples and those who will believe through their word (John 17:20). Since Jesus places no *terminus ad quem* on this request, it apparently includes his followers today. Consequently, it implies a unity that stretches not only through space, but also through time. Jesus grounds his request in the unity that exists between him and the Father. He notes that the Father is in him and he in the Father (v. 21). He asks that his followers may also be one "in us." The unity of Jesus' followers has a purpose. They are to be made one in order that the world may believe that the Father has sent Jesus. In some mysterious way, the unity of Jesus' followers is a necessary condition for the belief of the world. Very likely, the unity for which Jesus prayed is the same unity that comes from following Jesus (John 10). It is also the unity that comes from receiving Spirit baptism (1 Cor. 12:13). It is an inner, organic, invisible unity.

The fundamental unity of the church is invisible and intangible. It is an inward unity that comes with belief in the gospel. This observation does not imply that outward, visible unity is unimportant. Outward unity, however, can be enjoyed only where inner unity already exists. In sum, unity is always a function of what unites. Fellowship always involves something that is held in common. The quality of the thing held in common determines the quality of the fellowship or unity. The thing that is held in common by all Christians — the thing that constitutes the church as one church — is the gospel itself. Belief in the gospel is how people follow Jesus. Belief in the gospel is how people are Spirit-baptized into the one body. Consequently, the gospel is the essential ground of all genuinely Christian unity. Where the gospel is denied, no such unity exists. Even the most minimal Christian unity depends on common belief in the gospel.

## The Invisible Church and Visible Unity

What all Christians hold in common is the gospel. The fundamental unity that comes from the gospel, however, is essentially invisible, for both faith in the gospel and Spirit baptism are invisible. This invisibility presents a problem for determining the boundaries of visible, external Christian cooperation. How can invisible unity be relevant for questions of visible cooperation and fellowship? The answer is that external manifestations of fellowship are grounded in the real, internal unity that already exists between all genuine believers. Christians do not have the obligation to contrive unity or fellowship. God graciously gives these things.

Paul explicitly grounds visible unity on invisible commonalities in Ephesians 4. Believers are supposed to endeavor to maintain the unity of the Spirit in the bond of peace (v. 3). This external unity is founded in the seven invisible realities of one body, one Spirit, one hope, one Lord, one faith, one baptism, and one God and Father (vv. 4–6). The inner unity that believers have been granted ought to be reflected in their outer conduct.

How can Christians make judgments about Christian fellowship? Since God alone can see hearts, the test must be something other than perfect knowledge. God alone knows who genuinely *possesses* faith. What Christians can know, however, and what they must evaluate, is who *professes* faith. Christians are united by their faith in the gospel. When they profess the gospel, they announce their faith. Unless their profession is falsified by their behavior, they ought to be received as participants in the one flock and the one body.

Those who profess the gospel should be recognized as saints, provided that their lives do not contradict their professions. The Second London Confession, a Baptist document, states this principle: "All persons throughout the world, professing the faith of the Gospel, and obedience unto God by Christ, according unto it; not destroying their own profession by any Errors everting the foundation, or unholyness of conversation, are and may be called visible Saints."[6] As visible saints, such individuals are presumed to participate in the communion of the saints.

---

6. "Second London Confession," in W. L. Lumpkin, *Baptist Confessions of Faith*, 2nd ed. (Valley Forge, Pa.: Judson, 1969), 285. Virtually all branches of Protestant Christianity concur with this perspective. I have chosen a Baptist confession to illustrate this point, because some Baptists are uneasy with the notion of a "visible catholic church" as expressed, for example, in the Westminster Confession. The Second London Confession provides alternative language that has a similar theological effect.

Possession of faith in the gospel determines who really is a Christian. Profession of faith in the gospel determines who should be reckoned as a Christian. Profession of the gospel is the minimum requirement for visible Christian fellowship. The gospel is the boundary of Christian fellowship. The gospel defines fellowship, but that leaves another question: What exactly is the gospel?

## The Gospel, History, and Doctrine

The gospel is the primary category for understanding Christian fellowship. Therefore, a right understanding of the gospel is extremely important. Among those who name the name of Christ, however, definitions of the gospel vary widely. How do we know what the gospel is? If we want a biblical definition, then we ought to seek a biblical text that aims to give a definition. We find such a passage in 1 Corinthians 15. The chapter opens with Paul's statement that he intends to "make known" the gospel. In other words, Paul means to explain or define the gospel. What gospel? It was the gospel that he preached, that the Corinthians received and in which they presently stood, and by which they were being saved.

Its place in the epistle and, indeed, in the Pauline corpus underlines the importance of 1 Corinthians 15. Paul opens the epistle with a disquisition on the gospel. In 1 Corinthians 1:17–18, he explicitly ties the preaching of the gospel to the rationale (*logos*) of the cross. Unlike miraculous signs or human wisdom, the message of the crucified Christ has the power to save those who believe (1:20–24). In fact, Paul purposes to preach nothing but Jesus crucified so that people will trust God's power and not place their confidence in human wisdom (1 Cor. 2:1–5).

Paul returns to the subject of the gospel in 1 Corinthians 9. There he insists that he will surrender any privilege that hinders the effective proclamation of the gospel (v. 12). His reason is that he is duty-bound to preach the gospel, for the preaching of which he holds an administrative trust (vv. 16–17).

Paul also contrasts his gospel with other gospels. In 2 Corinthians 11:4, he mentions people who preach a different Jesus, receive a different spirit, and accept a different gospel. In one of his earliest epistles, he warns the Galatians about those who wish to pervert the gospel of

Christ (Gal. 1:6–7). He warns against being drawn away from the grace that is in Christ to a different gospel (Gal. 1:6–9).

Paul insists that his gospel is not one of human invention. He did not receive it from humans, but by direct revelation from Jesus Christ (Gal. 1:11–12). Only after Paul had begun to preach the gospel among the Gentiles did he review its contents with the other apostles (Gal. 2:2).

The gospel that Paul makes known, or defines, in 1 Corinthians 15 is the same gospel that he had been preaching. It was not new to the Corinthian congregation. They had heard it before. They had believed it. Now, however, it was coming under attack. In preparation for his counterattack, Paul clearly summarized the gospel.

In Paul's articulation, the gospel revolves around the death and resurrection of Jesus. It is news about specific events. Christ died. Christ arose. These are the decisive events of the gospel. Each of these events is attested by witnesses. The death of Christ is attested by the witness of his burial. The resurrection is attested by the witness of those who saw the risen Lord with their own eyes. If these events did not occur in just the way that Scripture says they did, then the gospel is false and without value.

By themselves, however, the events have no meaning. Christ was crucified, but the Romans crucified many criminals. Allowing that Christ did rise from the dead, why is this fact more than a scientific conundrum? The value of the events lies in their significance. When Jesus was crucified, he died for our sins. When he arose from the dead, he became the firstfruits of those who slept.

Paul's primary concern in 1 Corinthians 15 is with the resurrection of Christ. The resurrection was under attack. Paul uses the balance of the chapter to expound the significance of the resurrection. In contrast, he offers only the briefest explanation of Jesus' death: Christ died "for our sins." This explanation, however, is pregnant with meaning. It summarizes an understanding of Christ's death that was voiced, not only by Paul, but by other writers of the New Testament.

What does Paul mean when he says that Christ died for *our sins*? Certainly he means the kind of sins that he had discussed elsewhere in 1 Corinthians. These include matters such as incest, adultery, greed, idolatry, slander, homosexual conduct, stealing, drunkenness, the use of prostitutes, misapplication of gender roles, abuse of the Lord's Table, falsifying spiritual gifts, bickering with one's fellow Christians, judging the motives of others, preening over one's own superiority, engaging in crooked business dealings, suing fellow Christians, and even cursing Christ. These are the kinds of sins for which Christ died.

Such sins are all irreducibly personal. Granted, these sins do show up in the way that we treat other people (they have social dimensions). By committing them, we damage ourselves and others emotionally (they have psychological dimensions). They may even lead us to into twisted uses of the created order (they have environmental dimensions). Before they are anything else, however, they are personal. They involve the individual rejection of God's authority as moral lawgiver. They represent personal transgressions against his righteous demands.

The fundamental problem that sin poses is guilt, that is, injustice committed against the utterly pure judge of all. Even when sins have social, psychological, or environmental ramifications, they remain obstinately personal. The sins for which Christ died are personal sins entailing personal guilt and requiring personal salvation. In other words, the environmental, social, and psychological effects of sin are symptoms. The gospel is about personal redemption and the forgiveness of sins. In any articulation of human sin, personal guilt must remain primary.

What did Christ do about our sins? What does Paul mean that Christ died *for* our sins? Whatever other answers may be given, the New Testament definitely views the death of Christ in terms of penal substitution and the satisfaction of divine justice. This does not mean that other "theories" of the atonement are necessarily false in what they affirm. Each of them becomes false, however, if it is used to deny penal substitution. When Scripture declares that Christ died "for our sins," it means that God imputed the guilt of human sin to Christ on the cross and judged it there. It means that Christ's sacrifice propitiated God's wrath and satisfied the demands of his justice.

Paul's articulation of the gospel in 1 Corinthians 15 must be connected to his doctrine of justification. For Paul, God's justification of the ungodly includes two steps. First, it involves the imputation of their guilt to Christ, who bears retribution in their place. Second, it involves the imputation of Christ's righteousness to the believer. Reckoned to believers, this "alien" righteousness becomes the basis on which God declares them to be righteous. Fundamentalists unanimously insist that this double imputation is essential to the gospel.

The gospel presupposes a particular understanding of human sinfulness, rebellion, condemnation, and helplessness. It presupposes a future second coming at which Jesus Christ will pass judgment on resurrected humans. It presupposes a penalty so horrifying and inescapable that Jesus Christ is the only hope of deliverance. It includes the work that Christ did on the cross to satisfy the demands of God's justice and to deliver sinners from the penalty of their guilt. It includes his bodily resurrection from the dead.

The gospel necessarily presupposes Jesus' qualifications to be our sin-bearer. These qualifications entail his complete human nature, his complete divine nature, and the unity of his person. They entail his virgin birth and his perfect obedience to the Father. They entail his present session at the right hand of the Father as an intercessor for the believing sinner.

Furthermore, the gospel addresses the application of salvation. Scripture is clear, and evangelicals have agreed, that salvation is applied by grace alone through faith alone. In other words, salvation must be received as a gift without any admixture of work or merit.

The significance of the gospel cannot be known apart from revelation. To understand why Jesus died and why he rose again, humans require an authoritative explanation. That explanation has been vouchsafed to them in authoritative Scriptures that claim to be God-breathed (2 Tim. 3:16). Such inspiration necessitates inerrancy, because a God-breathed but errant Scripture would imply a God who was either mistaken or untruthful. A God who could make mistakes or who would knowingly mislead people is certainly a lesser God than the God whom the Bible presents. Such a God would not merit the kind of ultimate trust that Scripture requires for the salvation of the soul.[7]

---

7. Two words of explanation are in order. First, I am advocating verbal, plenary inspiration, but not dictation. Few fundamentalists have believed in the divine dictation of Scripture, but virtually all have affirmed verbal, plenary inspiration. Second, I am not suggesting that an inerrant Scripture is necessary in order to know the gospel. What is necessary is an authoritative Scripture. If Scripture is authoritative, however, then its claims about its own nature must be taken seriously. A verbally inspired Scripture that could err would imply a God who either could err or would deceive, but Scripture presents God as entirely truthful and trustworthy. Any theological construct that calls into question the veracity of God is necessarily committing a fundamental error. In other words, inerrancy is fundamental, not as an a priori

The gospel begins with events, but the events are not presented as brute facts. They are interpreted. The gospel discloses the meaning of the events, and that meaning explains why the good news is good. These explanations are doctrinal in nature. Therefore, the gospel has an irreducibly doctrinal component. The gospel is not only events; it is also doctrines.

Are people saved by trusting doctrines or by trusting Christ? The answer is that the only Christ who can save is the Christ whose person and work is doctrinally explained. To trust Christ as Savior is to trust a doctrinal Christ. To reject the doctrines is tantamount to rejecting Christ himself.

## The Gospel and the Fundamentals

The gospel is always doctrinal. Without doctrinal explanations, the death and resurrection of Jesus would be without significance. Those explanations, presuppositions, and implications on which the gospel depends are called *fundamental doctrines*, or simply *fundamentals*. Fundamental doctrines are essential to the gospel.

This does not mean that someone must explicitly know and affirm all of the fundamentals to be saved. Some of the fundamentals certainly must be known and accepted, while others are presupposed within or implied by the gospel. No fundamental can be denied, however, without implicitly denying the gospel itself.

Since the gospel functions as the boundary of Christian fellowship, fundamental doctrines are part of that boundary. The importance of boundary doctrines was recognized early in Christian history. Churches adopted increasingly complex formulae to indicate which doctrines could not be denied without damaging the gospel. What began as an orally confessed rule of faith eventually developed into the Apostles', Nicene, and Athanasian Creeds. These three creeds, together with the Symbol of Chalcedon, can be understood as early summaries of fundamental doctrines.

The chief creeds were not meant merely to provide abstract definitions. They were tests of fellowship. People who would not affirm

---

assumption (i.e., if Scripture were not inerrant, we could never know the gospel), but as an a posteriori inference (i.e., given the authority of Scripture and given what it teaches about its own nature, to deny inerrancy is to attack the truthfulness of God himself).

these creeds were not to be recognized as Christians or received into churches. People who contradicted the creeds were regarded as heretics and apostate teachers.

Each stage of church history brings denials that no one has thought of before. The chief creeds refuted denials of Trinitarian and christological dogmas. Before those questions were entirely resolved, attention had to be paid to the Pelagian denial of original sin. At a later stage, the Reformers responded to denials of justification through faith alone. Yet other denials have come, and some are still coming.

A current example may be the theology known as open theism. Fundamentalists have followed the evangelical debate over this new theology with considerable interest. Historically, some fundamentalists have actually entertained some of the ideas that now make up open theism. For example, J. Oliver Buswell, a noted fundamentalist theologian, argued rather vigorously against the notion that God is atemporal.[8]

Fundamentalists have watched with fascination as some evangelicals have denounced open theism as a denial of the gospel.[9] They have also followed the responses of open theists. They have listened as the discussion has come to focus on the denial of God's exhaustively definite foreknowledge of the future choices of free beings.[10]

Since open theism is completely absent from fundamentalism, fundamentalist theologians have felt little inclination to join the public fray. When they do, it is to reject the conclusions of open theists.[11] Though they do not often debate the subject publicly, fundamentalists strongly support those evangelicals who believe that the open theist understanding of foreknowledge implies a denial of the gospel.

---

8. James Oliver Buswell, *A Systematic Theology of the Christian Religion*, 3 vols. (Grand Rapids: Zondervan, 1962), 1:42–47.

9. To mention only one source, see three articles in John Piper, Justin Taylor, and Paul Kjoss Helseth, eds., *Beyond the Bounds: Open Theism and the Undermining of Biblical Christianity* (Wheaton: Crossway, 2003): Stephen J. Wellum, "The Inerrancy of Scripture," 237–74; Paul Kjoss Helseth, "The Trustworthiness of God and the Foundation of Hope," 275–307; and Bruce A. Ware, "The Gospel of Christ," 309–36.

10. In June 2002 the Evangelical Theological Society devoted an entire volume of its journal to the problem of open theism and evangelical boundaries (*JETS* 45, no. 2 [June 2002]). These articles provide some exceptional discussion from both sides of the question.

11. See, e.g., Rolland McCune's discussion of foreknowledge in his *Systematic Theology of Biblical Christianity*, 3 vols. (Allen Park, Mich.: Detroit Baptist Theological Seminary, 2008), 1:221–29.

## Fundamentals and Fellowship

Unity is a function of what unites, and fellowship is something that is held in common. The thing that Christians hold in common and that unites them is, minimally, the gospel itself. Those who profess the true gospel are to be accorded fellowship as Christians. Those who deny the gospel are to be excluded from Christian fellowship.

Applying this standard to someone who overtly follows a non-Christian religion is relatively easy. People who accept the teachings of Buddhism or Hinduism, for example, are necessarily denying the gospel. The same is true of an overt unbeliever. By denying the existence of God, an atheist unavoidably denies God's work in the gospel. Christian fellowship with such persons is not possible.

Furthermore, one of the oldest insights of Christianity is that not everyone who names the name of Christ professes the true gospel. Very early on, Christian churches had to find ways to distinguish themselves from groups like Gnostics and Arians. While such groups may profess to follow Christ, their message actually contradicts the gospel. Inasmuch as their message constitutes a denial of the gospel, their adherents are not to be accorded Christian recognition or fellowship.

Many theological systems (such as those of Jehovah's Witnesses or Mormons) claim to adhere to Christianity while they actually deny the gospel. What these groups preach as gospel contradicts the biblical gospel. Therefore, the adherents of these religions should not be recognized as Christians at all. They should be regarded as apostates.[12]

Fundamentalists believe that Roman Catholicism also denies the gospel. Catholicism attacks the gospel in at least two ways. First, it undercuts biblical authority by subjecting the Scriptures to an authoritative tradition and magisterium, not to mention an infallible papacy. Second, by confounding justification with progressive sanctification, it attacks the root of a gracious gospel and denies that salvation can be applied through faith alone. The result is a system of religion that mixes faith with works in the application of salvation.

Granted, Roman Catholicism, unlike Arianism or Mormonism, affirms Trinitarian orthodoxy. The Roman gospel, however, is false.

---

12. I am using the word *apostate* to denote persons who profess Christianity while denying the gospel.

Catholicism represents an apostate, rather than a Christian, system of religion. Christians cannot rightly extend Christian recognition or fellowship to those who endorse and proclaim the Roman Catholic gospel.[13]

Increasingly, evangelicals have become willing to do just that. In the document titled *Evangelicals and Catholics Together: Christian Mission and the Third Millennium*, the signatories contend that the unity for which Jesus prayed in John 17 includes Roman Catholics. The document states, "However imperfect our communion with one another, however deep our disagreements with one another, we recognize that there is but one church of Christ."[14]

More recently, a similar if somewhat more moderate attitude was evidenced in *The Manhattan Declaration: A Call of Christian Conscience*. This document presents itself as a declaration of "Orthodox, Catholic, and Evangelical Christians." Its signatories declare, "We are Christians who have joined together across historic lines of ecclesial differences to affirm our right—and, more importantly, to embrace our obligation—to speak and act in defense of [social and moral] truths."[15]

The problem consists in understanding how the declaration is using the word *Christian*. Does the use of this term imply the mutual recognition of genuine Christianity on the part of all signatories, or is it simply distinguishing them as participants in a moral tradition that traces itself to the moral system found in the New Testament? In other words, is the word *Christian* being used in a theological sense or a sociological sense?

At least some evangelical signatories understood it in the sociological sense. For example, Albert Mohler commented, "The Roman

---

13. This perspective is hardly unique to fundamentalism. One of the presidents of Fuller Seminary wrote, "If Christ is an authoritative revelation of the Father's will, Catholicism is anti-Christ. That much is lucidly clear. The gospel according to Christ and the gospel according to Rome cannot, in a rational universe, simultaneously be true. Romanism will fail." Edward John Carnell, *A Philosophy of the Christian Religion* (Grand Rapids: Eerdmans, 1952), 447–48.

14. "Evangelicals and Catholics Together: Christian Mission and the Third Millennium," in *Evangelicals and Catholics Together: Toward a Common Mission*, ed. Charles Colson and Richard John Neuhaus (Dallas: Word, 1995), xvi, xviii. If the point were simply that some Roman Catholics may trust Christ, receive salvation, and be united to the invisible body of Christ in spite of the teachings of their church, then this statement would be unobjectionable. That is not the point, however. The statement includes Roman Catholics *qua* Catholics within the orbit of Christian unity.

15. *Manhattan Declaration: A Call of Christian Conscience*, http://www.manhattandeclaration.org/the-declaration/read.aspx (accessed July 21, 2010).

Catholic Church teaches doctrines that I find both unbiblical and abhorrent—and these doctrines define nothing less than the Gospel of Jesus Christ. But the Manhattan Declaration does not attempt to establish common ground on these doctrines. We remain who we are, and we concede no doctrinal ground."[16] Mohler evidently recognizes Catholics as Christians only in the sense that they profess loyalty to Christ and not to Buddha or Muhammad.

The question is whether this distinction is really clear in the Manhattan Declaration itself. On the surface, at least, it does not appear to be. The document does acknowledge "ecclesial differences," but such differences would normally be construed as disagreements between genuine Christians. Moreover, if the word *Christian* were simply being used as a sociological category, then one might have expected signatories from, for example, the Church of Jesus Christ of Latter-day Saints. Consequently, without special explanation, a reader can only assume that the signatories are recognizing one another as Christians in the proper sense of the term. At the very least, the Manhattan Declaration creates confusion over the nature and boundaries of the Christian faith.

From a fundamentalist perspective, this confusion is alarming. Inasmuch as it denies the biblical gospel, Roman Catholicism is not Christianity. Traditionally, its view of God and its understanding of the person of Christ are correct, but its grasp of both the nature of spiritual authority and the application of salvation are fatally flawed. To extend Christian recognition to Roman Catholics is to circumvent the gospel as the boundary of Christian fellowship.

The same may be said of any system that denies a fundamental doctrine. Those who deny a fundamental doctrine deny the gospel. Those who deny the gospel must not receive recognition as Christians. The gospel draws the boundary of Christian fellowship. Those who are outside the boundary must not be recognized as Christians.

## The Idea of Fundamentalism and Maximal Christian Fellowship

Up to this point, the discussion has focused on minimal Christian fellowship. Minimal unity and fellowship among Christians is defined by

---

16. Albert Mohler, "Why I Signed *The Manhattan Declaration*," http://www.albertmohler.com/2009/11/23/why-i-signed-the-manhattan-declaration/ (accessed February 4, 2011).

the gospel itself. Where the gospel is held in common, unity exists and fellowship should be recognized. Where the gospel is denied (either directly or by denial of some fundamental doctrine), unity does not exist and fellowship should not be extended.

The Christian faith, however, is not simply about the gospel. The gospel functions as the boundary of Christianity, but within that boundary is an entire system of faith and practice. Where the gospel is essential to the being of Christianity, other aspects of the system are necessary for its well-being. Once minimal unity is realized (i.e., once the gospel is held in common), other levels of fellowship also become possible.

Within the boundary of the gospel, fellowship and unity may be greater or less. To understand why this must be so, we need only remember that unity is a function of what unites, and fellowship is something that is held in common. At minimum, Christians must be united by the gospel. At maximum, they may be united by the entire system of faith and practice, the whole counsel of God.

### Levels of Fellowship

Scripture implies different levels of fellowship. Not all fellowship relationships are equal. Different relationships bring with them different levels of accountability and responsibility. One level is simple personal fellowship: two believers rejoicing together in the gospel that they hold in common. Another level is discipleship. Ministry collaboration is a different level, as are both church membership and church leadership.

Personal fellowship requires only the gospel and a desire to please God. A discipleship relationship requires submission and accountability from the disciple and responsibility from the teacher. Collaboration requires yet greater responsibility and accountability. Inasmuch as most churches see themselves as covenanted bodies, church membership is much more serious than simple, personal fellowship. The most responsible level of fellowship is probably local church leadership, and the qualifications of overseers and deacons are correspondingly high (1 Tim. 3:1–13).

An individual may qualify for one of these fellowship relationships without qualifying for another. Not every person who qualifies for church membership necessarily qualifies for church leadership. Not everyone who qualifies for personal fellowship necessarily qualifies for ministry collaboration. If some Christians believe that amillennialism is an aspect of the whole counsel of God, then they may collaborate to promote their eschatology. Since their fellowship — their targeted collaboration — focuses on amillennialism, however, it stands to reason that a premillennial Christian will not be able to participate.

In sum, Christian fellowship is not all or nothing. Within the Christian faith, different levels of fellowship require different qualifications. Individuals may qualify for some levels of fellowship but not qualify for others.[17]

## Doctrinal Importance

The Christian faith includes both doctrines and practices. Some of these are more important than others. The distinction between fundamentals and nonfundamentals does not exhaust the possibilities for ranking their importance. Biblical teachings, whether theological or practical, can be evaluated according to their overall effect on the system of faith. An alteration or denial of some doctrines will make little difference to the overall system. Some doctrines, however, have significant implications for other doctrines, and their denial or alteration is much more likely to produce changes throughout the system.[18]

For example, one's opinion of the sons of God in Genesis 6 touches little else in the system of doctrine. Disputes over the nature of the kingdom, however, will affect one's view of the timing of the Lord's return, the present status of national Israel, the mission of the church, and the nature of Christian life and ethics during the present age. Of the two, one's doctrine of the kingdom is clearly more far-reaching.

Another factor that may increase importance, especially for practices, is their immediacy or urgency. Most Christians, for instance, agree that baptism is obligatory for a life of Christian obedience. If that

---

17. Two moderate fundamentalists who discuss levels of fellowship are Richard I. Gregory and Richard W. Gregory, *On the Level: Discovering the Levels of Biblical Relationships among Believers* (Grandville, Mich.: IFCA Press, 2005).

18. For a brief discussion of this phenomenon by a nonfundamentalist, see Robert A. Peterson, "Part Two: The Case for Traditionalism," in Edward William Fudge and Robert A. Peterson, *Two Views of Hell* (Downers Grove, Ill.: InterVarsity, 2000), 178–79.

is true, then knowing whether paedobaptism fulfills the requirement is clearly important.

Unity is a function of what unites. Fellowship is something that is held in common. What Christians ought to hold in common is not merely the gospel, but the whole counsel of God. Wherever Christians differ over some aspect of the whole counsel of God, their fellowship is in fact frustrated. They should not be surprised to discover that this may limit their ability to work together.

David Nettleton has suggested that when Christians differ over some aspect of the faith, they have two options. One is to limit their message. The other is to limit their fellowship.[19] If they limit their message, then they agree to ignore the difference. For the sake of cooperation, they mutually surrender all or part of their prerogative to proclaim some doctrine or practice. Sometimes, limiting one's message is the best thing to do.

When Christians limit their fellowship, however, they choose to work separately in areas that are affected by the difference. For example, a church cannot both permit and not permit infant baptism. If a church is committed to permitting infant baptism, and if some members are convinced that infant baptism violates Christian obedience, then those members have no choice but to organize a separate congregation.

To be sure, the most desirable Christianity would be one in which all believers agreed at all points of the whole counsel of God. Anything less than this perfect fellowship and unity is an evil, but it is less of an evil than a contrived or enforced unity. To force believers to violate their consciences is worse than erecting separate organizations in which all believers are free to obey God according to their best understanding.

Differences over the faith always affect fellowship, but they affect it to varying degrees. All other things being equal, cooperation and organization should be maintained wherever the differences do not preclude it. A difference should not preclude cooperation or common organization when it is sufficiently incidental that both sides can feel comfortable expressing their views without the other party feeling that an important aspect of the faith is being compromised. Sometimes,

---

19. David Nettleton, "A Limited Message or a Limited Fellowship," General Association of Regular Baptist Churches Archive Collection, http://wprnd.net/garbc/wp-content/uploads/2007/01/limited.pdf (accessed July 28, 2010).

however, a difference is sufficiently serious that it cannot be ignored. When that happens, conflict becomes inevitable at some level. Under such circumstances, greater harmony and outward unity may be maintained by separate organization.

## Separation among Christians

The discussion of maximal Christian fellowship is really about separation between Christians. This kind of separation is sometimes called "secondary" or "second-degree" separation. Most evangelicals and many fundamentalists, however, are uncomfortable with those labels. The idea is simply that believers must at times choose to limit their cooperation with some other believers.

How could a Baptist minister in good conscience sprinkle infants for a neighboring paedobaptist congregation? How could a Calvinist support an enterprise dedicated to the propagation of Arminianism? How could an amillennialist join a dispensationalist organization? None of these Christians has to denounce the others as unbelievers. At some level, they can and should fellowship. At other levels, however, they cannot. The question is not whether we should sometimes separate from each other. In fact, we cannot possibly cooperate with every other believer for every kind of Christian endeavor. The real question is how we can make God-honoring decisions about fellowship and separation.

Unfortunately, the New Testament lays down no simple rule. Rather, we must weigh a matrix of considerations. That matrix includes at least three sets of questions.

First, we should discover what level of fellowship is planned. The New Testament describes several levels, and we may encounter yet others. Decisions about cooperation require us to ask which aspects of the faith are affected by the fellowship that we envision. In what areas must we agree in order to work together in the intended way?

Second, we must ask frankly about our doctrinal and practical disagreements. We must evaluate those areas for their importance. We should try to understand what areas of cooperation they are likely to affect.

Third, we should be aware of one another's attitudes. We may weigh our disagreements differently. Some hold their position tenaciously, while others hold it tentatively. A difference that can be set aside by one person may be a central focus for another. Some are becoming more hardened in their view, while others are becoming less so. Certain forms of cooperation may run the risk of condoning an error, or at least of downplaying its importance. In short, some Christians may be able to limit their message, while others will have to limit their fellowship.

Fellowship and separation among believers is not all or nothing. It depends on properly weighing this matrix of considerations. Ultimately, Christians must make their own judgments for each unique case. Naturally, all Christians will not make the same judgment.

If more Christians recognized that decisions about fellowship and separation are judgment calls, their attitudes might change in two ways. First, some might be less critical of Christians who judge the situation differently. Second, others might become more willing to make decisions about limited cooperation. In any case, we need to allow one another liberty to apply the principles of Scripture to specific situations. On the other hand, judgments can be better or worse. In matters of fellowship and separation, Christians on both sides may exhibit patterns of poor judgment. Consistently poor judgment may itself become a reason to limit fellowship at some levels.

Separation between Christians need not be carried out in a petty or vindictive manner. We can love one another and pray for God's blessing on one another even when we cannot work together. We should conduct ourselves so that even in separation we are earnestly endeavoring to maintain the unity of the Spirit in the bond of peace (Eph. 4:3). Even in separation, we must be careful not to damage the possibility of cooperation in those areas in which we agree.

## Separation over Separation

Unity is a function of what unites. Fellowship is something shared in common. The gospel is the ground of all Christian unity and fellowship. Christian recognition ought to be extended to all those, but only those, who profess the true gospel.

This basic structure of fellowship and separation is itself one of the doctrines of the Christian faith. Consequently, it is one of the matters that must be weighed when making decisions about cooperation with other Christians. I have argued that Christians must never extend

Christian recognition and fellowship to people who deny the gospel, but some Christians do. That is an error—but how serious is it?

Paul knew people who taught a false gospel. He discusses them in Galatians 1:6–9. His attitude toward such persons is shocking in its bluntness. Paul says that if anyone—even heavenly angels or the apostles themselves—preaches a different gospel, then "Let him be damned!" (Gal. 1:8–9).[20] If Paul's attitude is the right one, then recognizing an apostate as a Christian would be a very serious error indeed. The error would be compounded if the apostate were promoted as a Christian leader and teacher.

The proper response to such false teachers is a major concern of John's second epistle. John is directly concerned with one particular way of denying the gospel, namely, refusing to confess that Jesus Christ has come in the flesh. John says that many people (presumably, people who view themselves as Christians) do not make this confession. Such persons, says John, are deceivers and antichrists (2 John 7). They do not have God (2 John 9).

John's teaching cannot be limited to only christological errors, however. The problem with denying that Jesus Christ has come in the flesh is that it eviscerates the gospel. This is a different way of denying the gospel than the one that Paul encountered among the Galatians, but the response of the two apostles is decidedly akin. The similarity of their reactions suggests that their attitude ought to be directed toward all those who profess Christ while denying the gospel.

John cautions his readers to beware lest they lose their full reward (2 John 8). At first glance, this caution is puzzling. How would such a loss be incurred? John hints at the answer to this question in his instruction about proper responses to those who teach apostasy. John tells his readers not to receive these teachers into their houses nor even to give them a civil greeting (2 John 10).

Most likely these prohibitions are intended to apply to ministry relationships rather than social interaction. Nevertheless, they probably seemed as severe to John's original readers as they do today. Then or now, what John required is a violation of basic civility. He demanded that no

---

20. This is not the normal way English translations handle the word *anathema*, but it approximates well enough the intent of Paul's thought. The NIV, for example, has "let them be under God's curse."

recognition or encouragement at all be given to someone who was teaching a false gospel, not even the encouragement of a civil greeting.

John had his reasons. Even the most insignificant encouragement to someone who is proclaiming a false gospel brings one into fellowship with the evil that follows (2 John 11). Apparently Christians can gain a share in the evil that apostates do. The apostate and the one who encourages the apostate have a common stake in the results of the false gospel. That is probably why John warned his readers about losing their reward. God would hardly reward someone for helping to spread apostasy.

We might debate some of the implications of this passage, and in a full discussion some qualifications would be appropriate. Still, I think that one thing is reasonably clear: Christians who make a habit of encouraging apostate teachers are hardly models of Christian discernment. We should treat them as people who have a share in the evil of apostasy.

That is why fundamentalists separate from Christian leaders who will not separate from apostates. It is not merely that such leaders are disobedient. The problem lies in the character of their disobedience. By refusing to break with apostates, such Christian leaders are losing reward by bringing themselves into fellowship with apostasy. The evil of apostasy becomes common property between them and the apostates.

Fundamentalists believe that separation from apostates is essential to the integrity of the gospel. Some evangelicals, however, insist on making common cause with apostates, bringing them into the Lord's work and recognizing them as Christians. From the fundamentalist perspective, this insistence is the most basic cause of the ongoing division between fundamentalists and the rest of the evangelical movement. Though they personally believe and preach the gospel, evangelicals who fellowship with apostates undermine the gospel's function and demean its importance. They remove the gospel from its position of privilege as the boundary between Christianity and non-Christianity.

## The Idea of Fundamentalism and the Fundamentalist Movement

Throughout this essay, I have distinguished the idea of fundamentalism from the fundamentalist movement. To this point, I have been most concerned to explain the idea. I now wish to turn attention to the fundamentalist movement.

Space does not allow a retelling of the story of fundamentalism. It must be said, however, that fundamentalists invented neither the idea of fundamentals nor the practice of separation. American Christians attended to these matters in detail during the decades on either side of the Civil War. The Old School Presbyterians, and particularly Charles Hodge, were very influential in articulating a theory of fellowship and separation that informed the beliefs of later fundamentalists.[21]

The core ideas of fundamentalism were not invented but inherited. As fundamentalists implemented these ideas, they mixed them together with other ideas. The varieties of the fundamentalist movement are the result of these combinations. This essay cannot offer a full taxonomy of fundamentalism. It would be incomplete, however, if it did not examine two deficient forms of the movement. The first of these is the result of combining fundamentalism and certain other ideas. The second is the result of a twisting of the idea of fundamentalism itself. Both are important for understanding the current status of the fundamentalist movement.

## Populist Revivalism

Populism and revivalism are related phenomena that have strongly affected segments of American Christianity. Not all revivalists or populists are fundamentalists, but their influence in certain segments of fundamentalism has been significant. Some of the most frequent criticisms of fundamentalism are often directed, not at fundamentalism per se, but at revivalistic versions of the movement.[22]

---

21. For a more thorough tracing of these ideas, see Kevin T. Bauder, "Communion of the Saints: Antecedents of J. Gresham Machen's Ecclesiastical Separatism in the Ecclesiology of Charles Hodge and the Princeton Theologians," PhD diss. (Dallas Theological Seminary, 2001). For a less detailed version of the argument, see Kevin T. Bauder, "What's That You Smell?" in *Pilgrims on the Sawdust Trail: Evangelical Ecumenism and the Quest for Christian Identity*, ed. Timothy George (Grand Rapids: Baker, 2004), 57–67, 215–19.

22. The term *revivalist* denotes more than someone who favors a revival. It involves a particular view of what revival is and how it can be achieved. The distinction can be explored in Iain H. Murray, *Revival and Revivalism: The Making and Marring of Modern Evangelicalism 1750–1858* (Carlisle, Pa.: Banner of Truth, 1994). Much of the philosophy of revivalism can be traced to Charles Finney, *Lectures on Revivals of Religion*, 2d ed. (Boston: Crocker and Brewster, 1835). For a critical fundamentalist perspective, see Gerald L. Priest, "Revival and Revivalism: A Historical and Doctrinal Evaluation," *Detroit Baptist Seminary Journal* 1 (1996): 223–52, http://dbts.edu/journals/1996_2/Revival.pdf.

Populism brought with it the attitudes of anti-intellectualism, antiecclesiasticism, and antitraditionalism. By the nineteenth century, these attitudes had gained a powerful hold in many circles of American Christianity. Not surprisingly, they were inherited by many fundamentalists.[23]

Revivalism assumes that the normal Christian life is one of decline. Left to themselves, Christians will backslide. Therefore, Christian living becomes an oscillation between habitual backsliding and moments of revival or "getting right with God." The turning point from backsliding to revival is typically a crisis decision, and the main responsibility of the preacher is to produce these crises. He does this by means of "hard preaching," which focuses on the plan of salvation, the importance of soul-winning, and whatever rules of conduct the backslider is presumed to be violating. A person who wishes to get right with God usually communicates this crisis decision by "going to the altar."

Revivalism produces several consequences. First, by emphasizing crisis decisions, it works against the notion that the normal Christian life is one of incremental growth. Second, it downplays or rejects the importance of biblical exposition in preaching, substituting confrontational exhortation. Third, it amplifies soul-winning as the key feature of being "right with God." Fourth, it lends itself to externalism: the spirituality of any believer can be judged by conduct, and the effectiveness of any minister can be judged by the number of decisions that are made under his ministry. Fifth, it fosters a philosophy of leadership that puts pastors in a near-dictatorial position (if the normal Christian life is one of decline, then important spiritual decisions cannot be left to ordinary Christians). Sixth, since numerical results are crucial, revivalistic churches tend to adopt methods that are calculated to draw crowds. Seventh, in these churches, congregational worship is depreciated or repudiated. Eighth, revivalism downplays the importance of theology and, consequently, of theological education.

Historically, revivalistic fundamentalism has been strongest in the South, where it has become the dominant version of fundamentalism. Nonrevivalistic fundamentalists emphasize the centrality of wor-

---

23. This story is told well by Nathan Hatch, *The Democratization of American Christianity* (New Haven, Conn.: Yale University Press, 1989).

ship and of expository preaching, aim for incremental growth through spiritual nourishment, teach theology, and reject a brittle emphasis on external conduct. Both sorts of fundamentalists have always existed. The tension between them has led to a lack of cohesiveness within the fundamentalist movement.

## Hyper-Fundamentalism

One version of fundamentalism goes well beyond the idea that I summarized earlier in this essay. It could be called hyper-fundamentalism. Hyper-fundamentalism exists in a variety of forms. Some of the characteristics of hyper-fundamentalism include the following.[24]

First, hyper-fundamentalists often understand fundamentalism in terms of loyalty to an organization, movement, or even leader. They equate the defense of the faith with the prosperity of their organization or its leader. Someone who criticizes or contradicts it is subjected to censure or separation.

Second, hyper-fundamentalists sometimes adopt a militant stance regarding some extrabiblical or even antibiblical teaching. For example, many professing fundamentalists are committed to a theory of textual preservation and biblical translation that leaves the King James Version as the only acceptable English Bible. When individuals become militant over such nonbiblical teachings, they cross the line into hyper-fundamentalism.[25]

Third, hyper-fundamentalists understand separation in terms of guilt by association. To associate with someone who holds any error constitutes an endorsement of that error. Persons who hold error are objects of separation, and so are persons who associate with them.

Fourth, hyper-fundamentalists are marked by an inability to receive criticism. For them, questioning implies weakness or compromise. Any criticism — especially if it is offered publicly — constitutes an attack. In other words, hyper-fundamentalism is often marked by extreme defensiveness.

---

24. A discussion of hyper-fundamentalism can be found in Jeff Straub, "The Fundamentalist Challenge for the 21st Century: Do We Have a Future?" (paper presented at the Bible Faculty Leadership Summit, July 30, 2009), http://www.sharperiron.org/article/fundamentalist-challenge-for-21st-century-do-we-have-future-part-1 (accessed February 7, 2011).

25. Cf. Roy E. Beacham and Kevin T. Bauder, eds., *One Bible Only? Examining Exclusive Claims for the King James Bible* (Grand Rapids: Kregel, 2001).

A fifth characteristic of hyper-fundamentalism is anti-intellectualism. Some hyper-fundamentalists view education as detrimental to spiritual well-being. This attitude produces a kind of pride of ignorance. Colleges, when they exist, are strictly for the purpose of practical training.

Sixth, hyper-fundamentalists sometimes turn nonessentials into tests of fundamentalism. For example, some hyper-fundamentalists assume that only Baptists should be recognized as fundamentalists. Others make the same assumption about dispensationalists, defining covenant theologians out of fundamentalism. Others elevate extrabiblical personal practices. One's fundamentalist standing may be judged by such criteria as hair length, musical preferences, and whether one allows women to wear trousers.

Seventh, hyper-fundamentalists occasionally treat militant political involvement as a criterion for fundamentalist standing. During the 1960s and 1970s, anticommunism was a definitive factor for some fundamentalists. Its place has now been taken by antiabortion and antihomosexual activism. Most fundamentalists do agree about these issues, but hyper-fundamentalists make militant activism a necessary obligation of the Christian faith.

Eighth and last, hyper-fundamentalists sometimes hold a double standard for personal ethics. They see themselves engaged in an ecclesiastical war, and they reason that some things are permissible in warfare that would not be permissible in ordinary life. They may employ name-calling, half-truths, and innuendo as legitimate weapons. They may excuse broken promises and political backstabbing.

Hyper-fundamentalism takes many forms, including some that I have not listed. Nevertheless, these are the forms that are most frequently encountered. When a version of fundamentalism bears one or more of these marks, it should be viewed as hyper-fundamentalist. It is worth noting that several of these marks can also be found in other versions of evangelicalism.

Hyper-fundamentalism is not fundamentalism. It is as a parasite on the fundamentalist movement. For many years it was simply a nuisance, largely ignored by mainstream fundamentalists. Ignoring the problem, however, permitted it to grow. While statistics are not available, hyper-fundamentalists now constitute a significant percentage of self-identified fundamentalists, perhaps even a majority. They have become the noisiest and often the most visible representatives of fundamentalism. They may be the only version of fundamentalism that many people ever see.

## Fundamentalism Today

Mainstream fundamentalists find themselves in a changing situation. One factor is that what was once the mainstream may no longer be the majority within self-identified fundamentalism. A growing proportion is composed of hyper-fundamentalists, who add something to the gospel as the boundary of minimal Christian fellowship. If the idea of fundamentalism is correct, then this error is as bad as dethroning the gospel from its position as the boundary.

Another factor is that some evangelicals have implemented aspects of the idea of fundamentalism, perhaps without realizing it. For example, both Wayne Grudem and Albert Mohler (among others) have authored essays that reverberate with fundamentalist ideas.[26] More than that, they and other conservative evangelicals have put their ideas into action, seeking doctrinal boundaries in the Evangelical Theological Society and purging Southern Baptist institutions.

Mainstream fundamentalists are coming to the conclusion that they must distance themselves from hyper-fundamentalists, and they are displaying a new openness to conversation and even some cooperation with conservative evangelicals. Younger fundamentalists in particular are sensitive to the inconsistency of limiting fellowship to their left but not to their right.

Furthermore, many fundamentalists have become impatient with revivalistic influences in their own movement. While they recognize that many revivalists genuinely love the Lord and wish to serve him, they see revivalistic methods as manipulative and pragmatic. These fundamentalists are deeply concerned about the revivalistic vision of worship, preaching, sanctification, and church leadership.

Many have grown weary of the crusading anti-Calvinism that has characterized revivalistic versions of fundamentalism. Few mainstream

---

26. Wayne Grudem, "When, Why, and for What Should We Draw New Boundaries?" in *Beyond the Bounds: Open Theism and the Undermining of Biblical Christianity*, ed. John Piper, Justin Taylor, and Paul Kjoss Helseth (Wheaton: Crossway, 2003), 339–70; Albert Mohler, "A Call for Theological Triage and Christian Maturity," *Baptist Press* (August 23, 2006), http://www.bpnews.net/bpcolumn.asp?ID=2359 (accessed August 16, 2010).

fundamentalists are thoroughgoing Calvinists, but many see value in some Calvinistic emphases. These fundamentalists are put off by the tendency of some revivalists to demonize even the most modest versions of Calvinism.

Furthermore, mainstream fundamentalists have rejected the anti-intellectualism that has characterized the populist wing of the movement. The days are long gone when mainstream fundamentalist schools refused accreditation. By the standards of the twenty-first century, mainstream fundamentalist institutions offer decent, postsecondary education. The better fundamentalist seminaries still lag behind evangelical schools in publication, but the level of their classroom instruction is comparable.

In recent years, mainstream fundamentalists have become sensitive to their dependence on one another. They have created forums for interchange among institutions and leaders. They have opened partnerships and networks that would have been unthinkable a generation past. They view themselves as collaborators rather than as competitors.[27]

The fact is, however, that mainstream fundamentalism is facing difficult times. Many who were once in the mainstream have drifted into the King James Only movement. Others, disgusted with the excesses of the Right or the triviality of revivalism, have left fundamentalism altogether. Today, what used to be mainstream fundamentalism is dwindling.

Whether this is a good thing or a bad thing depends on one's point of view. Many evangelicals are barely aware of the existence of fundamentalism to begin with. They would not miss it if it died. Alternatively, hyper-fundamentalists have been trying to co-opt fundamentalism for decades. The dissolution of the mainstream would give them clear title to whatever remains of the movement, though it would bear little resemblance to historic fundamentalism.

What if mainstream fundamentalism were simply to vanish? Would anyone miss it? I think the answer to that question lies in the value of

---

27. Examples of such collaborative organizations include the Fellowship of Missions and the American Association of Christian Colleges and Seminaries, both of which are the leading fundamentalist organizations in their fields. The Bible Faculty Leadership Summit is an annual academic meeting that was initially organized by Bob Jones University and Detroit Baptist Theological Seminary. For more than a decade, the National Leadership Conference (hosted by Calvary Baptist Theological Seminary in Lansdale, Pa.) provided a forum for the exchange of ideas among fundamentalists.

the idea. In my opinion, fundamentalism is a great idea. It is a necessary idea. More important, it is a biblical idea.

To be useful, however, even the best ideas must become incarnated in practice. Such an incarnation may begin with scattered individuals here and there, but ultimately it requires more. It requires mutual recognition, exchange, and cooperation among those who hold the idea. It requires vehicles of communication and venues for taking counsel. Eventually, it requires organizations and institutions. In short, if any idea, no matter how well worth believing and perpetuating, is going to endure and to affect human lives, it requires a movement of some sort.

The idea of fundamentalism is a great idea. Whatever its flaws, mainstream fundamentalism is the best incarnation of that idea that is presently available. To be sure, the fundamentalist movement bears the marks of human shortsightedness, inconstancy, and depravity. If it were to die, however, the only alternative would be to incarnate the idea of fundamentalism in a different movement—which would also bear the marks of human shortsightedness, inconstancy, and depravity.

Some version of fundamentalism is necessary. Granted, it needs to be a chastened fundamentalism. It needs to become even more serious about worship, preaching, devotion, and holiness. It needs to become more doctrinally careful. It desperately needs to distance itself from the excesses of its worst exemplars. If it cannot rid itself of hyper-fundamentalism and revivalism, and if it cannot learn sobriety, then the fundamentalist movement probably does not deserve to survive.[28]

What is the alternative? Those who hold the idea of fundamentalism cannot help having reservations about certain tendencies within evangelicalism. Admittedly, evangelicalism is even more diverse than fundamentalism. No individual evangelical or fundamentalist can be charged with all the faults of either movement. Still, fundamentalists register two concerns about evangelicalism in general.

The first concern is the tendency of some evangelicals to rethink and redefine the gospel. This redefinition is carried out in multiple ways. Newer theologies, such as open theism or the new perspective on

---

28. For a more complete description of what I think fundamentalism should become, see Kevin T. Bauder, "A Fundamentalism Worth Saving: An Address to the American Association of Christian Colleges and Seminaries" (February 2, 2005), http://www.aaccs.info/media/Bauder%20A%20Fundamentalism%20Worth%20Saving.pdf (accessed July 28, 2010).

Paul include teachings that threaten one or more of the fundamentals. Some evangelicals have shifted the emphasis of the gospel toward its putative social, psychological, and environmental effects, downplaying the centrality of personal guilt, penal substitution, and personal forgiveness. Some of the foregoing have begun to rethink personal conversion in favor of a rather vague notion of identifying with the work of the kingdom. Other evangelicals are reopening the issue of biblical inspiration by substituting narrative authority for propositional authority and by displaying a new openness to the more destructive perspectives of biblical criticism. Some evangelicals have even begun revising traditional moral perspectives, including (in some instances) the morality of homosexual relations. Fundamentalists see in these trends an incipient or actual denial of the gospel.

The second concern is that some evangelicals extend Christian recognition and fellowship to teachers who deny the gospel (i.e., to apostates). For example, some evangelicals have formally recognized Roman Catholics as Christians. Just as insidious is the practice of cooperative evangelism, in which evangelicals secure the sponsorship of ecumenical liberals by recognizing theologically liberal churchmen as Christian leaders. As long as some evangelicals cannot tell the difference between a person who professes the true gospel and one who denies it (i.e., between a Christian and an apostate), fundamentalists are not likely to view those evangelicals as thoughtful or perceptive Christian leaders. In fact, fundamentalists are not likely to follow their leadership at all.

The rift between fundamentalists and other evangelicals is more than a half century old. Do we stand on the brink of rapprochement between these two groups? Might we someday have *Evangelicals and Fundamentalists Together*?

If the above two concerns could be addressed, I think that room would exist for conversation. Fundamentalists think that these concerns are important because the gospel is at stake in both of them. Doubtless, evangelicals have their own concerns about fundamentalism. Mainstream fundamentalist leaders are ready to hear those concerns and in many cases may actually share them.

If some mutual understanding is to be achieved, however, it cannot be for the sake of mere show or political expedience. Any mutuality—

any *fellowship*—must manifest what is held in common. Unity is always a function of what unites. Fellowship is always something held in common. Any fellowship between fundamentalists and other evangelicals must grow out of what they hold jointly, and it must not ignore their differences.

Wherever fundamentalists are wrong, evangelicals have a right to confront them and to ask them to abandon their errors. By the same token, wherever fundamentalists are right, they have a right to challenge evangelicals and to ask them to adopt ideas and practices that conform to Scripture. The better sort of fundamentalist will take an evangelical's rebukes as the wounds of a friend. I hope that some evangelicals will also receive this essay as the entreaty of a brother. The idea of fundamentalism is worthy of consideration. It is capable of defense. It merits discussion. So let's talk.

# A CONFESSIONAL EVANGELICAL RESPONSE

## R. ALBERT MOHLER JR.

What hath Murfreesboro to do with Wheaton? A chapter on fundamentalism in a book about evangelicalism? Kevin Bauder's chapter is one of the most promising essays I have read in a long time, and I am thankful for his contribution.

Kevin's honest and energetic defense of fundamentalism will be, I believe, an important part of the history of the fundamentalist movement in America. He and his colleagues are trying to rescue fundamentalism from cultural obscurity and institutional fratricide. At the same time, evangelicals in this generation need to rethink the distinctions between evangelicalism and fundamentalism that we have taken for granted for over half a century.

The received evangelical tradition holds that conservative Protestantism in North America was saved from intellectual obscurantism and cultural disaster only by the emergence of the "New Evangelicals" in the middle of the twentieth century, thus providing an escape from the great embarrassment of fundamentalism.

That account is not wrong, but it isn't really right either. I took it as truth as a college and seminary student. As a teenager, I had occasionally visited fundamentalist churches at the invitation of friends. On one occasion, I later discovered that my attendance was a means toward my friend's goal of earning a prize for bringing a friend. No worry—he got a hamster, and I got an earful of fundamentalist preaching.

My surprise was that what I heard was not markedly different from the sermons I heard in my own Southern Baptist congregation. Same gospel, same urgency—even the same invitation hymn. Nevertheless, I did spot a preoccupation with matters never raised in my church, ranging from hemlines to haircuts.

As a college religion major, I visited an independent Baptist church in order to hear John R. Rice preach. I felt that I knew him already, since a dear woman in my home church bought me a subscription to

*The Sword of the Lord.* I must admit that I did not read it reverently. My favorite feature was the advice column for young "preacher boys." It wasn't exactly what I was hearing at my Baptist college.

When I arrived at seminary, I quickly learned that the great goal of my ministerial life was to do whatever was necessary to prove beyond a shadow of a doubt that I was not a fundamentalist. The faculty of that day represented a generation of Southern Baptists who feared any association with fundamentalism and were doing their dead-level best to prove that they were not fundamentalists. They were spectacularly successful in achieving that goal. So much so, in fact, that many openly embraced liberal theology. Accepted into the theological tribe of that school, I knew that my first concern must be to prove my nonfundamentalist identity.

But problems ensued. In the first place, I began to see that an aversion to fundamentalism could (and before my very eyes *did*) quickly lead to an embrace of heterodoxy. All I knew were fundamentalist stereotypes, and they were easy enough to confirm when I observed many fundamentalist churches, organizations, publications, and schools. I didn't want any part of that spirit, the tendency to elevate peripheral matters as central concerns, the anti-intellectualism, the KJV-onlyism, and the cultural awkwardness.

But then I read Harry Emerson Fosdick's infamous 1922 sermon, "Shall the Fundamentalists Win?" Fosdick preached:

> I know people in the Christian churches, ministers, missionaries, laymen, devoted lovers of the Lord and servants of the Gospel, who, alike as they are in their personal devotion to the Master, hold quite different points of view about a matter like the virgin birth. Here, for example, is one point of view that the virgin birth is to be accepted as historical fact; it actually happened; there was no other way for a personality like the Master to come into this world except by a special biological miracle. That is one point of view, and many are the gracious and beautiful souls who hold it. But side by side with them in the evangelical churches is a group of equally loyal and reverent people who would say that the virgin birth is not to be accepted as an historic fact.[29]

29. Harry Emerson Fosdick, "Shall the Fundamentalists Win?" *Christian Work* 102 (June 10, 1922): 716–22.

Louisville, we have a problem. If Fosdick framed the issue rightly, then count me as a fundamentalist. I later read J. Gresham Machen's *Christianity and Liberalism*,[30] and came to know that there was more than one way to be fundamentalist. Not all were obscurantist, theologically eccentric, or anti-intellectual.

In the course of my doctoral work, I devoted years to understanding the evangelical movement, and I grew to identify with leaders like Carl F. H. Henry, who attempted to forge an identity for conservative Protestantism that was genuinely orthodox but never obscurantist. I came to appreciate the effort of these "New Evangelicals" to create a new movement that would separate itself from the perceived anti-intellectualism, doctrinal preoccupations, antagonism to the culture, and vitriolic stance associated with fundamentalism.

And yet I have also come to see the inherent instabilities of that experiment. This very project serves to underline the failure of evangelicalism to define itself with anything close to adequacy. Add to that the fact that, as it happens, if you are a theological conservative who seeks to defend theological orthodoxy, you will be called a fundamentalist anyway. When Roger writes of "the tug of resurgent fundamentalism among us,"[31] he is not talking about a burgeoning enrollment at Bob Jones University—he is talking about evangelicals like me. In his essay in this project, he writes of some evangelicals "slipping back into the old fundamentalism." We know who he means.

Add to this the fact that the media have tremendous difficulty knowing the difference between an evangelical and a fundamentalist and often seem to distinguish along attitudinal rather than theological lines.

And now, along comes Kevin Bauder to argue that fundamentalism "is a serious attempt to wrestle with the nature of the church as the communion of the saints." I never expected John R. Rice to say that, and Kevin instantly captured my attention. Is that what fundamentalism is about?

Kevin's narrative of the gospel, the Scripture, and the necessity of cognitive knowledge to salvation is lucid and helpful. That is just classic

---

30. J. Gresham Machen, *Christianity and Liberalism* (Grand Rapids: Eerdmans, 2009).

31. Roger E. Olson, *How to Be Evangelical without Being Conservative* (Grand Rapids: Zondervan, 2008), 20.

Christianity. When he states, "One of the oldest insights of Christianity is that not everyone who names the name of Christ professes the true gospel," who can argue?

On all of those issues, evangelicals and fundamentalists *should* stand in common agreement. The turning point in his argument is when he shifts from a discussion of *minimal* Christian fellowship to *maximal* Christian fellowship. This is where we encounter Kevin's concern with "the nature of the church as the communion of the saints." He writes, "At minimum, Christians must be united by the gospel. At maximum, they may be united by the entire system of faith and practice, the whole counsel of God."

Now, *this* is an argument worth a close consideration. But should our goal be maximal fellowship through agreement concerning "the whole counsel of God"? That allows for no disagreement on any theological issue, as if all are of equal importance. Hold that thought.

Kevin first qualifies his argument with reference to different levels of fellowship and doctrinal responsibility. He then qualifies his argument once again with the affirmation that not all doctrinal issues are of equal importance. He writes with care: "Biblical teachings, whether theological or practical, can be evaluated according to their overall effect on the system of faith. An alteration or denial of some doctrines will make little difference to the overall system. Some doctrines, however, have significant implications for other doctrines, and their denial or alteration is much more likely to produce changes throughout the system." This is a very good argument, and, if I read Kevin rightly here, it is in keeping with the theoretical framework I set out in my proposal for "theological triage" in my essay. Some issues and doctrinal differences impinge upon the gospel and its central doctrines and can quickly lead to theological disaster.

On the other hand, Kevin explains, "A difference should not preclude cooperation or common organization when it is sufficiently incidental that both sides can feel comfortable expressing their views without the other party feeling that an important aspect of the faith is being compromised." I am a bit surprised by Kevin's use of the category of affections here. He writes with hope that both sides can *feel* comfortable without the other party *feeling* compromised. See, fundamentalists have feelings too.

As I read his argument, I am sure that Kevin intends this to mean a serious theological analysis that issues in both judgment and emotional comfort. His language is helpful, even as we might wonder exactly how a responsible fundamentalist would make such a judgment. I am fairly certain that there would be arguments over the relative status of disagreements, and that is not necessarily a sign of confusion. It can be a sign of a vital movement fulfilling its theological responsibility.

The next turn in Kevin's argument is where the sparks will fly. When maximal Christian fellowship breaks down, what then? This is where the doctrine of separation (held by all faithful Christians) and the doctrine of secondary separation (characteristic of fundamentalism) enter the picture. Brace yourselves.

At the first level, Kevin's argument is classically Protestant. He acknowledges a fellowship among faithful Calvinists and Arminians, Baptists and Presbyterians, or amillennialists and dispensationalists. But fellowship has its limits. Kevin provides a rubric for analyzing when a difference must produce separation. He calls it a "matrix" that includes the level of fellowship proposed, an honest assessment, an attitudinal analysis, and a proper "weighing" of these matters.

He concludes by stating, "Ultimately Christians must make their own judgments for each unique case. Naturally, all Christians will not make the same judgment."

Really? The fundamentalist position leaves us with that much possible variance?

Then he turns to "separation over separation," or secondary separation. Some evangelicals, he charges, "insist on making common cause with apostates, bringing them into the Lord's work, and recognizing them as Christians." He then writes:

> From the fundamentalist perspective, this insistence is the most basic cause of the ongoing division between fundamentalists and the rest of the evangelical movement. Though they personally believe and preach the gospel, evangelicals who fellowship with apostates undermine the gospel's function and demean its importance. They remove the gospel from its position of privilege as the boundary between Christianity and non-Christianity.

Now, that is a serious, if predictable, charge against evangelicals. Part of it rings true, and many nonfundamentalist evangelicals have spoken with equal concern. But the other side of this question is also pressing—how far is this to be taken? At face value, this would seem to imply that orthodox believers would never seek to rescue or redeem wayward institutions and wavering Christians. Had this principle been strictly followed, there would have been no conservative resurgence in the Southern Baptist Convention and no reformation of its institutions.

Perhaps I misunderstand how this principle would operate, strictly applied, but I think I have observed enough to know that some fundamentalist leaders might even charge Kevin with violating this principle by participating in this project. Thanks for taking the risk, Kevin.

Kevin ends by offering a bracingly honest assessment of contemporary fundamentalism and its future prospects. I greatly admire his honesty and candor. "Some version of fundamentalism is necessary," he believes. Nevertheless, "If it cannot rid itself of hyper-fundamentalism and revivalism, and if it cannot learn sobriety, then the fundamentalist movement probably does not deserve to survive."

If fundamentalism does survive, it will owe a great deal to Kevin Bauder and others who share his concerns and courage. I believe that fundamentalists like Kevin and conservative evangelicals are experiencing a convergence of concerns. This will encourage many but frighten both hyper-fundamentalists and the evangelical left.

Kevin has convinced me that distinctions remain between conservative evangelicals and our fundamentalist friends. A few quick changes to our cultural context could render those distinctions to contain little difference.

### JOHN G. STACKHOUSE JR.

Kevin Bauder shows a remarkable humility in recognizing that fundamentalists have not interpreted themselves to themselves or to anyone else very well either historically or theologically. So we want to pay careful attention to what he says, as he is clearly both historically and theologically informed. Still, in what follows, I will suggest—and I hope with evident goodwill—that Brother Kevin's depiction of fundamentalism and of evangelicalism suffers from a narrowness of focus that almost certainly paints him and his "tribe" less accurately and less positively than it should. In fact, I intend to indicate that Brother Kevin's kind of fundamentalists are better evangelicals and, indeed, better Christians than they might appear to be here.

Brother Kevin says, "While purity is important to fundamentalists ... the primary motive of fundamentalism is the unity and fellowship of the church." I think his essay also shows that among the core values of fundamentalists is *clarity*: clarity about what the gospel says and doesn't say, clarity about what the church is and isn't, clarity about what we ought to do and ought not do, clarity about who is in and who is out, clarity about those with whom we should have fellowship and those with whom we should not, and so on.

These fundamentalist values compel Brother Kevin to say certain things I wouldn't say. For example, "The church cannot both permit and not permit infant baptism." But why not? A church could show how the sacrament of baptism is understood differently at certain levels by different Christians, teach that basic gospel principles yet inform both views, and then invite Christians to practice Christian liberty by allowing each other to enjoy baptism as they understand it. To say, "Those members have no choice but to organize a separate congregation" perhaps makes sense in a fundamentalist understanding, but it doesn't make obvious sense in mine.

Moreover, I agree with Brother Kevin that it is impossible for someone to be rightly called a Christian who disbelieves in the gospel—in the good news about Jesus. One would not be a "good" Muslim if one did not believe that "there is only one God and Muhammad is his prophet," nor could one sensibly be called a "good" Buddhist if one were to deny the Four Noble Truths. But why focus so much—in fact, almost exclusively—on Christian doctrine? Where are the traditional Christian—indeed, the traditional evangelical—emphases on mission and piety? Why is there no equal emphasis on orthopraxy (correct practice) and what I'm calling orthopathy (right affections)?

A particularly key passage reads as follows:

> The most desirable Christianity would be one in which all believers agreed at all points of the whole counsel of God. Anything less than this perfect fellowship and unity is an evil, but it is less of an evil than a contrived or enforced unity. To force believers to violate their consciences is worse than erecting separate organizations in which all believers are free to obey God according to their best understanding.

I respectfully suggest that "the most desirable Christianity" is not characterized by cognitive agreement on the contents of the Bible. Indeed, it is not obvious to me that such agreement would automatically produce a "perfect fellowship and unity." What about fervency and appropriateness of worship and spiritual experience? What about faithfulness in caring for each other within the body of Christ? What about effectiveness in pursuing God's mission to the world? Aren't these necessary elements of "the most desirable Christianity"? I'm sure Brother Kevin thinks they are. So why aren't they mentioned? And how are they properly connected to orthodox belief—since I doubt he actually thinks they emerge immediately from mere correctness of theology?

Let me underline my agreement with Brother Kevin's concern that any "generous orthodoxy" be truly "orthodox" as well as "generous." I wonder, however, where he would draw the line in regard to indisputably orthodox individuals who fail to practice love for the neighbor—especially the poor neighbor, or the neighbor with a different color skin, or the female neighbor—or who fail to practice humility, gentleness, forbearance, forgiveness, and other virtues I am sure he would agree are nonnegotiably part of basic Christian practice. Aren't these practices and affections rightly viewed as "fundamentals" as well?

I further want to say that outside of the fundamentalist frame it doesn't follow that to ask believers to tolerate differences of opinion and practice within a Christian fellowship is tantamount to forcing them to "violate their consciences." The apostle Paul spends quite a bit of time asking the strong to bear with the weak. He even articulates a key paradox as he suggests that those with "strong" consciences may not in fact be superior Christians, but are simply more scrupulous, even more fastidious, than others. And he indicates that people with such consciences, if they will not exercise their Christian liberty to tolerate and even support fellow Christians who think differently and act differently than they do, thus impede the work of the Holy Spirit. I confess I am not yet clear on Brother Kevin's stance on this crucial principle of cooperation-despite-difference *within a congregation*.

This question leads to another, regarding the definition of "second-degree separation." I previously thought, having read the standard historians of fundamentalism, that it is the general fundamentalist practice of separating from those who do not themselves separate from the impure. But according to Brother Kevin, this practice is expected only of leaders, and particularly that they must not associate with heretics for fear of confusing their own flocks as to what is acceptable doctrine. Ordinary fundamentalists apparently do not have to observe this practice and should certainly avoid judging each other in what Brother Kevin calls the "hyper-fundamentalist" practice of attributing "guilt by association." But is Brother Kevin truly representing the mainstream fundamentalist tradition here? Or is his narrowing of this practice in fact a softening—albeit a commendable softening—of what used to be a universal requirement?

I'm glad to see that Brother Kevin tries to distinguish among levels of fellowship corresponding to various levels of doctrinal agreement. Ironically, however, without a clear discussion of what the gospel actually is and the methodological grounds for determining what the gospel is, it isn't clear how fundamentalists are supposed to follow his advice about making good "judgment calls." Alas, judgment calls, therefore, are likely going to be referred to popular leaders who will decide on behalf of everyone else. Each of the other essays in this volume asserts that evangelicalism has no magisterium. But that is true only at the most general levels. All over evangelicalism, thanks to its populist nature, there are little popes deciding these things for the people — sometimes few, sometimes very many — who agree to abide by their authority. I hope Brother Kevin will succeed in educating his flock as to just how we can properly sort out these matters without resorting to mini-magisteria.

Speaking of magisteria, I agree with Brother Kevin that there are grave problems in Roman Catholicism. I agree, particularly, that Roman Catholicism incorrectly elevates tradition to a place of revelation with authority equal to that of the Bible. I also agree that the papacy enjoys far more authority than any human office ever should.

Where we importantly disagree, however, is on whether these two important beliefs amount to a denial of the gospel. I think they don't. The Roman Catholic Church does not deny the authority of the Bible. It adds too much authority to Catholic theology, some of which is good and true and helpful, while some of it isn't. But the same thing happens in certain Baptist circles in regard to Baptist theology over the centuries. And I believe that deferring too much to Catholic tradition — or Baptist tradition — does not amount to denying the gospel. Nor does following the pronouncements of a human leader amount to a denial of the gospel, whether that leader is Catholic or Baptist. To be clear: these ideas and practices are wrong, and they are importantly wrong. But they do not keep someone from believing that God was in Christ reconciling the world to himself. They do not keep anyone from confessing Jesus as Lord and Savior, nor do they interfere with someone living a fruitful Christian life. I wish Roman Catholics didn't teach these things — just as I wish certain Baptists and other evangelical groups did not function in exactly the same way as Brother Kevin depicts Catholicism functioning. But I hope he would not excommunicate Baptists of this sort. And, if he would not, then I hope he will not excommunicate Catholics either.

As for grounds for excommunicating fellow evangelicals, I will linger just a moment over Brother Kevin's mistaken belief that the doctrine of inerrancy is entailed by the doctrine of God. To say that the Bible contains information that is not strictly accurate does not imply, as he says it implies, "a God who is either mistaken or untruthful." It could be, as John Calvin himself suggested, the work of a God who accommodates himself to the severe limitations of his human listeners. Just as a wise driving instructor does not try to teach all of the rules of the road and all of the variations on those rules necessary to handle every possible driving situation, but instead simplifies his instruction to match the learning ability of her student, so God takes us by the hand and leads us into truth.

Torah is not a law for all time. The Proverbs, like all extensive collections of wisdom sayings, seem to contradict each other in places as two complementary generalizations overlap. Numbers can be rounded off or can be used for dramatic or symbolic effect, rather than provided for reportorial accuracy. And the epistle to the Hebrews stands as a literary monument to the principle of "That was then; this is now." The Bible is a complex phenomenon, and we must attend to what it actually is, rather than confine it to what we, in the grip of our deductive presuppositions, *expect* it *must* be.

In my own essay I stoutly defend penal substitutionary atonement. Where Brother Kevin and I would disagree is over his reduction of the problem of sin to a question of guilt before a "moral lawgiver." I frankly don't see the Bible as depicting God as fundamentally a moral lawgiver. The Bible depicts God as fundamentally *God*—in *all* that "I AM WHO I AM" actually entails. To see God fundamentally as a divine legislator who expects to be obeyed and punishes those who disobey is to oversimplify. Indeed, God is fundamentally the creator, sustainer, and redeemer of the world who gives moral laws as instructions on what the world actually is and how to negotiate it properly. To disobey God's laws is to run against the grain of the universe. Sin incurs God's wrath, yes—but that is simply God's resolute holiness, his settled attitude and constant action of resistance to all that is not good. The forensic imagery is appropriate, therefore, but much too limited to serve as our basic picture. God is a disappointed father, a shamed suitor, a betrayed husband, a badly used master, a wronged monarch, and more. In fact, to restrict our focus so severely to the categories of morality and guilt plays directly into the hands of the critics of the doctrine of penal substitutionary atonement.

Having been raised a fundamentalist myself, however, may I say that it is, sadly, in keeping with the core values of fundamentalists—purity, orthodoxy, clarity—to view sin as primarily guilt before a divine lawgiver? Among the worst themes of fundamentalist religion is this: *correctness is all.* I hope Brother Kevin will help his fellow fundamentalists escape the burden of having to be right all the time. His manifest intelligence, charity, piety, and good sense give me hope that he will.

Brother Kevin remarks on both Wayne Grudem and Albert Mohler publishing "essays that reverberate with fundamentalist ideas." I entirely agree. In fact, I think we see in this book only three versions of evangelicalism. But I'll press that point further in my response to Brother Al's essay.

## ROGER E. OLSON

I applaud Kevin Bauder's clarity and courage in setting forth his vision of fundamentalist evangelicalism. Seldom have I read a more lucid account of fundamentalism and rigorous defense of separationism. At the same time, reading it brought back some painful memories and raised some important questions.

I grew up Pentecostal near a large fundamentalist church and Bible college. Inevitably my path crossed the paths of some of the fundamentalists. I was told that I was not a real Christian and might even be demon-possessed. When attending a Billy Graham crusade, I saw some of them picketing outside the stadium with signs that criticized Graham and his ministry as "compromised." Perhaps these were examples of Bauder's "hyper-fundamentalists," but they called themselves simply fundamentalists; I'm sure they thought of themselves as "mainstream fundamentalists." This is the image of fundamentalism I grew up with.

Much later, some years ago, I taught theology at a mainstream evangelical liberal arts college and seminary in the same metropolitan area where Bauder teaches. I invited a professor of theology at his seminary to speak to one of my classes about fundamentalism, and he did an excellent job. His talk was entitled "Will the Real Fundamentalists Please Stand Up?" and it overlapped significantly with Bauder's chapter. He emphasized the unity and diversity of fundamentalism in the United States.

After his lecture, I offered to return the favor by speaking to one of his classes. I'll never forget his cold look as he said firmly, "We won't be inviting you." I knew what he meant. My very presence at his seminary would pollute it, because I enjoyed fellowship with people he considered apostates, such as my open theist colleague.

Bauder's essay pulls no punches; it is a defense of separatistic fundamentalism in all its strangeness to most nonfundamentalists, including most other evangelicals. Let me say up front that I agree with him that fundamentalists of the kind he represents and defends are my fellow evangelicals. I believe in and defend a "big tent" view of evangelicalism that includes some who might not want to be included there (because it is too inclusive). Some evangelicals draw boundaries around the movement (something I argue is impossible) that exclude the kind of fundamentalists Bauder represents — to say nothing of the hyper-fundamentalists he criticizes. I don't think that's historically or theologically tenable. Post–World War II, postfundamentalist evangelicalism, as a movement, has been critical of separatistic fundamentalism. Fuller Seminary president E. J. Carnell (1919–67), whom Bauder quotes sympathetically, called it "*orthodoxy gone cultic*."[32] However, fundamentalists and evangelicals share much in common, including common historical roots. In fact, in many cases they believe exactly the same things (except secondary separation). Both share a passion for the gospel. So what's the difference between them?

It seems to me the main differences between Bauder's "moderate" or "mainstream" fundamentalists and postfundamentalist evangelicals (labeled "neo-evangelicals" by fundamentalists in the 1940s) lie in how much doctrine they pack into "the gospel" and exactly when and how they practice separation from apostates and heretics — people who claim to be Christians but reject the gospel or perceived orthodox doctrines — and from other evangelicals. Virtually all evangelicals practice some degree of separation; that is not unique to fundamentalists. And even fundamentalists do not agree among themselves about how exactly to believe in or practice it.

Some evangelicals, including probably most fundamentalists, consider me left of center if not outright liberal. However, even I do not have Christian fellowship with those I believe to be apostate or heretical. The difference seems to me to lie in *who is considered apostate and heretical* and *how one should treat them*.

When I taught a course on America's cults and new religions ("unsafe sects") at an evangelical liberal arts college, I invited spokespersons from many alternative religious groups to speak to my students.

32. E. J. Carnell, *The Case for Orthodox Theology* (Philadelphia: Westminster, 1959), 113 (italics in original).

Of course, I gave the students lots of information about the groups, including why they are generally considered heretical or even apostate by mainstream Christians. And we prayed for the cults' representatives before and after they came to class. I encouraged the students to show them Christian love when they came. Never, however, did we pray with them or invite them to worship or have devotions with us. (Sounds pretty fundamentalist and even separatistic, doesn't it?) (I should mention that such was not the case with the fundamentalist speaker, whom I invited to a different class on church history, with whom I would gladly have Christian fellowship!)

A young man who had spoken to my class about his Asian-based group that regards its leader as "the Lord of the Second Advent" called me. He asked me if I would deliver the invocation at their messiah's personal appearance in Minneapolis. I gently but firmly declined and told the shocked minister that I do not consider his sect Christian and that, in my opinion, the man he regarded as messiah is a false prophet preaching a false gospel. But I did take some of my students to hear him speak. Much to my shock and dismay, a Baptist minister delivered the invocation before the Korean spiritual leader spoke and asked for God's blessing on his "prophet from Korea." I did not think that minister was practicing proper discernment or separation.

I tell that story simply to illustrate that I, like most or all evangelicals, draw the line of fellowship somewhere. It's not as if we nonfundamentalist evangelicals are simply unaware of the biblical truth of separation or ignore it. To the best of my knowledge, *all* evangelicals recognize and practice it. It's just a question of when and how.

Kevin Bauder's colleague drew the line at inviting me to speak to his students. I drew the line at giving the invocation at (what I and all evangelicals consider) a false prophet's public speech. Even the Baptist minister who gave the invocation at the Korean's talk probably draws the line somewhere. (I personally think he was simply unaware of the man's teachings or his church's doctrines.) I have family members who probably fit Bauder's profile of hyper-fundamentalists. One of them told me, "There's no salvation apart from the King James Bible." Another one asked me if I believe healing evangelist Kathryn Kuhlman was an "agent of the pope." When I said no, he got up and walked away from me and refused to speak to me afterward. Everyone draws the line of fellowship somewhere and somehow. My relatives would probably not enjoy Christian fellowship with Bauder!

E. J. Carnell called fundamentalism *"orthodoxy gone cultic"* because he believed it made too much of relatively minor aspects of truth. He didn't accuse it of wrong doctrinal beliefs, but he accused it of making an ideology out of doctrine and refusing to recognize areas where Christians can legitimately disagree and still have warm Christian fellowship.

Bauder and I agree that the Roman Catholic Church teaches false doctrines and rejects true doctrines. Where we probably disagree is about whether these doctrinal aberrations require rejection of Catholics as apostates. (Actually, I found his qualification about individual Catholics interesting and puzzling. How would he decide whether to have fellowship with an individual Roman Catholic? Maybe we don't disagree about this; it's hard to tell.) Personally, I would not invite a Catholic priest to participate in a union Thanksgiving service even if his church was next door to mine. Nor would I attend his Mass except as an observer. But that doesn't mean I consider him or his parishioners apostates. I have attended ecumenical dialogue events with Mormons at Brigham Young University without worshiping with them. Like most evangelicals (and even so-called mainstream Protestants), I consider the Church of Jesus Christ of the Latter Day Saints a heretical sect and not a Christian denomination (to say nothing of the "fourth branch of Christianity"!) However, engaging in face-to-face dialogue with them has proven beneficial to me; I have had to revise some of my opinions about them, which is good because holding wrong opinions of others is a bad thing even if they are apostates or heretics.

Bauder considers open theists apostates. There we definitely disagree. I would like to know on what grounds he considers them apostates. They might believe everything he does except about the nature of the future. Does the gospel itself hinge on that? I don't think so. The ones I know are God-fearing, Bible-believing, Jesus-loving Christians. Oh, but he might say they can't be Bible-believing. And therein lies another difference between Bauder's fundamentalism and my evangelicalism. It seems to me that fundamentalists confuse their own interpretations of the Bible (e.g., penal substitution atonement) with the Bible itself. For example, he pronounces, "When Scripture declares that Christ died 'for our sins,' it means that God imputed the guilt of human sin to Christ on the cross and judged it there. It means that Christ's sacrifice propitiated God's wrath and satisfied the demands of his justice" as if all of that is actually stated in Scripture. He doesn't seem aware that this is an *interpretation* of Scripture; he equates this doctrine with the gospel itself, which the Bible does not do.

Now, interestingly, I happen to agree with Bauder that that is a correct interpretation of Scripture. But I recognize a "gap" between this interpretation, correct as I think it is, and the gospel itself. The gospel itself is that God was in Christ reconciling the world to himself. Is someone who denies the penal substitution theory of the atonement denying the gospel? Not automatically—simply by virtue of rejecting the penal substitution theory. I worry that in this case as in many cases, Bauder and his fundamentalists pack an entire system of theology (e.g., Charles Hodge's or B. B. Warfield's) into the gospel. The result is a distinct lack of humility with regard to theology and charity with regard to Christians who disagree about secondary doctrines.

Of course, that last statement begs the question, "What are primary and secondary doctrines?" Fundamentalists tend to empty the "nonessentials" category and overfill the "essentials" category. The only doctrine Bauder states that is clearly incidental and therefore not a "deal breaker" in terms of fellowship is the meaning of the "sons of God" in Genesis 6. I suspect he would acknowledge others, but it would be good to know what they are. Views of the millennium? William Bell Riley, longtime pastor of First Baptist Church of Minneapolis, of which Bauder's seminary is a distant offshoot, famously added premillennialism to the fundamentals of the faith. Does Bauder? If he doesn't, many fundamentalists do and would accuse him of "compromise" for not doing so.

What exactly is the litmus test for Christian fellowship? Saying just "the gospel" isn't sufficient—especially when one appears to regard "the gospel" as including many doctrines that developed through the history of Christian theological reflection. And what degree of Christian fellowship and cooperation is appropriate with those who disagree over points of "the whole counsel of God," and who decides that? After all, Bauder acknowledges that nobody speaks for all fundamentalists. Is this why fundamentalists are divided into so many camps that have trouble talking to each other? Is there truth to the suspicion that a spirit of dissension and division lies in the DNA of fundamentalism?

I suspect the one clear line of demarcation between fundamentalism and the rest of evangelicalism is the doctrine and practice of "secondary separation." As I have argued, all evangelicals practice some degree of separation from some other self-identified Christians. I know of no evangelical leader (holder of a responsible position) who goes around having Christian fellowship with everybody in sight, practicing no discernment whatsoever. So "biblical separation" is not unique to fundamentalism. It's a matter of degree. Fundamentalists like Bauder simply see apostasy where many other evangelicals don't.

I know of no nonfundamentalist evangelicals, however, who practice secondary separation. Where in Scripture are we told to avoid fellowship with those who have fellowship with apostates or heretics? And why not go further? Why not insist on tertiary separation—refusal of fellowship with those who have fellowship with those who have fellowship with apostates and heretics? And so on. Billy Graham started out a fundamentalist but was rejected because he allowed Catholics and Protestant ministers of National Council of Churches denominations to cooperate in his evangelistic crusades. This was and remains one of the main reasons for the division between fundamentalists and evangelicals and, in my opinion, justifies Carnell's label *orthodoxy gone cultic.*

# CONFESSIONAL EVANGELICALISM

## R. ALBERT MOHLER JR.

The evangelical movement in America emerged in the twentieth century as conservative Protestants sought to perpetuate an intentional continuity with biblical Christianity. While the roots of the movement can be traced through centuries prior to its emergence in twentieth-century America, its organizational shape appeared mainly in the years after World War II. And as anyone who considers the movement with a careful eye understands, evangelical definition has been a central preoccupation of the movement from the moment of its inception.

## Defining Evangelicalism

The word *evangelical* long predates the coalescence of the evangelical coalition of the last century. The word has been applied to Methodism in the eighteenth century, to nonconformists and low church Protestants in Great Britain in the nineteenth century, and to a host of groups, churches, and movements ever since. As early as the nineteenth century, frustration and confusion arose over the use and misuse of the term. The seventh Earl of Shaftesbury expressed frustration in the late nineteenth century when he declared, "I know what constituted an evangelical in former times.... I have no clear notion what constitutes one now."[1]

In this light, one is tempted to identify with the late justice Potter Stewart who, during deliberations of the U.S. Supreme Court in a 1964

---

1. E. Hodder, *The Life and Work of the Seventh Earl of Shaftesbury, K.G.*, cited in David W. Bebbington, *Evangelicalism in Great Britain: A History from the 1730s to the 1980s* (London: Unwin Hyman, 1989), 1.

case concerning pornography, simply declared, "I know it when I see it." In the most common usage of the term, it works in almost this very sense. An evangelical is recognized by a passion for the gospel of Jesus Christ, by a deep commitment to biblical truth, by a sense of urgency to see lost persons hear the gospel, and by a commitment to personal holiness and the local church. In any event, this is what we should hope to recognize as authentically evangelical.

But there is more to the question, of course. Honesty requires that the term be defined by its necessity. In this sense, *evangelical* has been and remains a crucial term because we simply cannot live without it. Some word has to define what it means to be a conservative Protestant who is not, quite simply, a Roman Catholic or theological liberal. While Catholics and liberal Protestants may speak of themselves in terms of an evangelical spirit (and both have), the term makes no sense as applied to a movement unless it is held to be clearly distinct from both Roman Catholicism and Protestant liberalism. Yet there is more to the story, of course, since the evangelical movement was also born out of a deep concern to identify a posture distinct from Protestant fundamentalism.

Attempts have been made to replace the term *evangelical* with something more useful, but such efforts have met with little success. The reason for this is quite simple: the word really does accomplish what it sets out to do. The word identifies those who find their primary identity as a gospel people. It functions as a descriptor for many millions of Christians for whom no other aggregate denominator is appropriate. The word has enduring value precisely because we cannot operate without it.

That is not to say that its use is uncontroversial. Dissatisfaction with the term was evident among many of the young leaders of the "New Evangelicalism" that emerged with great energy in the years just after World War II. Driven by a determination to distinguish themselves from separatist fundamentalism on the one hand and Protestant liberalism on the other, these ambitious founders of contemporary evangelicalism laid hold of the only term that seemed to describe their identity and aspirations. What other term would serve so well?

During the 1970s and 1980s, laments over the word and its usage led figures such as William J. Abraham to argue that the word is an "essentially contested concept"—a term borrowed from the world of philosophy. Abraham, a leading intellectual figure on the evangelical Left, argued that the term was almost always used in the context of theological judgment. Nevertheless, he asserted, "There is no single essence or one particular condition that captures the achievement concerned or will be agreed upon by all evangelicals."[2] Of course, even in making his argument, Abraham had little choice but to use the term *evangelicals* even as he argued that the concept is "essentially contested."

Evangelical definition must be placed within three distinct but overlapping contexts. We should consider evangelicalism in historical, phenomenological, and normative senses. None of these can stand alone; all three are needed in order to understand evangelicalism and to consider the question of evangelical identity.

### Evangelicalism in a Historical Sense

In the English-speaking world, the term goes back at least to the early eighteenth century. David W. Bebbington traces evangelical history to the spiritual awakenings of that era and to the famed ministries of figures such as George Whitefield and the brothers John and Charles Wesley. In this sense, the earliest evangelicals were British Methodists and their spiritual cousins, whose infectious love for the gospel, concern for social justice, and commitment to holy living shaped the religious life of both the British Isles and North America.

Later the term was applied to the nonconformists and low church Anglicans who stood apart from the influence of Anglo-Catholicism in the Church of England and from the developing theological liberalism that had already reached into both Anglican and nonconformist churches and institutions. In this sense, a figure like Charles Spurgeon, the great Baptist preacher of nineteenth-century London, is a paradigmatic evangelical type — and one who was already deeply concerned about theological compromise within evangelical circles.

In the United States, the term was often applied as it had been in European contexts — as a synonym for *Protestant*. The heirs of the Reformation were simply described as evangelical as a way of stressing a positive identity other than just being known as non-Catholic.

---

2. William J. Abraham, *The Coming Great Revival: Recovering the Full Evangelical Tradition* (San Francisco: Harper and Row, 1984), 73–74.

In the early twentieth century, the term was often applied to a spirit of evangelism and gospel energy. But as the nation was rocked by the fundamentalist-modernist controversy in so many churches and denominations, the word caught the attention of some conservative Protestants who steadfastly opposed theological liberalism but who also wanted to distinguish themselves from fundamentalism.

The controversies and church battles between the fundamentalist and modernist forces in the early decades of the twentieth century revealed rival understandings of the Christian faith. The modernists claimed to be saving Christianity by accommodating Christian theology to the antisupernaturalism that increasingly shaped the thought life and worldview of the intellectual classes. They adopted higher-critical approaches to the Bible and its interpretation, revised virtually all of Christianity's core doctrines, and transformed the life of denominations, institutions, and churches that had formerly held to far more conservative beliefs. They relativized the creeds and gained control of the organizational infrastructures of most of the mainline Protestant denominations.

The fundamentalists pledged themselves to oppose this theological revolution and return to the "fundamentals of the faith." They sought to resist and to reverse the liberal trends within their churches and denominations, and battle after battle ensued. The fundamentalists mounted a massive movement, holding Bible conferences and establishing networks of preachers and laypersons. But in the end, battle after battle was lost. The governing structures of the mainline denominations were filled with either liberals or their "moderate" supporters.[3]

In the years between the two great wars, the fundamentalists generally separated from the established denominations, forming their own universe of Bible colleges, seminaries, publishing houses, and even denominations. After the public humiliations of the Scopes Trial and other developments, fundamentalism began to drop out of the nation's intellectual conversation. Liberals controlled the denominations, the established denominational colleges and seminaries, and the prestigious pulpits. The fundamentalists were relegated to a constellation of Bible

---

3. See Bradley J. Longfield, *The Presbyterian Controversy: Fundamentalists, Modernists, and Moderates* (New York: Oxford University Press, 1991).

colleges, newspapers, Bible conferences, and publishing houses. They also seized on new technologies, particularly radio, to convey their message to a mass audience.

After World War II ended, a movement of young leaders, pastors, theologians, evangelists, and organizers came together to create a new conservative alternative to fundamentalism. They were, in fact, the founding fathers of modern evangelicalism — men such as Billy Graham, Harold John Ockenga, Carl F. H. Henry, and Charles Fuller. Some, including Henry, E. J. Carnell, Gleason Archer, and Kenneth Kantzer, pursued doctoral degrees at prestigious universities to gain access to the larger intellectual conversation. These "New Evangelicals," as they styled themselves, were determined to maintain a clear and unquestioned commitment to theological orthodoxy and to oppose theological liberalism in all its forms. Yet they also wanted to distinguish themselves and their movement from fundamentalism, which they identified with anti-intellectualism, a lack of serious theological engagement, a withdrawal from social responsibility, and an eccentric list of theological preoccupations.

Over time, these leaders created their own constellation of churches, evangelistic associations, colleges and universities, theological seminaries, publishing houses, and mission agencies. They sought to unify conservative Protestants into a coherent and credible movement. In their view, the movement should appeal to conservatives still remaining within the liberal denominations as well as to fundamentalists who had grown weary of the debates and factionalism of the fundamentalist movement. They established a central periodical, *Christianity Today*, launched in 1956 as a conservative alternative to the liberal *The Christian Century*. As founding editor Carl F. H. Henry made clear, *Christianity Today* would engage the issues of the day from a posture of intellectual engagement and credibility.

Over the last half of the twentieth century, these leaders and their heirs built a massive evangelical movement that, by the last quarter of that century, had captured the attention of the larger public, even if it failed to make much headway toward the recovery of the mainline denominations. Through their colleges and seminaries, publishing houses and periodicals, media empires and extensive networks, the evangelicals created a major "third force" in American life, distinguished from both a newly assertive Catholicism and the mainline Protestant denominations then in marked numerical decline.

By the 1970s, it was impossible to speak knowledgably about religion in America without acknowledging the existence and influence of the evangelicals. This did not mean, however, that observers of the movement had a clear grasp of what constituted evangelical identity.

## Evangelicalism in a Phenomenological Sense

The phenomenological definition of evangelicalism is rooted in observation. It is descriptive rather than normative. In terms of theological distinctives, David W. Bebbington has offered what must be the most widely influential summary: "There are the four qualities that have been the special marks of Evangelical religion: *conversionism*, the belief that lives need to be changed; *activism*, the expression of the gospel in effort; *biblicism*, a particular regard for the Bible; and what may be called *crucicentrism*, a stress on the sacrifice of Christ on the cross. Together they form a quadrilateral of priorities that is the basis of evangelicalism."[4]

Bebbington's "quadrilateral" has become a generally accepted description of evangelical identity, and it is hard to imagine that any individual, institution, or entity that falls short of these "qualities" could fairly be considered as evangelical. But as is so often the case with phenomenological definitions, these criteria are so vague as to be fairly useless in determining the limits of evangelical definition. Construed in such general terms, it is hard to see how many Roman Catholics and liberal Protestants would not consider themselves included. They, too, believe that lives need to be changed, hold "a particular regard for the Bible," place a stress on the sacrifice of Christ on the cross, and seek an activist demonstration of their faith.

So, even as Bebbington's descriptive argument is helpful, it hardly solves the problem of evangelical identity and definition. Similarly, a lack of precise definition is evident within the public mind. The national media, for example, seems to use the term *evangelical* to refer to anyone associated with Christianity who is neither a theological liberal or a Roman Catholic. Nevertheless, even this cannot be counted on. In 2005

---

4. David W. Bebbington, *Evangelicalism in Modern Britain: A History from the 1730s to the 1980s* (London: Routledge, 1989), 2–3.

*TIME* magazine published a cover story and photo essay with a list of the twenty-five "most influential evangelicals in America," and the list included two Roman Catholics.[5]

## Evangelicalism in a Normative Sense

A phenomenological definition of evangelicalism turns out to serve a necessary but quite limited purpose. It points toward the definition of what an evangelical believes, but only in the most general of theological terms. It utterly fails to identify in any helpful sense who is *not* an evangelical.

Such confusion abounds. During the heyday of Protestant liberalism, figures such as Harry Emerson Fosdick, a paradigmatic theological liberal, continued to claim to be evangelical and refused to surrender the word. He was hardly alone. In more recent times, individuals who hold to theological positions hardly distinguishable from Protestant liberalism — even those theological positions explicitly named by the founding fathers of the movement as positions to be excluded — claim evangelical identity.

Part of the problem is the absence of a credentializing authority. Roman Catholicism is defined by the magisterium of the Roman Catholic Church. If you want an authoritative definition of Catholic identity, ask the Vatican. But evangelicalism has no magisterium, no pope, and no Vatican. Evangelical definition is dependent on a continual conversation and debate among evangelicals, association with evangelical institutions or churches, and identification with core evangelical beliefs.

As the current and continuing confusion makes clear, this is not enough. A merely descriptive definition of evangelical identity cannot provide an adequate foundation for evangelical coherence or credibility. The integrity of evangelicalism requires a normative definition of evangelical identity. Such a definition will be informed by the historical understanding and shaped by the descriptive approach, but it cannot stop with these.

To that end, evangelicalism refers to that movement of Christian believers who seek a conscious convictional continuity with the theolog-

---

5. "The 25 Most Influential Evangelicals in America," *TIME* (June 30, 2005), http://www.time.com/time/covers/1101050207/photoessay/. The Roman Catholics were the late Richard John Neuhaus and former senator Rick Santorum.

ical formulas of the Protestant Reformation. In so doing, these believers, like the Reformers, seek also to embrace the faith "once for all delivered to the saints" and cherished by the faithful throughout the centuries. With the Reformers, this movement of believers seeks conscious convictional continuity with the apostles. Confessing this faith, evangelicals embrace and affirm the historic creeds of the Reformation churches in their respective communions, even as they seek to engage the larger world of life and thought with a reason for the hope that is in them.

Thus, evangelicalism is a movement of confessional believers who are determined by God's grace to conserve this faith in the face of its reduction or corruption, even as they gladly take this gospel to the ends of the earth in order to see the nations exult in the name of Jesus Christ.

This movement of believers does indeed hold, as David Bebbington suggests, to "a particular regard for the Bible," "a stress on the sacrifice of Christ on the cross," an activist faith, and the need for individual conversion. But each of these requires much more elaboration and definition, or else the term *evangelical* will die the death of a thousand equivocations. It is to that larger task that I now turn.

## Evangelicalism: Both Centered and Bounded

In the quest for evangelical identity, some have turned to mathematical set theory in order to borrow from that field a conceptual understanding that might offer assistance. As variously construed, sets are defined as bounded, centered, and center-bounded. Some in the field of mathematics also employ the notion of a "fuzzy" or ambiguous set.

### Bounded Set

As applied to the question of evangelical identity, the bounded set would be defined more clearly and forcefully by accepting agreed-on boundaries. This type of set is defined in terms of the lines dividing insiders from outsiders — those who belong inside the set as defined by its boundaries and those who do not belong.

The application of this model of set to the question of evangelical identity points most clearly to the structures of American fundamentalism. That movement is most classically defined by its attention to boundary beliefs and maintaining clearly defined borders between acceptable and unacceptable forms of belief.

## Centered Set

The centered set, on the other hand, applies most clearly to the evangelical Left—to reformist and revisionist models of evangelical identity. These forces within the movement have argued that evangelical identity is not found in defined theological and doctrinal boundaries, but in common commitments to the center of evangelical faith, theology, and experience. This set is defined by attraction to the center, not by concern for a boundary.

## Center-Bounded Set

Of course, most sets are defined by both a center and a definable or discernible boundary. While evangelicals are first and foremost defined by love for Christ and enthusiasm for the gospel, there is no question that conscious and deliberate attention to the boundary of acceptable belief is also necessary. A singular obsession with the establishment and maintenance of boundary beliefs would produce a sterile and lifeless faith—orthodox but spiritually powerless. On the other hand, the center must itself be defined, and the moment the center is defined, boundaries necessarily appear.

Just consider the affirmations that Jesus Christ is Lord and that Jesus saves. These, along with other essential affirmations of biblical Christianity, form the center. But these twin affirmations are not mere slogans or evangelical mottos—they are theological declarations that require definition lest they become mere tropes or statements of emotional import.

Seen in this light, set theory is indeed useful as we seek to understand evangelical identity, but we must be careful that we do not misrepresent rival models of evangelical understanding by reducing the question to three types of sets. Fundamentalists have gained their name by a public preoccupation with the policing of doctrinal boundaries, but it would be slander to suggest that fundamentalist Christians placed their faith and hope in these boundaries or trusted them for their salvation. They loved Christ and believed the gospel. Convinced and alarmed that the very gospel by which they had been saved was being subverted by modernist theological concession and doctrinal subterfuge, the fundamentalists felt that they had no choice but to rally the troops and issue a battle cry to establish a catalog of doctrines integral to true Christianity.

On the other hand, the evangelical revisionists, repulsed and embarrassed by the boundary preoccupations of the fundamentalists, sought to define evangelicalism in terms of shared beliefs at the center. Without doubt, some of the boundary preoccupations of the fundamentalists were eccentric and hard to justify. Eschatological timetables and the doctrine of second-degree separation are but examples of how the fundamentalist movement invested an undue priority and almost creedal authority in the wrong affirmations.

Yet the larger problem, the more pressing urgency, lies in the failure of the revisionist evangelicals to adequately define the movement and its core theological affirmations. To the contrary, in many cases the doctrinal boundaries that these figures oppose are those that evangelicals have long considered to be central rather than peripheral. In truth, the doctrinal formulations and theological trajectories championed by many in this camp resemble nothing as closely as the Protestant liberalism against which the early evangelicals defined evangelical identity.

By now it should be clear that I will argue for a model of evangelical identity that directs constant attention to both the center and the boundary. I do not believe that we can have one without the other. If evangelical is to mean anything coherent, it must refer to Christians who are first marked by their devotion to Christ and the gospel, but who are also constantly aware of the need to be specific about who Christ is, what the gospel is, and on what authority we can even claim to know these truths.

Attention to the boundary is not a matter of mere doctrinal policing. It is necessary for our faith to resemble and represent what the Bible reveals. Attention to the boundary lines is essential lest the evangelical movement forfeit its responsibility to make our own confession of Christ clear.

## Theological Triage

For some years now I have been arguing for another conceptual model of understanding our theological responsibility and the task of defining which doctrines are central and essential to our faith. I discovered this model in a hospital emergency room, where medical personnel have to make decisions very similar to those we face in the theological task.

Emergency medical personnel practice a discipline known as triage — a process that allows trained personnel to quickly evaluate relative medical urgency. Given the chaos of an emergency room reception area, someone must be armed with the medical expertise to make an immediate determination of medical priority. Which patients should be rushed into surgery? Which patients can wait for a less urgent examination? Medical personnel cannot flinch from asking these questions and taking responsibility to treat the patients with the most critical needs, since those patients are the top priority.

The word *triage* comes from the French word *trier*, which means "to sort." Thus, the triage officer in the medical context is the frontline agent for deciding which patients need the most urgent treatment. Without such a process, medical personnel would treat a scraped knee and a gunshot wound to the chest with the same urgency. The same discipline that brings order to the hectic arena of the emergency room can also greatly assist Christians in defining the faith in the present age.

A discipline of theological triage would require Christians to determine a scale of theological urgency that would correspond to the medical world's framework for medical priority. With this in mind, I suggest three different levels of theological urgency, each corresponding to a set of issues and theological priorities found in current doctrinal debates.

## First-Level Doctrines

First-level theological issues are most central and essential to the Christian faith. These include the Trinity, the full deity and humanity of Jesus Christ, justification by faith alone, and the authority of Scripture.

In the earliest centuries of the Christian movement, heretics directed their most dangerous attacks on the church's understanding of who Jesus is and in what sense he is the very Son of God. Other crucial debates concerned the question of how the Son is related to the Father and the Holy Spirit. The earliest creeds and councils of the church were, in essence, emergency measures taken to protect the central core of Christian doctrine. Historic turning points, such as the councils at Nicaea, Constantinople, and Chalcedon, vindicated orthodoxy and condemned heresy—and these councils dealt with doctrines of unquestionable first-order importance. Christianity stands or falls on the affirmation that Jesus Christ is fully man and fully God.

The church quickly moved to affirm that the full deity and full humanity of Jesus Christ are absolutely necessary to the Christian faith. Any denial of what has become known as Nicaean-Chalcedonian Christology is, by definition, condemned as a heresy. The essential truths of the incarnation include the death, burial, and bodily resurrection of the Lord Jesus Christ. Those who deny these revealed truths are, by definition, not Christians.

The same is true with the doctrine of the Trinity. The early church clarified and codified its understanding of the one true and living God by affirming the full deity of the Father, Son, and Holy Spirit—while insisting that the Bible reveals one God in three persons.

In addition to the christological and Trinitarian doctrines, the doctrine of justification by faith alone must also be included among these first-order truths. Without this doctrine, we are left with a denial of the gospel itself, and salvation is transformed into some structure of human righteousness. The truthfulness and authority of the Holy Scriptures must also rank as a first-order doctrine, for without affirming the Bible as the very Word of God, we are left without any adequate authority for distinguishing truth from error.

These first-order doctrines represent the most fundamental truths of the Christian faith. Denying these doctrines represents nothing less than eventually denying Christianity itself.

## Second-Level Doctrines

What distinguishes first-level and second-level doctrines is that evangelicals may disagree on the second-order issues, though this disagreement creates significant boundaries between believers. These boundaries become evident when Christians organize themselves into congregations and denominational forms.

Second-order issues include the meaning and mode of baptism. Baptists and Presbyterians, for example, fervently disagree over the most basic understanding of Christian baptism. The practice of infant baptism is inconceivable to the Baptist mind, while Presbyterians trace infant baptism to their most basic understanding of the covenant. Standing together on the first-order doctrines of evangelical faith, Baptists and Presbyterians eagerly recognize each other as believing Christians and authentic evangelicals but recognize that disagreeing on issues of this importance prevents fellowship within the same congregation or denomination. There are any number of issues that are properly seen in this light—whenever disagreement does not imply a denial or subversion of the gospel. No one should deny that those who stand together on the core evangelical affirmations are truly evangelical.

### Third-Level Doctrines

Third-order issues are doctrines over which evangelicals may disagree and yet remain in close fellowship, even within local congregations. I would put most of the debates over eschatology, for example, in this category. Christians who affirm the bodily, historical, and victorious return of the Lord Jesus Christ may differ over timetable and sequence without rupturing the fellowship of the church or the integrity of the evangelical movement. Christians may disagree over any number of issues related to interpreting difficult texts. Nevertheless, standing together on issues of more urgent importance, evangelicals should be able to accept one another without compromise when third-order issues are in question.

In this light, the goal of applying a discipline like theological triage would be to avoid doctrinal collapse in terms of first-order doctrines, on the one hand, and doctrinal preoccupation and schism over third-order doctrines, on the other. In this model, we expect debates over the second-order issues to be the most difficult in terms of definition and identity. Placed alongside set theory, exercising theological triage supports evangelicalism as a center-bounded set. Some theological divergences and debates are possible within the circle of evangelical identity. Others are clearly outside that circle.

## My Evangelical Pilgrimage in the Southern Baptist Convention

My own evangelical pilgrimage reflects a continual struggle with these questions. I was raised in a home and church environment that can be described only as classically evangelical, though I cannot remember ever hearing of that term when I was young. I grew up within the Southern Baptist Convention (SBC), a denomination of churches that is at the center of the evangelical movement in one sense but marginal in another sense. In terms of piety, beliefs, and program, the SBC appears almost quintessentially evangelical. Nevertheless, organizationally the SBC remained detached from the developing evangelical infrastructure. The SBC never joined the National Association of Evangelicals, despite repeated overtures. Throughout much of the twentieth century, Southern Baptists were reluctant to describe themselves as evangelicals because they considered that movement to be organizationally concentrated in the North.

In my teenage years, I experienced a sense of theological crisis. I made a public profession of faith in the Lord Jesus Christ at age nine, but in the context of intellectual foment during my high school years, I encountered serious objections to Christianity that required a substantial apologetic response. Guided by kind figures who counseled me during these years, I was directed to theological resources that emerged from those who were explicitly identified as evangelical. Most significantly, I was rescued by the writings of figures such as Francis Schaeffer and a host of authors who were clearly identified as evangelicals teaching largely within evangelical institutions. At a very strategic point in my life, I discovered that I was, indeed, an evangelical.

Though I remained then, and now, fully committed to Baptist theology, I found myself at home within the universe of American evangelicalism—nourished by its thinkers, energized by its passions, and at home in its convictions. I went to college thoroughly convinced that I was both a Southern Baptist and an evangelical and that there was no inherent contradiction or conflict in this dual identity.

My graduation from college and arrival at the Southern Baptist Theological Seminary for theological education coincided with the advent of controversy within the SBC. That controversy, later known as the conservative resurgence within the convention, represented a massive reversal of denominational direction and a recovery of a clear confessional identity within the life of the denomination. Though many theological issues were important to the debate, the issue of biblical inerrancy was front and center.

In itself, the issue of biblical inerrancy reveals the essential evangelical identity of the SBC. At the same time, the SBC had operated in a largely insular environment, and it lacked internal resources to deal adequately with the theological challenge of the inerrancy controversy.

As a seminarian, I quickly discerned that the needed resources were found within the larger evangelical movement—a movement that had been dealing with controversies and debates over biblical inerrancy long before the issue erupted within the SBC. As the inerrancy controversy dominated the SBC in the 1980s, Southern Baptists turned naturally and eagerly to the larger evangelical context, looking for and finding theological resources that were necessary to define and defend the inerrancy of Scripture.

In seeking to understand the Southern Baptist conflict, I recognized that Southern Baptists were divided into two polarized parties defined by their opposing positions on biblical inerrancy. I could clearly see, even at that time, that the fundamental dynamic driving each of these two parties was dissimilar on grounds that were far more basic than a single doctrinal controversy. I saw that Southern Baptists were divided between a truth party that defined Baptist identity first and foremost in terms of shared theological convictions and a libertarian faction that defined Baptist identity in terms of certain freedoms that included a freedom *from* creeds and confessional statements.

I soon discovered that a very similar dynamic operated within the world of American evangelicalism. Throughout the 1970s, 1980s, and well into the 1990s, American evangelicals were divided into parties that appeared to be incredibly, and not accidentally, similar to those so easily identified within the Southern Baptist conflict. The truth party sought to locate evangelical identity in a doctrinal consensus that the creeds and confessions of the Reformation explicitly established and in a common effort to define and defend the faith in the face of modern challenges. As in the SBC, a more libertarian party sought to define itself in terms of freedom from doctrinal and creedal constraints.

Then, as now, the situations within the SBC and the larger evangelical movement appeared not only as parallels, but also as repetitions of the same theological conflicts. I became convinced that only a conscious and wholehearted embrace of biblical doctrine could establish an adequate foundation for evangelical identity. In other words, it became apparent to me that the integrity of evangelical witness required careful and faithful attention to both the center and the boundaries of evangelical conviction.

## Evangelical Solidarity and Recent Tensions

An ethos of cooperation across denominational lines was central to the evangelical movement in its inception. The new evangelicals who appeared on the scene after World War II represented diverse denominational identities and institutions. Those early evangelicals needed to cooperate and create what they called "a united evangelical front," partly because more liberal leaders within the established churches and denominations largely marginalized conservatives. Evangelicals had a constellation of Bible colleges, publishing houses, evangelistic organizations, and various institutions, but they did not control the massive denominational bureaucracies that more liberal leadership had taken over decades before. Thus, leaders such as Carl F. H. Henry and Harold John Ockenga set out to establish an evangelical platform that minimized denominational differences — those pesky second-order doctrines — and established a common ground based in a primary identification as evangelical and only a secondary identification with a denomination.

That dynamic was one of the central reasons the SBC did not join the evangelical movement in any institutional sense during those years. Creating a common evangelical platform helped create a movement larger than would have been possible within any of the denominations alone. But the movement had to minimize denominational distinctives in order to maintain institutional solidarity.

Evangelicals who could trace their roots directly to the Reformation dominated the evangelical movement of the mid-twentieth century. At the same time, evangelicals drawn from Bible churches and denominations such as the Evangelical Free Church joined the Presbyterians and Baptists. A look at issues from the early years of *Christianity Today*, for example, reveals a good representation of leaders from those denominations and traditions along with Lutherans and Methodists. At another level, the evangelical movement was diverse because it included conservatives who remained within the established mainline denominations — often working with renewal movements — and those who were in evangelical denominations or no denomination at all.

A new dynamic emerged in the last half of the twentieth century as the charismatic and Pentecostal movements also began to participate in the larger evangelical world. By the end of the century, observers would often describe the evangelical movement in terms of Reformed, Baptist, Wesleyan, and charismatic traditions.

## Evangelicals and Catholics Together

This approach to evangelical solidarity works relatively well as long as the parties involved are drawn from clearly Protestant contexts. New tensions arose in the 1990s, most evident in controversy over a 1994 statement known as *Evangelicals and Catholics Together* (*ECT*). The background to that document was a sense of urgent concern that brought together leading figures from both evangelical and Roman Catholic ranks. Largely led by Chuck Colson and Richard John Neuhaus, the movement produced a manifesto that declared a new unity that existed between evangelicals and Roman Catholics on a host of issues.

The originating purpose behind *Evangelicals and Catholics Together* was driven by a sense of cultural and theological crisis. The massive social, cultural, and moral revolutions of the 1960s and 1970s, combined with the theological revolts that had occurred within both liberal Protestantism and the more liberal wings of Catholicism, produced an urgent climate that leaders such as Colson and Neuhaus seized on to establish a publicly declared commonality of purpose or "cobelligerency" in the light of massive new challenges. These challenges were as basic as the existence and knowability of truth and the value and sanctity of human life.

These leaders declared a new spirit of cobelligerency in the light of the "culture wars" over fundamental questions of human dignity and flourishing. In the words of Timothy George, dean of Beeson Divinity School, the new unity between evangelicals and Roman Catholics was best understood as "an ecumenism of the trenches."

More was going on here than first met the eye. Both sides were motivated by a sense of cultural and theological emergency. Both sides brought a considerable force of motivated adherents to the conflict. But the evangelicals lacked something that the Catholics had by massive weight—a long and sustained tradition of moral reasoning and teaching. Confronting a moral rebellion set loose within the culture, a joining of evangelical and Roman Catholic forces seemed only natural. At an even deeper level, these evangelicals and Catholics stood together in a defense of truth against the antirealism and postmodern relativism that threatened to subvert all claims to truth.

The problem with the ECT movement and its statements became clear in a first reading of the first document. Conservative evangelicals and conservative Roman Catholics commonly believe in doctrines as basic as the Trinity and the full deity and humanity of Christ, but the ECT document seemed to imply or to require far more — a virtual recognition in some sense of the validity of both evangelical churches and the Roman Catholic Church. How could evangelicals square this with the centrality of justification by faith alone?

Making matters even more difficult, the ECT movement later released statements on justification and Mary that pressed their ecumenical arguments even further. I could not in good conscience sign the ECT statement, nor the later statements, precisely for this reason. I am thankful for the Catholic witness to the reality of revealed truth and the sanctity of human life, but I cannot recognize the Catholic Church as a true church. I am a convictional heir of the Reformers.

Fifteen years later, I did sign the Manhattan Declaration, a statement of common concern on the issues of the sanctity of human life, the integrity of marriage, and the defense of religious liberty. I had been present in meetings leading up to the document's release, and I was thrilled with its masterful defense of those three endangered affirmations. I was moved by its affirmation that we will not bend the knee to any earthly power that calls us to deny the faith. I was instructed by the quality of the document's theological, biblical, and moral thinking.

I had great hope that the document and the movement would steer a new path that would accomplish a brave moral consensus without confusing the theological issues at stake. Nevertheless, in light of subsequent statements, I came to believe that the Manhattan Declaration had also crossed the line into an unwarranted and unbiblical recognition of the Roman Catholic Church. We should not be embarrassed to state that we stand together when indeed we do — and on these crucial issues of concern it is especially important that we stand together with courage. But no sense of cultural crisis should blind us to the priority of the gospel. The moral arguments presented in the Manhattan Declaration are eloquent and powerful statements of Christian moral conviction and discernment. The statement is a brave call for men and women of conviction to defend life, marriage, and religious liberty with courage. When it comes to evangelicals and Roman Catholics, the difficulty lies in crafting a statement that acknowledges the Christian truths that are expressed and commonly cherished without requiring a mutual recognition of churches.

## Revisionist Evangelicalism: A New Form of Protestant Liberalism

Taken together, all of these considerations point directly to the unavoidable issue of boundaries. Who is and is not an evangelical? With whom should evangelicals cooperate in gospel efforts, and with whom not? Which theological expressions are truly evangelical, and which are beyond the pale?

These questions are central to the ongoing crisis of evangelical identity. In 1989 Carl F. H. Henry spoke to the urgency of answering these questions: "The term 'evangelical' has taken on conflicting nuances in the twentieth century. Wittingly or unwittingly, evangelical constituencies, no less than their critics, have contributed to this confusion and misunderstanding. Nothing could be more timely, therefore, than to define what is primary and what is secondary in personifying an evangelical Christian."[6]

Just a year after Henry offered those words, Robert Brow called for a complete transformation of evangelical theology—and did so within the pages of *Christianity Today*, the flagship periodical once edited by both Carl Henry and Kenneth Kantzer. Brow's manifesto was a clarion call to abandon the Augustinian-Reformation model in favor of a new Arminian and postmodern model. Brow declared that the intellectual context of postmodernity made such an exchange necessary. He argued that doctrines such as the omnipotence, omniscience, and sovereignty of God would have to be radically reinterpreted in light of current thinking. He explicitly rejected doctrines such as the substitutionary atonement, a penal understanding of the cross, forensic justification, and imputed righteousness. With remarkable boldness, he called for the rejection of the traditional doctrine of hell, and he denied both a dual destiny after judgment and the exclusivity of the gospel. As he

---

6. Carl F. H. Henry, "Foreword," in *Evangelical Affirmations*, ed. Carl F. H. Henry and Kenneth Kantzer (Grand Rapids: Zondervan, 1990), 17.

made these demands, he informed his readers of the inevitability of an evangelical "megashift" because "a whole generation of young people has breathed this air."[7]

In short order, Brow was joined by Clark Pinnock and a corps of fellow revisionists who called for a thoroughgoing reformulation of evangelical theology from top to bottom. Pinnock would call for embracing what he called the "openness of God" — his own version of a radical reconstruction of theism. Pinnock argued that the traditional evangelical doctrine of God is overly dependent on Greek philosophy. In the style of Adolf von Harnack, Pinnock attempted what he styled as a radical de-hellenization of Christian doctrine. He explicitly denied the omniscience of God by arguing that God cannot know the future decisions of free human creatures.

With Brow, Pinnock called for the affirmation of "creative love theism" in the place of traditional theological frameworks. This new model of theism would redefine all doctrines in terms of a radical human libertarianism and a denial of any direct mode of divine sovereignty. They replaced the traditional understanding of divine sovereignty with an affirmation of divine "effectiveness" — an "ad hoc sovereignty."

Pointedly, they also rejected the exclusivity of the gospel of Christ, arguing that evangelicalism had long been captive to a "fewness doctrine" that slanders God's character. There was more, of course. They denied the ontological trinity and redefined the inspiration of the Bible in an effort to avoid inspiration being "over-supernaturalized."[8]

Similar calls were issued by Stanley Grenz, among others. Grenz called for a "postfundamentalist shift" in evangelical theology that would reconceive theology as a practical discipline rather than as a system of propositional truth. Roger Olson has encouraged the revisionists, even as he has called for forming a new center for evangelical theology.[9] More recently, leaders of the emergent church such as Brian McLaren have called for rejecting the way evangelicals (and virtually all Christians) have read the Bible's metanarrative or story line. McLaren

---

7. Robert Brow, "Evangelical Megashift," *Christianity Today* (February 19, 1990): 12–14.

8. Clark H. Pinnock, *Tracking the Maze: Finding Our Way through Modern Theology from an Evangelical Perspective* (San Francisco: Harper and Row, 1990), 175.

9. Roger E. Olson, "The Future of Evangelical Theology," *Christianity Today* (February 9, 1998): 40–48.

does not want to modify the traditional rendering of the story line of creation-fall-redemption-new creation. He demands that we replace it after "calling the entire scheme into question."[10]

McLaren does indeed call the entire structure of Christian theology into question, and he eventually dismisses belief in virtually all of the major doctrines of classical Christianity. He reduces the Bible to a "library" of human documents in which we can seek wisdom, and he dismisses the entire account of the salvation of sinners through the atonement accomplished by the Lord Jesus Christ as an erroneous reading of the biblical tradition.

It is by now apparent that the reformist evangelicals are not actually calling for a reformation of evangelicalism as a movement of conscious continuity with the classical Christian tradition. At least some of them are calling for the abandonment of the very theological foundations on which the evangelical tradition was established.

The old "two-party" system of American Protestantism recognized the polarities of Protestant liberalism on one end and evangelicalism at the other end. In terms of the larger culture, little distinction was made between evangelicalism and fundamentalism within the conservative party of Protestantism. The early evangelicals did not seek to abandon the classical Protestant paradigm, and they made this abundantly clear in almost every way imaginable. They rejected the limited theological preoccupations of some fundamentalists, their withdrawal from theological and intellectual engagement, and the development of battle lines over secondary and tertiary issues.

But the founders of the evangelical movement sought only to defend the crucial doctrines of biblical inerrancy and infallibility, the plenary verbal inspiration of the Scriptures, the Nicaean and Chalcedonian consensus on Christology, the substitutionary character of Christ's atonement, and the entire structure of the classical Christian tradition. They saw themselves as protecting this doctrinal inheritance from marginalization on the right and from accommodation on the left. They feared that fundamentalism was fighting over many of the wrong issues even as the liberals were tearing down the house.

---

10. Brian D. McLaren, *A New Kind of Christianity: Ten Questions That Are Transforming the Faith* (New York: HarperOne, 2010), 35.

The emergence of revisionist or reformist evangelicals raises all the questions of evangelical identity anew. Put bluntly, their proposals amount to what can be described only as a new form of Protestant liberalism. Their proposals, though informed by various intellectual movements that emerged in recent decades, are really quite at home within the world of Protestant liberalism that the early evangelicals explicitly rejected as subevangelical.

The early evangelicals painfully and courageously left the mainline denominations and their institutions precisely because those churches and denominations had been lost to liberalism. They left positions, pulpits, and pensions behind as they did what they believed fidelity to Christ and the substance of biblical Christianity required. Now all that the early evangelicals sought to defend is under sustained subversion from within the movement they gave their lives to build.

A strange new ground has appeared on the theological landscape. A postliberal movement has emerged from within Protestant liberalism, influenced by postfoundationalist thought and elements of postmodernism. Leading figures such as George Lindbeck and Colin Gunton are clearly distinct from the older liberal models they dismiss as hopelessly mired in modernism, but they are not seeking to return to what theologian Edward Farley has called the old "House of Authority."[11] At the same time, the same intellectual currents have deeply influenced many of the revisionist evangelicals. Moving from the right, these reformist evangelicals now meet the postliberals in something of a new third way in Protestant theology.

# Contested Questions

Clearly, there are crucial issues on which the question of evangelical identity will be determined. These include, but are by no means limited to, the trustworthiness of the Bible, the exclusivity of the gospel, the integrity of theism, and the nature of justification and the atonement.

## The Trustworthiness and Truthfulness of Scripture

Debates over the nature and authority of Scripture have roiled the waters of the Christian world for centuries. The Reformation formula

---

11. Edward Farley, *Ecclesial Reflection: Anatomy of Theological Method* (Philadelphia: Fortress, 1982).

of *sola scriptura* was not born out of a theological symposium, but in the crucible of the life-or-death effort to determine authentic Christianity from its counterfeits. In more recent times, the emergence of higher-critical views of Scripture came with the rise of modern consciousness. The dividing line between Protestant liberals and evangelicals came at this very point. The conservatives rejected the accommodation of the doctrine of Scripture to the norms of secular thought.

Revisionist evangelicals have argued that the doctrine of the Bible's inerrancy can or should be abandoned in light of modern challenges or postmodern structures of thought. Heated and costly battles over biblical inerrancy marked evangelicalism in the 1970s and thereafter. The strident warning issued in the 1970s by Harold Lindsell, a former editor of *Christianity Today*, in *The Battle for the Bible* presaged the battle lines that continue today.[12] Though Lindsell was often criticized as alarmist at the time, developments within the evangelical world vindicated his warnings in short order.

In the late 1970s, a significant movement to define and defend biblical inerrancy appeared in the form of the International Council on Biblical Inerrancy. In 1978 the group adopted the Chicago Statement on Biblical Inerrancy and presented it to the evangelical movement as an attempt to reestablish the evangelical consensus on the high ground of the Bible's total truthfulness and trustworthiness.

But challenges to biblical inerrancy have continued, even as some evangelical seminaries and colleges explicitly revised statements of faith and hiring guidelines to accommodate noninerrantists. A recent call for abandoning the claim of the Bible's inerrancy has come from Kenton L. Sparks of Eastern University, who argues that this claim has led evangelicalism into an "intellectual cul-de-sac" and has been an "intellectual disaster."[13]

What becomes clear, however, is that abandoning biblical inerrancy requires some new model for understanding the Bible's truthfulness and the nature of its inspiration, and that new model accommodates to some degree the secular assumptions of the Bible as a human artifact marked by the frailties of human finitude.

---

12. Harold Lindsell, *The Battle for the Bible* (Grand Rapids: Zondervan, 1978).

13. Kenton L. Sparks, *God's Word in Human Words: An Evangelical Appropriation of Critical Biblical Scholarship* (Grand Rapids: Baker, 2008). See also http://biologos.org/blog/after-inerrancy-evangelicals-and-the-bible-in-a-postmodern-age-part-1/.

Evangelical leaders such as Carl F. H. Henry vigorously sought to defend biblical inerrancy while preventing evangelical fratricide. In Henry's formulation, inerrancy should be considered a measure of evangelical consistency rather than evangelical authenticity. But the trajectory of the debate quickly revealed that abandoning inerrancy and a verbal model of the Bible's inspiration required adopting some other model that could not undergird evangelical authenticity.

Affirming the total truthfulness, trustworthiness, and authority of the Bible is a first-order theological issue. Without an unqualified confidence in the Bible as the revealed Word of God, we are left without any means of knowing what the gospel is and what we are to believe and to teach. And without affirming biblical inerrancy, we are left without any adequate way of expressing our confidence in the Bible's truthfulness and trustworthiness.

## The Exclusivity of the Gospel

The question of the exclusivity of the gospel of Jesus Christ arises within the New Testament itself, and necessarily so. The declaration that salvation is found in the name of Jesus, and in no other name, is central to the faith of the church. Paul's teaching that "faith comes from hearing, and hearing through the word of Christ" (Rom. 10:17 ESV) drives the theology and urgency of Christian missions and evangelism.

Protestant liberalism was marked by a rejection of the gospel's exclusivity and by the growing affirmation of redemptive revelation within other world religions. By the midpoint of the twentieth century, mainline Protestantism was headed into a self-declared moratorium on conversionist missions and evangelism. The evangelicals, on the other hand, were steadfastly convinced that salvation is to be found only through the gospel of Christ. The contrast between the moratorium of conversionist missions within mainline Protestantism and the energetic and ambitious conversionist impulses of the evangelical movement was apparent to any observer, made clear in global events such as the World Congress on Evangelism held in Berlin in 1966 and the Lausanne Congress on World Evangelism held in 1974. *The Lausanne Covenant* adopted at that congress stated, "We affirm that there is only one Saviour and only one gospel, although there is a wide diversity of evangelistic approaches. We recognise that everyone has some knowledge of God through his general revelation in nature. But we deny that this can save, for people suppress the truth by their unrighteousness."[14]

Revisionist and reformist evangelicals have rejected this exclusivity. Most have argued for adopting some form of inclusionism, whereby Christ appears and functions salvifically in some way through non-Christian revelation. Some, however, argue for what can be described only as forms of universalism.

The gospel of Jesus Christ is a first-order theological issue, and affirming that gospel requires explicitly acknowledging that, as *The Lausanne Covenant* states, "there is only one Saviour and only one gospel."

## The Integrity of Theism

At the heart of Christianity lies a distinctive theism, and that understanding is irreducibly Trinitarian and necessarily bold. This theism must affirm how God has revealed himself to be and to act in the Bible. In recent years, some revisionist evangelicals have called for reformulating theism, arguing that the classical Christian tradition overly depends on Greek modes of thought.

Specifically, some have denied God's exhaustive foreknowledge. In the name of "creative love theism" and the "openness of God," proponents of open theism have argued that God simply cannot know what cannot be known, and this includes the future decisions of his free creatures.

Of course, open theism also requires embracing contingency within the understanding of God's means and mode of relating to his creation. So it is not only the future decisions of humans that cannot be known, but the contingencies of the cosmos that are both related and unrelated to those decisions.

The motivations behind open theism are explicit. This proposal emerges from the intersection of desires to resolve difficult questions of theodicy and affirm a radical model of human libertarian freedom. The concern for theodicy is clear in the claim of proponents of open theism that their rendering of God's limited foreknowledge frees him from direct responsibility for tragic events, both in the natural world

---

14. The Lausanne Covenant, adopted 1974, http://www.lausanne.org/covenant.

and in the realm of human action. But the theological cost of such a reformulation is disastrous to biblical Christianity. Open theism flies in the face of the Bible's repeated claim that God does indeed know what the open theists claim that he cannot know: the future decisions of his human creatures. Open theism is rooted in a radical claim of human libertarian freedom, namely, that humans cannot be truly free if their decisions are perfectly known by God in advance and thus fixed by that perfect knowledge.

Unsurprisingly, open theism has emerged from within the Arminian wing of evangelicalism. Yet classical Arminians, as did Arminius himself, explicitly affirm God's perfect and exhaustive foreknowledge.

Biblical theism requires that we affirm that God is "infinite in all his perfections," as the creedal consensus has affirmed. This is a first-order theological issue.

## The Nature of Justification and the Atonement

Recent debates over the nature of justification have emerged in many quarters, from the movement known as the Federal Vision to the influential work of Anglican theologian and biblical scholar N. T. Wright. Proponents of these arguments assert that forensic notions of justification that were themselves grounded in a misreading of Judaism in the first century misdirected the Protestant tradition. But this argument strikes at the heart of what was nothing less than the central concern of the Protestant Reformers—just how is it that a sinner can be declared to be justified before a holy God?

Justification by faith *alone* is an evangelical essential, a first-order issue. Those who set themselves against this doctrine set themselves against the central thrust of the Reformation. While they are certainly free to make their arguments, it is difficult to see how they can make them from within the house that the Reformation built. If evangelical means anything, it means a bold assertion that sinners are justified only on the basis of what the Reformers called an alien righteousness—the righteousness of Christ imputed to all who believe in him.

The substitutionary character of the atonement of Christ has also been a primary focus of the revisionists, who call for abandoning substitution as a category, primarily on moral grounds. The debate over the substitutionary character of Christ's atonement for sin cannot be severed from the efforts to revise the doctrine of justification. In this case, those who contend for abandoning substitution as a category argue, in the main, that the assertion that God demanded the blood sacrifice of his Son to satisfy his divine wrath and display his righteousness is a slander against God's own character. The implication and outright claim is that such a rendering of God is immoral. Some have gone so far as to claim that a substitutionary rendering of the atonement amounts to a form of divine child abuse.

While the Bible reveals the atonement of Christ in many dimensions and models for our understanding, substitution stands at the heart of the Bible's revelation of the cross and its meaning. Once again, we face the fact that the Bible clearly reveals the reality that Christ is our substitute and that God required the cross precisely in order to display his own righteousness (Rom. 3:21–26). Furthermore, the calls for reformulating the doctrine of atonement rarely stop even with this. In most cases, the proposal amounts once again to what Protestant liberalism argued earlier. The doctrine of substitutionary atonement lies at the heart of the gospel, and the gospel is a first-order issue.

## Conclusion: Confessing, Conserving, and Cherishing the Faith

The future of evangelicalism is not a theoretical question. It will be hammered out in very real debates over unavoidable questions of evangelical belief and evangelical identity. The cultural and intellectual pressures experienced by evangelicals in late modernity are powerful and seductive. Over two decades ago, sociologist James D. Hunter warned that a generation of younger evangelicals was marked by a pattern of "cognitive bargaining" in which theological claims were up for varying degrees of negotiation. Central to his assessment was the diminishing confidence in the exclusivity of the gospel even then measurable among evangelical college students. Those college students are now old enough to be the parents of today's college students, who face even stronger pressures to accommodate the secular mind. As Christian Smith and his team of researchers have revealed, today's evangelical youth and emerging adults are marked, rather overwhelmingly, by a theological posture defined by the researchers as "moralistic therapeutic deism" — a religious mode that is, if anything, only vaguely Christian.

In rather short order, evangelicals will be tested and perhaps divided over debates about the social character of the gospel and the demands of justice and over questions such as the moral status of same-sex relationships and marriage. Behind all of these debates will be more fundamental issues such as the nature of the gospel and the authority of Scripture.

All of this points to the fact that evangelicalism must be seen as both a centered and a bounded set. The center of evangelical faith is devotion to Christ and joyful confidence in the gospel. These are and must be the animating energies and passions of evangelicals as individual believers and churches, as well as the evangelical movement as a whole. But evangelicalism is coherent as a movement only if it is also known for what it is not. Attention to the boundaries is as requisite as devotion to the center.

David Bebbington's quadrilateral of conversionism, activism, biblicism, and crucicentrism points to the center of evangelical faith. But these cannot be left defined in terms as general as "a particular regard for the Bible" and "a stress on the sacrifice of Christ on the cross." Left in these general terms, we know something of what an evangelical believes, but hardly enough to know who then is not an evangelical. Such a definition would surely include a large percentage of Roman Catholics and some who would openly associate with Protestant liberalism. Mormons claim to believe in the necessity of conversion, faithful activism, "a particular regard for the Bible," and "a stress on the sacrifice of Christ on the cross." Much greater specificity is needed, or the term *evangelical* becomes useless — even dangerous.

Roger Olson has proposed that evangelicals are those who affirm the trustworthiness of Scripture, the deity of Christ, and the necessity of grace for salvation.[15] But while these three principles are well stated as beliefs central to evangelical faith, they are hardly unique to evangelicals when left in this generalized form.

The center, rightly understood, defines the boundary. The boundary does not exist for its own sake, but as the necessary correlate to the center. Any coherent group or movement is known for what it is not, even as its central passions define what it is.

---

15. Roger E. Olson, "The Future of Evangelical Theology," *Christianity Today* (February 9, 1998), 47.

Evangelical identity is, in the end, a matter of evangelical integrity. Our passion and joy are to proclaim the gospel of Jesus Christ, for we are above all a gospel people. But as was true of the apostles — the first ambassadors of the gospel — our task is to be clear about what the gospel is and is not. Far more than the question of evangelical identity rides on that task.

We must develop the skill of discerning different levels of theological issues in order that we not divide over the wrong issues and betray the gospel. But when the issues are of the first order, we must be clear and determined lest we lose the gospel.

## KEVIN T. BAUDER

Perhaps I should begin my response to Al Mohler with a word of condolence and commiseration. Some of Al's opponents would rather dismiss him than respond to his arguments, and one of their favorite tactics is to accuse him of being a virtual (or actual!) fundamentalist. As a term of theological opprobrium, *fundamentalist* is about as bad as it gets. Al is naturally eager to distance himself from the caricatures that the term evokes. Aren't we all?

Nevertheless, I have two reasons for not teaching Al the secret fundamentalist handshake. The first is that he is doing a good work, and that work would be hindered if I were to lend credibility to the accusation that he is a fundamentalist. The second and more important reason is that Al is really not a fundamentalist in the proper sense of the term. Genuine differences remain between historic fundamentalism and his version of confessional evangelicalism. The format of this book obligates me to point out some of those differences (after all, who would buy the book if we simply congratulated ourselves on our agreement?).

They are not exactly the differences that Al and others seem to suppose. As is well known, the fragmentation of modern evangelicalism began when the neo-evangelicals broke with fundamentalism during and after World War II. The stated reasons for the divide, as they are given by evangelicals, are typically the ones that Al lists. These include (as he puts it) "anti-intellectualism, lack of serious theological engagement, a withdrawal from social responsibility, and an eccentric list of theological preoccupations."

In my opinion, the split between neo-evangelicals and fundamentalists was only marginally about these matters (e.g., if the neo-evangelicals objected to anti-intellectualism, then why did they court First-Wave Pentecostals?). The rupture was primarily over a different question: whether the gospel should be recognized as the boundary of

Christian fellowship. Fundamentalists insisted that no Christian fellowship could exist with those who denied the gospel. Neo-evangelicals suggested that it could and should, at least under some circumstances.

Some of the most pointed criticisms of the new evangelicalism came from evangelicals who were not fundamentalists. For example, Cornelius Van Til produced a seventy-six-page paper that sharply criticized neo-evangelicalism.[16] This paper is especially interesting in view of the fact that a few years earlier, Van Til had been cited along with several neo-evangelical theologians in a pivotal article on how evangelical theology was changing.[17]

For Van Til, neither fundamentalism nor neo-evangelicalism had the answer. He was not alone in this opinion. In a recent history of Dallas Theological Seminary, John D. Hannah shows how John Walvoord steered that institution down a middle way between neo-evangelicalism and fundamentalism.[18] In one of his late works, Francis Schaeffer also positioned himself between a loveless fundamentalism and an evangelicalism that had disastrously surrendered truth.[19]

The Dallas Seminary of Walvoord and the Westminster Seminary of Van Til were prominent institutions. Schaeffer was one of the most successful evangelical authors of the 1970s. Voices like theirs probably represented a majority position within the evangelicalism of their generation.

In other words, more than two positions existed in the evangelicalism of the 1950s and 1960s. On the one pole was separatist fundamentalism, some representatives of which were becoming increasingly extreme. On the other pole was the new evangelicalism, the public face of which was the ecumenical evangelism of Billy Graham. In between, however, stood a very large number of evangelicals (I think a significant majority) who felt comfortable with neither extreme.

---

16. Cornelius Van Til, "The New Evangelicalism" (unpublished paper), Westminster Theological Seminary, n.d. (c. 1962).

17. "Is Evangelical Theology Changing?" *Christian Life* 17 (March 1956): 16–19.

18. John D. Hannah, *An Uncommon Union: Dallas Theological Seminary and American Evangelicalism* (Grand Rapids: Zondervan, 2009), 153–59.

19. Francis Schaeffer, *The Great Evangelical Disaster* (Wheaton: Crossway, 1984). A history of Schaeffer's relationship with fundamentalism needs to be written. He sided with Machen, then with Carl McIntire, and was apparently ridden out of fundamentalism by McIntire during the late 1940s and early 1950s. To all appearances, Schaeffer never rejected the idea of fundamentalism, even though he had been bruised badly by the institutional movement.

The difference between the three groups can be roughly characterized as follows.

- Neo-evangelicals believed that under some circumstances, some people who denied fundamentals could be recognized as Christians and should be the objects of Christian cooperation.
- Separatist fundamentalists believed that the gospel (and therefore the fundamentals) constitutes the boundary of Christian recognition and fellowship, and they were determined not to extend fellowship or recognition to anyone who denied the gospel. They saw neo-evangelicalism as a scandalous betrayal (not a denial) of the gospel, and they refused to recognize neo-evangelicals as wise or insightful Christian leaders.
- The middle group (shall we call them *confessional evangelicals*?) also rejected the ecumenism of the neo-evangelicals, but they could not bring themselves to censure or refuse cooperation with the neo-evangelicals themselves.

Envisioning evangelicalism as a three-party phenomenon goes far toward explaining the events of the 1960s through the 1980s. Fundamentalists and neo-evangelicals found themselves competing for the loyalty of the "silent majority" of evangelicalism. Neo-evangelicals emphasized evangelism, fellowship, and Christian unity, while fundamentalists focused on doctrinal purity and separation. The problem for fundamentalists, however, lay in deciding how far to take separation. They began by withdrawing all Christian recognition from apostates (whom they saw as denying the gospel). Then they withdrew public cooperation from neo-evangelicals (whom they saw as betraying the gospel). But what about confessional evangelicals?

This was the point at which fundamentalism itself began to fragment. Some adopted a binary approach to fellowship and separation. Either one was a fundamentalist (which often meant *their kind* of fundamentalist) or else one was a neo-evangelical. If one was a neo-evangelical (i.e., not the right kind of fundamentalist), then that one became an object of separation, and separation itself became absolute. While this kind of binary thinking did not characterize all fundamentalists, it was sufficiently widespread to foster a popular caricature of the movement.

The strategy was disastrous for fundamentalists. From the mid–1960s through the mid–1980s, confessional evangelicals were driven further and further from fundamentalism and into closer cooperation with neo-evangelicalism. For their part, fundamentalists became increasingly estranged from the rest of the evangelical movement. The result was the creation of a fundamentalist subculture within what was already an evangelical subculture, followed by the hardening of the fundamentalist subculture into its own ecclesiastical universe.

At the same time, alarming things were happening on the fringes of the new evangelicalism. Reports began to circulate that the inerrancy of Scripture was being questioned in some evangelical institutions. Then rumors of even worse denials began to surface. The situation came to a breaking point with what Harold Lindsell called for the "battle for the Bible" in 1976.

The International Council on Biblical Inerrancy and kindred organizations represented a coalition between confessional evangelicals and the more conservative remnant of the original neo-evangelical movement. This coalition was a kind of last, best effort to rearticulate the boundary and to exclude the new Left from the evangelical movement. The failure of that effort has led to the present uncertainty over evangelical identity.

Fundamentalists bear part of the responsibility for this uncertainty. Because they did not always adequately distinguish varieties of evangelicals and because their responses were sometimes excessive, they helped to create confusion and to poison the ecclesiastical atmosphere. Detailing those offenses is a task for a separate venue, but fundamentalists certainly did respond wrongly on some occasions; and even those who did not participate in those wrong responses nevertheless often failed to challenge those who did.

Still, fundamentalists were responding to a real problem. Either the gospel is the boundary of Christian recognition and fellowship, or it is not. If it is, then refusal to recognize that boundary constitutes, in some meaningful sense, a betrayal of the gospel. Extending Christian recognition and fellowship to people who deny the gospel is a grave matter. Yet that is what the neo-evangelicals did. Especially beginning with Billy Graham's first New York City crusade, they did it visibly and noisily.

The new evangelicalism represented the same phenomenon that J. Gresham Machen called *indifferentism.* For Machen, an indifferentist was an individual who personally believed the fundamentals of the gospel but who extended Christian recognition to others who did not. Machen's first use of the term occurred in his comments on the letters to the seven churches in Revelation: "It will be observed that the sin of the churches at Pergamum and Thyatira was not limited to those who actually accepted the Nicolaitan teaching. Even to endure the presence of the guilty sect was the object of the Lord's rebuke. Toward the works of the Nicolaitans only hatred was in place, Rev. 2.6. That is a solemn lesson for modern indifferentism."[20]

Their attitude toward indifferentists was the principal difference between fundamentalists and confessional evangelicals. Without denying that neo-evangelicals were brothers, fundamentalists saw them as indifferentists who had earned the Lord's rebuke. Confessional evangelicals were not entirely comfortable with neo-evangelicals but could not bring themselves to deliver public admonitions to them or to withdraw publicly from their programs.

For a generation or more, the litmus test of fundamentalism was whether one would cooperate with Billy Graham. This attitude was motivated, not by personal dislike of the evangelist, but by a sense of scandal over his methods. By extending Christian recognition to liberals, Catholics, and other apostates, and by sending new converts back into their churches, Graham defined himself as a quintessential indifferentist. Even today, fundamentalists are virtually united in their rejection of Graham's methods and their refusal to cooperate in them. While they admit that Graham accomplished much good by his presentation of the gospel, fundamentalists also insist that he has gained a share in the evil of the apostates whom he recognized as Christian leaders.

Some confessional evangelicals will privately agree that Graham's methods were wrong, and they also quietly decline to support Graham-style crusades. Nevertheless, they are rarely willing to offer public reproof to those who employ Graham's methods or to denounce those methods publicly. In fact, Al was willing to chair the last Billy Graham

---

20. J. Gresham Machen, *The New Testament: An Introduction to Its Literature and History*, ed. W. John Cook (Carlisle, Pa.: Banner of Truth Trust, 1976), 278. The essays in this volume were originally published as Sunday school lessons; idem, *A Rapid Survey of the Literature and History of the New Testament Times*, teacher's manuals and student textbooks, pts. 1–4, in *The Westminster Graded Lessons*, ed. John T. Faris (Philadelphia: Presbyterian Board of Publication and Sabbath School Work, 1914–15).

crusade in Louisville, and he has a Billy Graham School of Missions and Evangelism on his campus.[21]

At the time of this writing, Billy Graham has retired from public ministry, but that does not really change the question. The issue was never the person, but his practices. The issue is indifferentism. Fundamentalists reject indifferentism and refuse to recognize indifferentists as insightful Christian leaders. While not indifferentists themselves, confessional evangelicals have certainly been slower to distance themselves from indifferentism or to warn against it publicly.

Perhaps I have said enough to explain why confessional evangelicals like Al should not be accused of fundamentalism. Let me hastily add that I do not wish to minimize the areas of agreement. Mainly, both groups agree that the gospel (including the fundamentals) is the boundary of Christian faith and fellowship. In fact, confessional evangelicals have labored to implement that boundary.

Al himself has been a leader in the resurgence of conservatism in the Southern Baptist Convention, and that resurgence is all about gospel-bounded Christian fellowship. Frankly, I doubt that any of us in fundamentalism believed that conservatives could ever gain control of the convention and its institutions. Nevertheless, Al and his allies in the SBC have largely reclaimed these assets for biblical Christianity. We fundamentalists are eager to see the conservative resurgence completed, among other ways by implementing a doctrinal test that would disfellowship heterodox churches and that would bar heterodox messengers from the convention floor.[22]

---

21. Please note that I am not accusing Al of being an indifferentist or of extending Christian recognition to non-Christians. As a condition of chairing the Graham crusade, Al insisted that no theological liberals or Roman Catholics would serve in the crusade organization, be featured on the platform, or be given decision cards from the crusade. In other words, though Al agreed to chair the crusade, he succeeded in doing what fundamentalists had never managed to do, that is, to turn the Graham organization (in this instance) away from ecumenical evangelism. It is also true that, in a sense, Al inherited Billy Graham, who was already very important in the life of the Southern Baptist Theological Seminary. For Al to distance himself from Graham would be far more personal and difficult than it would be for the average fundamentalist today. Nevertheless, the choices that fundamentalists faced in the 1950s through the 1970s were just as personal and difficult, and they chose in the opposite direction. I believe that fundamentalists acted on biblical principle when they made the more difficult choice.

22. Fundamentalists have always recognized that biblical separation could (and preferably would) involve expelling non-Christians from Christian work. In principle, we have no problem with purging a Christian institution of anti-Christian leadership. Indeed, Minnesota Baptists (among whom I work) did exactly that, retaining control of the Minnesota Baptist

Incidentally, I deeply appreciate the remarks that Al has made about the Manhattan Declaration in his chapter. In my original essay, I expressed concern that his signature on that document seemed to grant some recognition to Roman Catholicism as a Christian system of teaching. His essay will go far toward allaying these concerns.

Al and I also agree on the notion of theological triage. Indeed, a legitimate fundamentalism virtually requires some calculus of doctrines and of levels of fellowship. To state that some doctrines are fundamental is automatically to recognize that others are not. If anything, many fundamentalists (including me) would want to add a few additional levels of reckoning for both doctrinal importance and for fellowship relationships.

Where we disagree is in our assessment of indifferentists. From the perspective of confessional evangelicals, it is apparently possible to be an indifferentist and still be a respected Christian leader. From the perspective of fundamentalism, to be an indifferentist is to commit one of the most serious possible errors short of outright apostasy. If we are going to do theological triage, then the error that the neo-evangelicals committed is a grave one indeed.

Many fundamentalists (and I am among them) are growing in their appreciation of the contributions that confessional evangelicals have made. We do not consider them enemies, opponents, or even mere allies, but friends. Yet differences remain between us, the largest of which is our assessment of indifferentism. What, then, should our relationship be?

My response is to repeat a comment from one of Al's friends, Baptist pastor Mark Dever. Speaking to fundamentalists, he said something like this: "There is nothing wrong with our having fences. But let us keep our fences low and shake hands often." That remark nicely summarizes the sense of a growing number of fundamentalists.

---

Convention and of an educational institution. Most of us sincerely doubted, however, that the feat could ever be repeated in an agency as unwieldy as the Southern Baptist Convention. Some of us still question whether the work can actually be completed, though we certainly wish that it might. For fundamentalists, leaving the institutions was a last resort after the attempt to expunge the anti-Christian leadership had failed. Such failures, however, became the pattern to such a great extent that recent fundamentalism has focused more on "coming out" than on "purging out."

## JOHN G. STACKHOUSE JR.

Al Mohler's essay confirms my sense that he is not only my brother in Christ, but a fellow evangelical. We evidently share many convictions and concerns. We also disagree, however, about a few things—including whether his form of evangelicalism differs significantly from that of Kevin Bauder.

Brother Al denotes his position as "confessional," not fundamentalist. But to be a "confessional" Christian, you actually have to adhere to, and draw your theological direction from, confessions. Confessional Lutherans have the Augustana and the Formula of Concord. Confessional Presbyterians have the Westminster Standards, while the Reformed have Dordt, the Belgic Confession, and the Heidelberger. In his essay, however, Brother Al quotes from no confession at all, nor does he refer to any "greats" in any tradition.

I respectfully suggest that his position is not "confessional" so much as it is "conservative," and in exactly the way American fundamentalists understand "conservative": conserving what they understand to be the basics of the Christian faith, regardless of when or by whom in church history they might have been formulated. As far as they are concerned, what they defend is simply what true Christians have always affirmed—and it comes right out of the Bible. But that's not confessionalism: that's primitivism—the same outlook that the Churches of Christ have, or the Plymouth Brethren, or the Anabaptists. And we encounter it here in a militant sort—a sort that sees "compromise" as a bad word and is quite willing instead to split congregations, agencies, schools, and denominations—and thus is fundamentalist. To say so is neither to praise nor to blame. It is simply to call things by their right names in the hopes of improving understanding.

It is thus entirely predictable that Brother Al's definition of "evangelical" is confined to three elements: information about God and a desire that other people learn that information about God, a commitment to keeping oneself pure, and a commitment to the well-being of one's local church. Those are good things to care about, of course. But where we see in his definition "a passion for the gospel of Jesus Christ," I would rather see a passion for Jesus Christ himself. Where there is an interest in declaring the gospel, I would rather see a commitment to the much more holistic, and difficult, work of making disciples (Matt. 28). "A deep commitment to biblical truth" is much narrower than a commitment to respond to the Bible in the various ways it expects us to respond as it offers us not just truth but command, promise, warning, assurance, prophecy, and more. And we see nothing at all in his definition about fervent piety beyond the vague category of holiness.

Later in the essay, Brother Al, like Brother Kevin, again focuses on doctrine as the key to Christian life: "only a conscious and wholehearted embrace of biblical doctrine could establish an adequate foundation for evangelical identity." No mention is made of liturgy, personal piety, evangelism, care for the poor, working for justice, stewarding creation, and other great concerns of Christianity. Why not?

Brother Al describes the "new evangelicals" as characterizing fundamentalism by way of "anti-intellectualism, a lack of serious theological engagement, a withdrawal from social responsibility, and an eccentric list of theological preoccupations." He's right about that, so I am particularly interested to know what he feels "social responsibility" should look like for evangelicals nowadays, since he devotes precious little time to that question. As for whether the evangelicals he represents are "anti-intellectual" and whether they engage in "serious theological engagement" would depend on whether one sees them to be undertaking fruitful theology that raises and answers important questions and coordinates those inquiries well with the best learning of other academic disciplines — or whether he and others like him instead spend their academic resources on the doctrinal barricades making sure that their version of evangelicalism is secure and that everyone is clear as to who belongs inside those barricades and who belongs outside them. And as for whether he and his sort have "eccentric" preoccupations — that is, they have driving concerns about matters not in the center of theology — one might ask about his campaign to elevate a particular view of gender to a core teaching of his own denomination.[23]

Brother Al thinks we need a much more thorough definition of evangelicalism than the historians give us, calling David Bebbington's criteria "fairly useless in determining the limits of evangelical definition." We might, however, examine those criteria as carefully as David Bebbington set them out for us—in page after page of exposition, not in a few vague phrases. We would then see immediately how Roman Catholics and liberal Protestants would not be included as, for just one example, Bebbington says that evangelicals preached justification by faith alone according to the free grace of God.[24] So I will continue to think that we can build well on Bebbington's foundation.

Brother Al is concerned to find a definition with both a center and a boundary. He never actually shows, however, what difference it would make if there were to be a borderland between evangelicalism and theological liberalism, or evangelicalism and Catholicism, or evangelicalism and fundamentalism. In fact, Brother Al seems not to understand the relationship of a center and a boundary when it comes to sets. He asserts that "the center must itself be defined, and the moment the center is defined, boundaries necessarily appear." Yes, when a set's center is defined, those who do not agree with the center are necessarily no longer members of the set. But that has nothing to do with boundaries. The notion of boundaries has to do with whether there must be sharp definition at the edges, not whether there is clear definition at the core.

Like Brother Kevin, Brother Al seems incapable of imagining Christians organizing themselves into congregations and denominations if they disagree on second-order issues. Understandably for a Baptist, he uses baptism as his example. But in my response to Brother Kevin's essay, I have suggested that it is not self-evident to everyone, at least, that baptism must be the "water that divides." Indeed, it just isn't true that "Baptists and Presbyterians ... fervently disagree over the most

---

23. My question here is not about his particular view of gender, an issue over which he and I clearly disagree, but over *any* particular view of gender being required as part of the "Baptist Faith and Message"—especially in a denomination that prizes congregational autonomy and "soul competence" as much as this one says it does.

24. David W. Bebbington, *Evangelicalism in Modern Britain: A History from the 1730s to the 1980s* (London: Unwin & Hyman, 1989), 6.

basic understanding of Christian baptism." In my view, they agree quite strongly on the most basic issues in Christian baptism: on the necessity and prevenience of God's saving grace and on our inability to save ourselves; on the requirement of faith alone in responding to God's gift of salvation; on the demand that we consciously and continually give our lives to God in daily submission and service; on baptism being the mark of initiation into the Christian community in its symbolism of dying and rising with Christ; and on and on. So why must churches divide over baptism—or many other second-order issues, for that matter?

When we move to third-order questions, having grown up in dispensationalist circles, I can understand Brother Al's impatience with certain squabbles over eschatological details. Yet eschatology itself is a crucial category for theology and ethics, to take only the question of just how "realized" is the kingdom of God in our era and how we therefore should act in the light of that eschatological understanding. Again, without a clear presentation of what is primary, secondary, and tertiary in the Christian faith and how we can arrive properly at such distinctions, believers are rather at the mercy of this or that evangelical "magisterium" to say what's what.

It's time now to take up what may seem to be incidental matters of history, but I trust the reader will see some crucial points emerge.

Brother Al represents them correctly when he says, "Southern Baptists were reluctant to describe themselves as evangelicals because they considered that movement to be organizationally concentrated in the North." But he seems quite unembarrassed that they had no interest in identification with (other) evangelicals, because that might entail them relating to, horrors, northerners. In Christ, apparently, there is neither Jew nor Greek, but there continues to be a war between the states.

I think Brother Al is wrong, however, when he claims that the new evangelical leaders strongly downplayed denominational loyalty and that this was "one of the central reasons the SBC did not join the evangelical movement in any institutional sense during those years." I believe instead that the National Association of Evangelicals simply distinguished between denominational loyalty and the political concern to form a "united evangelical front." Furthermore, it is evident instead that the SBC long championed denominational loyalty to the complete exclusion of any other association, cooperating with almost no other

*Baptist* groups, let alone groups of any other tradition. To implicitly blame the new evangelicals for the SBC's lack of cooperation strikes me as a self-justifying way to read the history.

More significantly, however, Brother Al sees the later conflict in the Southern Baptist Convention, in which he himself played a major part, as a culture war between two "polarized parties defined by their opposing positions on biblical inerrancy." Belonging as I did to a Southern Baptist church during this time, I find this to be a grossly oversimplified view of what was happening in that denomination. To say "Southern Baptists were divided between a truth party ... and a libertarian faction ... that defined Baptist identity in terms of certain freedoms that included a freedom *from* creeds and confessional statements" rather breathtakingly insults the latter group, ignoring their manifest commitment to the vast common ground between these groups on such basic matters as the lordship of Jesus Christ, faithfulness to the Southern Baptist Convention, devotion to global mission, and more. Indeed, devotion to Jesus, the SBC, and mission are what most Southern Baptists felt were the key elements of SBC identity and purpose, not one or another view of the Bible and correct theological method.

Bad enough, then, that Brother Al paints this picture of his own denomination. But he goes on to suggest a parallel among American evangelicals, and once again he is on the side of truth over against the side that wants to "define itself in terms of freedom from doctrinal and creedal constraints." Yet I don't know any evangelical theologian who sees himself or herself utterly free of doctrinal and creedal constraint. For to see oneself this way is by definition to see oneself as a theological liberal. To be sure, Brother Al says outright that those who oppose him and his party are, in fact, liberals. But, again, that's the sort of thing a fundamentalist would say: "There are only two kinds of people in the world. We stand for faithfulness to tradition; we have opponents; they therefore must feel no attachment to tradition."

The situation is actually stranger than that. Does a Baptist, or any evangelical, or even any Protestant, really want to imply that he is *constrained* in some absolute way by doctrine and creed, even if he were to believe that the Bible teaches otherwise? Surely not. And if instead he construes "constraint" less severely, as I trust Brother Al does, then how is he different in kind, not just in degree, from those he opposes, who also value tradition and dogma but do not feel (absolutely) *constrained* by them?

Despite my several differences with Brothers Al and Kevin, however, I share much of their worry about evangelical theological revisionism. Our late brothers Brow and Pinnock did tend to speak in extravagant language as they sought to emancipate evangelicals from what they believed to be stultifying conservatism and to enthuse them toward refreshing alternatives. Brothers Grenz and Olson have sometimes spoken of spiritual experience and contemporary culture in ways that make me wonder if they are giving too determinative a role for these elements in theology. I don't know Brother McLaren personally, but I'm not terribly sympathetic to his agenda of raising many more questions than he satisfactorily answers.

I differ with Kevin and Al, however, in response. Worries about liberalism are not best answered by becoming more conservative. Rather than steering left or right, I would rather we go deeper: deeper into the Christian tradition, deeper into the best deliverances of contemporary reason and experience, deeper into imagination and intuition, and deeper most of all into the Bible. The Holy Spirit speaks to us through all of these means—although I, like all evangelical Christians, give priority to the Bible and the way the Spirit particularly loves to speak in it and through it. I hope all evangelicals will go deeper into the resources God has given us so that we may avoid extremes of both left and right and explore the vast riches of God's revelation as best we can.

# A POSTCONSERVATIVE EVANGELICAL RESPONSE

ROGER E. OLSON

On at least one thing Al Mohler and I agree: "An evangelical is recognized by a passion for the gospel of Jesus Christ, by a deep commitment to biblical truth, by a sense of urgency to see lost persons hear the gospel, and by a commitment to personal holiness and the local church." Our differences begin to appear after that.

My main complaint about Mohler's account of evangelical identity is that it is too narrow. While at first seeming to limit Christian (and evangelical) essentials to the core doctrines of historical orthodoxy, he goes on to pack much more into that category, almost as much as a fundamentalist would.

If Mohler is right, Catholics cannot be Christians, let alone evangelicals. Nor can open theists or those who deny the penal substitution theory of the atonement be evangelicals. I suspect, although I may be wrong, that he thinks they cannot be Christians either. Where does this stop? It seems that Mohler wants evangelicalism, if not Christianity itself, to be a very exclusive club populated only by those who agree with him — at least with regard to whatever he says is an essential of Christian belief.

As should be obvious from my essay, I prefer a "big tent" view of evangelicalism under which people of many persuasions can gather and have fellowship and cooperate. For me, what holds them together as a relatively coherent movement is the center, and that center is stated fairly well in the quote at the beginning of this response.

Mohler seems very concerned with knowing who is "in" and who is "out" of evangelicalism. I'm not as concerned about that, although I admit at times that becomes an issue that cannot be avoided. I prefer to decide based on relationship to the center rather than based on some rigidly imposed boundaries. After all, who sets the boundaries? Mohler? He admits that evangelicalism has no magisterium and no pope. So it seems there really is no one to set the boundaries or enforce them. I don't think he quite grasps the meaning of evangelicalism as a movement. By their very nature, movements cannot have boundaries. The only thing a person is doing who insists on identifying a movement's boundaries is expressing his or her preferences and hoping others will agree.

Of course, as I argue in my chapter, history is helpful in discovering evangelical identity. We can look back across several centuries of evangelicalism and see what most evangelicals have agreed on—a sort of evangelical consensus. But one thing we notice immediately is that inerrancy, for example, is not one of those. I wonder what Mohler thinks about the great Scottish evangelical theologian James Orr (1844–1913), who explicitly denied biblical inerrancy? And yet the eminent Princeton champion of inerrancy, B. B. Warfield, embraced him as a fellow evangelical. And he was invited to contribute to the booklets *The Fundamentals* (1910–11). Also, I would ask him about the leading Nazarene theologian H. Orton Wiley (1877–1961), author of the magisterial Wesleyan three-volume systematic theology *Christian Theology* (1940). He didn't believe in inerrancy. And what about the fact that the National Association of Evangelicals statement of faith does not mention inerrancy? Or that it also doesn't mention substitutionary atonement?

If we go by history, as we really must when attempting to identify evangelicalism, many of the things Mohler wants to pack into the essentials category have been considered nonessentials by evangelicals of the past. Could it be that Mohler is simply uncomfortable with evangelical diversity and now wants to limit it by asserting a narrower definition?

Problems arise mainly when evangelicals attempt to define their movement normatively, because there really is no authority that can do that. Normativity can be recognized only historically. We can look to historians such as George Marsden (b. 1939) for help. In his groundbreaking and often considered authoritative volume *Understanding Fundamentalism and Evangelicalism*, Marsden underscores evangelical diversity (past and present) and says,

> Evangelicals might agree in a general way on the essentials of evangelicalism: "that the sole authority in religion is the Bible and the sole means of salvation is a life-transforming experience wrought by

the Holy Spirit through faith in Jesus Christ." Other than that, they represent largely independent, even if related, traditions.[25]

Is it possible that Mohler and certain other conservative evangelicals want to impose one tradition—their own—on all evangelicals? If so, their only hope is to emphatically assert that evangelicals must all agree with them and hope people believe them. But they are going against history, which highlights a greater evangelical diversity.

For Mohler and many other conservative evangelicals, the enduring essence of evangelicalism is doctrine—orthodoxy. That's one strain of evangelicalism. But there has never been unanimous agreement about exactly what doctrines or how they should be expressed. True, most, if not all, informed and studious evangelicals have affirmed the deity of Jesus Christ, the Trinity (after some fashion), the authority of the Bible, Jesus' death and resurrection as the basis of salvation, and perhaps some other beliefs. But they have interpreted these in different ways. And simply to label those who call for new interpretations "liberals" is a shortcut, if not a copout. That hardly takes seriously the arguments of people like myself, Stanley Grenz, N. T. Wright, and others who argue for revisioning doctrines in the light of fresh and faithful biblical interpretation.

What seems ironic to me is that while Mohler and other conservative evangelicals pay lip service to the sole, supreme authority of Scripture, they undermine it by elevating traditional doctrinal formulations to the status of incorrigibility. That is, they implicitly bring something like a Catholic elevation of tradition (but in this case the "received evangelical tradition") back into Protestantism. But if Scripture is supreme, then all doctrines must be judged by it, and if fresh and faithful interpretation of Scripture requires reform of doctrine, then so be it; evangelicals must be open to that.

Mohler simply dismisses open theists (among others he castigates as false evangelicals) as if they do not argue their case from Scripture. They do, and he ought to acknowledge that and meet them on that ground rather than simply wave them off as incipient liberals. Furthermore, it is wrong to say they deny God's omniscience; they do not. They interpret

---

25. George M. Marsden, *Understanding Fundamentalism and Evangelicalism* (Grand Rapids: Eerdmans, 1991), 65.

it differently. The argument is over the nature of the future, not over what God knows. Nobody thinks God knows the DNA of unicorns or that denial of that is tantamount to denying God's omniscience. Mohler and other conservative evangelical critics of open theism continue to caricature it. And to argue that open theists aren't Christians or even evangelicals just seems ludicrous to me.

I'm amazed that a person can give an account of normative evangelicalism and never mention the born-again experience. While it may have been trivialized by the media, the experience of being born again, regenerated by God's Holy Spirit, is central to the evangelical cause. At the very least, it is odd to ignore it when describing evangelical identity. Conversion-regeneration and a personal relationship with Jesus Christ (conversional piety) would seem to be more crucial to defining the evangelical ethos than doctrines. If Mohler is right, evangelicalism is compatible with a dead orthodoxy and a sterile Christian experience. Whatever happened to the "warmhearted" aspect of evangelicalism? Mohler seems to make evangelicalism mainly a matter of commitment to causes and doctrines.

My own pilgrimage in evangelicalism is different from Mohler's, which may explain some of our differences of opinion about evangelical identity. I grew up in and was spiritually nurtured by Pentecostalism and the Youth for Christ movement. (But my uncle, president of our Pentecostal denomination, was on the board of the NAE, so I knew we were most definitely evangelicals!) Together these experiences communicated to me that authentic Christianity is mainly about having a right relationship with Jesus Christ that surpasses mere doctrine. It also involves personal transformation by the Holy Spirit through faith in Jesus Christ that is heartfelt. I grew up knowing many wonderful evangelical Christians who understood very little about doctrine and were sometimes, in my later opinion, doctrinally confused. But because of their obvious heartfelt love for the Lord and daily walk with Jesus Christ that manifested in a passion for holiness, evangelism, and discipleship, I never questioned the authenticity of their evangelicalism.

Contrary to what some may think, I am not arguing that doctrine doesn't matter. It's just that I can't think of it as a litmus test of evangelical identity. Perhaps because of my upbringing, I am not as concerned about who is in and who is out as Mohler and other conservative evangelicals seem to be. I sometimes wonder why they are concerned about excluding people from what one emerging church leader calls the "e-club." I'm always delighted when I discover that someone I thought wasn't evangelical actually is! I've met charismatic Catholics, for example, who I am sure are very evangelical in their faith. And I have never met a true liberal Christian who has a genuinely personal relationship with Jesus Christ in the evangelical sense. And I have met people who are perfectly orthodox in their doctrinal beliefs who are spiritually dead. They are no more evangelical in the true sense of the word than is the liberal. And the charismatic Catholic is much more evangelical than those caught up in orthodoxy (or liberalism) without a vibrant personal faith in Jesus Christ.

What it seems to come down to is this: Mohler and I are simply thinking of different things when we utter the words *evangelical* and *evangelicalism*. Of course, our understandings of them overlap; they are not entirely incommensurable. When I utter these terms, I am thinking of all genuinely God-fearing, Bible-believing, Jesus-loving Christians who have a vibrant personal relationship with Jesus Christ that began with conversion-regeneration by faith in response to the gospel. When he utters them, he seems to be thinking of people who believe certain doctrines in the right way and are not open to reconsidering them even if biblical research requires that. His approach, so it seems, is much about excluding people from the evangelical movement. Mine is not compatible with anything and everything, but it is more about including as many real believers in Jesus Christ as possible than in identifying exclusive boundaries and keeping the company of faithful evangelicals doctrinally pure.

Much to Mohler's dismay, I'm sure, I don't sign or swear allegiance to any man-made creed or confessional statement. I respect the early church's creeds and the Baptist Faith and Message and the National Association of Evangelicals statement of faith. But if someone wants to know what I believe, I have my own written confession of faith to show them. However, when someone asks me if I'm an evangelical and asks me to prove it by trotting out my doctrinal beliefs, I suspect they have things backward. My testimony of conversion to Jesus Christ and faith revealed by a personal, daily walk with him is much more important to my evangelical identity than my doctrinal confession, as important as that is.

At the end of the day, evangelicalism really cannot be anything other than a spiritual movement marked by affinities between very diverse Christians. Affinity is different from uniformity; it simply designates common interests and goals. Marsden and other historians of evangelicalism are right; it has always been very diverse, and people like Mohler simply need to become more comfortable with that diversity and the ambiguity resulting from it. Otherwise they are going to continue shouting their denunciations of fellow evangelicals whom they suspect of doctrinal drift or deviation into the wind, hoping others will hear and agree. But people who hear and read them need to realize that not one of them is the pope of evangelicalism and that there is no headquarters of all evangelicals. Ultimately, each individual who cares will have to decide for himself or herself who is truly evangelical.

# GENERIC EVANGELICALISM

**JOHN G. STACKHOUSE JR.**

My thesis in this chapter is simple: the position outlined here is the most authentically evangelical of the four positions represented in this book. Of course, that is also what my coauthors think about their respective positions. But they are mistaken, sadly, as I shall now try to show, and they are mistaken, strangely, in exactly the same way. Each of my good brothers in this project has developed a definition of evangelicalism that fits himself quite well and the rest of us not so well, leaving one of us a better evangelical than the others. I will offer instead a definition of evangelicalism that lets us all feel we are authentic evangelicals, without defining evangelicalism so broadly that it becomes useless as a descriptor of a particular kind of Christianity, which I think it is.[1] In short, I intend to set out *generic evangelicalism.*

## Defining "Evangelical"

The word *evangelical* comes, of course, from the Greek word for "good news." This *evangel* is a message about the life, work, and significance of Jesus Christ as God reconciling the world to himself and how we can participate in that salvation.[2]

---

1. I responded earlier to certain binary typologies, notably Millard Erickson's and Roger Olson's, in "The Perils of Left and Right," *Christianity Today* (August 10, 1998): http://www.christianitytoday.com/ct/article_print.html?id=1461.

2. I am passing over other historic uses of *evangelical,* such as "Protestant" (versus Roman Catholic) in the Reformation, "Lutheran" versus "Reformed" in Germany (thus the word *Evangelical* in the titles of various North American Lutheran denominations), and so on, in order to focus on the uses most in view in this book. For a more thorough account of these and yet other uses of *evangelical,* see John G. Stackhouse Jr., *Canadian Evangelicalism in*

Thus the word *evangel* hovers interestingly among three key terms: Jesus, Bible, and church. For the evangel is centrally *about* Jesus, and he is the one who matters most. Evangelicalism in this fundamental sense is *Christian* first, last, and always. Evangelicalism is not, that is, properly concerned primarily about the Bible or the church, as important as they are, and certainly not about itself, but about Jesus — even as sometimes we evangelicals get confused and do preoccupy ourselves with one of these other things as if it does matter most.

The evangel, moreover, is an epitome of the teaching of the Bible, God's written Word to humanity by which we can, with the help of God's Spirit, learn what the evangel fully means. Furthermore, we receive this gospel epitome, this "rule of faith," not directly from the pages of Scripture (for it is nowhere thus summarized), but from the church that has summarized it and since has taught us the whole Bible. So to be evangelical literally by definition means to be grateful for, and necessarily involved in, both the tradition of the church and its ongoing life as it mediates, again with the help of God's Spirit, the good news of Jesus to us and to the rest of the world. (Critics both within and without evangelicalism have disparaged its lack of church-awareness, but such a lack was not characteristic of the original evangelicals. Nor can the church be ignored, I am suggesting, by any basic understanding of what evangelicalism essentially is.)

So far, however, there seems nothing particularly distinctive about evangelicalism. Isn't it just *Christianity?*

Well, yes. At least, we evangelicals think so. But let's proceed to define evangelicalism more carefully, and we will see how it is both true and not quite true that evangelicalism is merely Christianity.

Religious groups of any sort can be defined helpfully according to three components: tenets, affections, and practices — that is, what they believe, what they care about, and what they do. Evangelicalism has always been an initiative of renewal and mission. It has generally not sought to be a separate kind of Christianity on the same level as denominations or broader traditions (such as "Reformed" or "Anabaptist"). Quite the contrary: it emerged in the eighteenth century and continues

*the Twentieth Century: An Introduction to Its Character* (Toronto: University of Toronto Press, 1993), 6–17.

today as a desire to stir up the Christian church to fidelity in doctrine, fervency in piety, and faithfulness in mission.

This basic concern for authentic Christianity has meant that evangelicals have been neither reflexively conservative nor innovative, but instead have been selectively both. Evangelicalism has thus been literally *radical*: concerned to (re)connect with the *roots* of genuine Christianity, to cut away all that hinders its vitality and to develop anything that will help it flourish. Evangelicals therefore have defended certain traditional teachings while modifying or jettisoning others (such as emphasizing substitutionary atonement while being less particular about a theology of baptism); have cared deeply about some matters and scandalized others by ignoring what their critics have held sacred (such as holding a much higher affection for the person of Jesus than has been true in some traditions while maintaining a relatively low regard for the Eucharist); and have felt free to innovate in a wide range of practices (such as preaching in the open air instead of "properly" in a pulpit).

Historians have worked hard to understand why some aspects of the Christian religion received more attention, passion, and action from evangelicals than others. Much of their analysis has been to do with noticing where the church was *lacking in a particular time and place*. As a renewal movement, that is, evangelicalism would naturally seek to remedy what was deficient by a corresponding emphasis.

Given that historical situatedness, however, it is striking that over several centuries evangelicals have continued to emphasize a few characteristic teachings, concerns, and practices, which I will detail below. Perhaps the modern world has needed these emphases everywhere and always. Perhaps they are simply crucial for healthy Christianity no matter what the context. It is difficult for a lifelong modern North American evangelical such as I am to get some interpretative distance on this question! Perhaps, instead, modern evangelicals in other countries will be emphasizing other concerns as the gospel continues to move in quite different cultural contexts. Indeed, one sees in the worldwide spread of Christianity over the last century a remarkable emphasis on the person of the Holy Spirit, on spiritual gifts, and on spiritual warfare not typical of historic evangelicalism — so different, in fact, that many Pentecostals and charismatics see their kind of Christianity as something other than evangelicalism. And some evangelicals, in turn, have worried that these movements risk becoming merely "spiritual" and only nominally *Christian*. The next century's conversations should show whether evangelicalism ought to incorporate more of these emphases or instead ought to maintain its traditional foci for the good of all concerned.

For the present discussion, however, we can revert to more familiar ground. In the scholarly literature so far, there have appeared basically two related types of definitions for *evangelical, evangelicalism*, and the like.

## Definition 1

*Evangelical* denotes a type (quite literally, a type — a particular, distinct variety) of Christian ethos, of "Christian being." This definition is what is indicated by British historian David Bebbington's oft-cited criteria of crucicentrism, biblicism, conversionism, and activism:[3]

1. *Crucicentrism.* Evangelicals focus on Jesus Christ and particularly champion the doctrine of the atonement with a focus on the sacrificial, substitutionary death of Christ on the cross.
2. *Biblicism.* Evangelicals love the Bible as the Word of God written and place it in the center of our corporate worship (literally, in terms of church architecture, such as the central place accorded the pulpit, and liturgically, in terms of the order of service focusing on the sermon), spiritual exercises, theological method, and epistemological outlook.
3. *Conversionism.* Evangelicals believe that each person must be converted from sin to salvation (not necessarily in a dramatic "conversion experience") and must press on toward full holiness of life — to be "fully converted."
4. *Activism.* Evangelicals commit themselves to participating with God in his saving mission in and to the world, particularly in the proclamation of the gospel but also in charitable work and in caring for all of creation.

This sort of definition is also the type of definition used by pollsters, sociologists, and others who go out into the world seeking evangelicals:

---

3. David W. Bebbington, *Evangelicalism in Modern Britain: A History from the 1730s to the 1980s* (London: Unwin Hyman, 1989), 6.

"Do you believe the Bible is...?" "Do you attend church regularly?" "Have you had an experience of...?" and so on. Those people who correspond to their abstract definition they count as evangelicals. And *evangelicalism* thus is the noun meant to describe this way of being Christian.

Alas, some pollsters and sociologists have used oversimplified versions of Definition 1. Such definitions usually have been defended as easier to deploy in the field than the cumbersome jargon of the academicians. I suggest instead that a simple, but not simplistic or truncated, definition can be formulated for such surveying, and such a definition will help prevent some unhappy outcomes — not least among which have been the wildly varying totals for "evangelicals" in Canada or the United States.

Worse, some observers of evangelicalism, armed with such compromised "data," have gone on to make characterizations of "evangelicals" that miss the mark, to put it mildly. George Barna is particularly guilty on this count, and Ron Sider's *The Scandal of the Evangelical Conscience*, heavily indebted to Barna and Barna-type methodology, is a key example of one led astray by their methods. Starting out with a bad definition, they then find the wrong set of people and thus derive wrong conclusions about evangelicals, such as that evangelicals are just as sinful, worldly, and miserly as everyone else — which, better research has shown, is manifestly not true *as long as you define* evangelical *properly*, say, as in a way that John Wesley or Billy Graham would recognize as a proper definition. Evangelicals of *that* sort — that basic sort — do in fact live demonstrably different, and better, lives than the North American population at large: better marriages and families, better volunteering and donating to charity (and not just Christian charities), and so on.[4]

A classic case of this mistake of analysis built on a faulty definition in Canada is instructive. The George Rawlyk/Angus Reid/*Maclean's* magazine national poll of the 1990s found large numbers of what Rawlyk called "Catho-Evangelicals" — Catholics who were also evangelicals. But all that the survey actually found were, in my view, reasonably faithful Roman Catholics. How did this happen? The poll questions failed to distinguish between Protestant and Roman Catholic views of the

---

4. See Christian Smith, "Evangelicals Behaving Badly with Statistics," *Books & Culture* 13 (January 2007): 11; John G. Stackhouse Jr., "What Scandal? Whose Conscience? Reflections on Ron Sider's *Scandal of the Evangelical Conscience*," *Books & Culture* 13 (July 2007): 20–21, 41–42; Bradley R. E. Wright, *Christians Are Hate-Filled Hypocrites ... and Other Lies You've Been Told* (Minneapolis: Bethany, 2010).

authority of the Bible versus church tradition, namely, that Protestants see the Bible as supremely the written revelation of God, while orthodox Catholics see tradition as equally inspired revelation—a significant distinction observed by both sides since, well, the sixteenth century.[5]

Bebbington's quartet of criteria must be supplemented, however, with American historian George Marsden's fifth element: *transdenominationalism*, recognizing authentic Christianity in other denominations sufficiently strong as to warrant working together on projects of mutual concern. Such an attitude made possible the cooperation of evangelicals in the eighteenth-century revivals, which were the defining moment of the emergence of evangelicalism, as Definition 2 indicates below, and the vast range of evangelical cooperation ever since.[6]

The criterion of transdenominationalism also helps to mark off evangelicals from the more generic category of what we might call "observant Protestants," a category that would include, say, conservative Lutherans or conservative Anglicans, who generally have little to do with any other kind of Christian. And this transdenominationalism is possible only because of the trait of evangelicals we noticed earlier, namely, the valuing of some beliefs, affections, and practices as more central than others—a distinction not observed in Christian organizations that insist on conformity all the way down. Indeed, evangelicals often have scandalized their brothers and sisters in this or that denomination or movement precisely because they were willing to make distinctions among matters of primary, secondary, and tertiary importance and, when the primary concerns were met, would offer to cooperate with others of different secondary and tertiary convictions.[7]

Marsden's criterion of transdenominational cooperation in fact leads us to the second definition.

---

5. See the account in George A. Rawlyk, *Is Jesus Your Personal Savior? In Search of Canadian Evangelicalism in the 1990s* (Montreal and Kingston: McGill-Queen's University Press, 1996).

6. George M. Marsden, "Introduction: The Evangelical Denomination," in *Evangelicalism and Modern America*, ed. George M. Marsden (Grand Rapids: Eerdmans, 1984), vii–xvi.

7. The classic statement of this attitude is the tract by John Wesley, widely anthologized as it is here: "The Character of a Methodist," in *A Burning and a Shining Light: English Spirituality in the Age of Wesley*, ed. David Lyle Jeffrey (Grand Rapids: Eerdmans, 1987), 232–38. Notice, however, that Wesley's punch line ("Is your heart … as my heart…?") is often ripped out of context, usually by those who want to enlist him on behalf of a vague mysticism as the "true core" of religious life. Wesley does not simply ask for similarity of affection, but for similarity also of a range of beliefs and practices. But once those things are agreed, Wesley says, we can cooperate. In this he shows himself again to be an exemplary evangelical.

## Definition 2

*Evangelical* denotes an individual or a corporate entity that belongs to a historical movement known as *evangelicalism*. This definition is based on the eighteenth-century revivals as the site of the emergence of a historical phenomenon: evangelicalism. For this sort of definition to be useful today, we must speak carefully. Evangelicals today would be:

1. those individuals and groups who descend from those revivals;
2. *and* who have not departed from the characteristic emphases of those revivals (which is where definition 1 does help us, if it is rooted in historical description, as Bebbington's and Marsden's definitions are);
3. *or* are individuals and groups who have since identified themselves with this evangelical tradition and thus connect with other evangelicals beyond their own denominational lines.

North American examples of (1) and (2) would be most Baptists, some Presbyterians, and a minority of Anglicans/Episcopalians. Examples of (1) and *not* (2) would be most of the United Methodist Church in the United States and the United Church of Canada. Examples of (3) would be the Mennonite Brethren and the Christian Reformed Church.

We might usefully pause to acknowledge that there have been several ulterior motives in defining evangelicals in particular ways.

Some leaders of the National Association of Evangelicals (NAE) in the United States and of the Evangelical Fellowship of Canada (EFC), in my view, have employed Definition 1 *without* the "transdenominational" element and thus have presented themselves as representing many groups that they did not, in fact, represent. Such groups included such large denominations as the Southern Baptist Convention and the Missouri Synod of Lutherans (= the Lutheran Church – Canada), which had no actual relationship with the NAE or EFC and generally stuck to themselves. Thus, such leaders passed themselves off as (let us be frank) more important than they really were in their quest to present a "united evangelical front" (as the NAE used to put it).[8]

---

8. John G. Stackhouse Jr., "The National Association of Evangelicals, the Evangelical Fellowship of Canada, and the Limits of Evangelical Cooperation," *Christian Scholar's Review* 25 (December 1995): 157–79.

Others have wanted to marginalize evangelicals from public life and so have asked questions about creation science, biblical literalism, apocalyptic beliefs, or speaking in tongues in order to identify evangelicals as those with "strange" beliefs or practices, even though none of these is central to evangelicalism, nor are any of them held by all evangelicals.

Still others would like to have claimed evangelical identity and credentials for themselves while departing from orthodoxy in doctrine or practice. (I have in mind here a wide range of examples, such as those who would combine evangelicalism with New Age spirituality, those who would like to maintain an evangelical identity while converting to Roman Catholicism, et al.) Definitions of evangelicalism that are too simple may well unintentionally or, in this case, *intentionally* include heterodoxy and heteronomy.

To summarize, then, by this definition evangelicals are defined by the following cluster of convictions. But before I set out this summary, let's pause to make a couple of key qualifications that pick up themes previously sounded.

First, these criteria describe evangelicals' own professed values. They are not meant to suggest that other Christians do not share some of these values: of course they do. Precisely because they do share many values with evangelicals (as I am defining them here), in fact, they have been counted as evangelicals by many historians, sociologists, pollsters, and others. Observing carefully the definition summarized below would (finally) yield study of *evangelicals*, and not just conservative or orthodox or observant or enthusiastic or evangelistic or revivalistic Christians.

Therefore, second, this set of criteria functions properly only as a set. There is nothing peculiarly evangelical about any of them singly, of course. It is only this set that helps scholars, pollsters, leaders, and interested others "pick out" evangelicals from Christians in general, or observant Christians in general, or observant Protestants in general, and so on. Thus, it must be employed as a set, without compromise, versus the common polling practice of counting as evangelicals those who score only "highly" but not absolutely on some scale derived from such criteria. Evangelicals, I maintain, do not compromise on any of these values: they don't think it's okay to fudge on the atonement or the Bible, or to neglect churchgoing, or to avoid evangelism.

Thus the promised summary of evangelical characteristics:

1. *Crucicentric.* Evangelicals are Christocentric in their piety and preaching, and emphasize particularly the necessity of Christ's salvific work on the cross.
2. *Biblicist.* Evangelicals affirm the Bible as God's Word written, true in what it says and functioning as their supreme written guide for life.
3. *Conversionist.* Evangelicals believe that (1) everyone must trust Jesus as Savior and follow him as Lord; and (2) everyone must cooperate with God in a life of growing spiritual maturity.
4. *Missional.* Evangelicals actively cooperate with God in his mission of redeeming the world and particularly in the proclamation of the gospel and making of disciples.
5. *Transdenominational.* Evangelicals gladly partner with other Christians who hold these concerns, regardless of denominational stripe, in work to advance the kingdom of God.

In previous attempts to define evangelicalism, however, I have added a sixth criterion: evangelicals are orthodox and orthoprax.[9] By including that sixth criterion, I have attempted to explicate what would have been assumed by evangelicals all along, namely, that evangelicals share the primary beliefs, affections, and practices of their particular traditions (Baptist, Methodist, or whatever). Indeed, to be rigorous in our nomenclature, we might say that evangelicals are to be orthodox, "orthopath," and orthoprax. (Curious that there is currently no English word for "having the correct feelings/affections.")

George Whitefield or John Stott would never have expected to count as an evangelical someone who was truly "crucicentric" or Christocentric but who denied the Trinity—as in "Jesus-only" Pentecostalism. And much is taken for granted as being entailed by one or more of the other criteria, whether regular churchgoing as part of "a life of growing spiritual maturity" or caring for the poor as part of what it means to "cooperate with God in his mission of redeeming the world."

But here is where my fellow authors and I may disagree, namely, on *just how* orthodox, orthopath, and orthoprax one must be to count as a

---

9. John G. Stackhouse Jr., "Defining 'Evangelical,'" *Church & Faith Trends* 1 (October 2007): 1–5.

genuine evangelical. And the "how" can be measured along at least two axes: *how many items* are on the list of "entailments" of evangelical belief and *how correctly* one holds to any of those items.

Can one be an (authentic) evangelical and, say, hold that covenantal domestic and romantic partnerships between homosexuals should be recognized by the church as sanctioned by God? Certainly there are people today who claim to fit all five criteria and hold yet to this opinion (and, indeed, have the corresponding affections and practices). Can one be an (authentic) evangelical (and I am going to stop inserting "authentic" in what follows, since the point of these essays is, indeed, to discuss authentic evangelicalism) and hold to the "prosperity" teaching that Jesus intends his disciples to enjoy health and wealth and success on all other fronts if they will only be faithful? Again, it is evident that there are such people who would claim to meet all five criteria, whether the actual "Word-Faith" movement or other preachers and churches of this sort around the world—and conspicuously in places where evangelicals like to claim great success for their cause, such as sub-Saharan Africa, Korea, and Latin America.

The customary answer from many evangelicals to the claims of such unorthodox/unorthopath/unorthoprax folk is to say, "Well, you might claim that you meet the five criteria, but you don't." You don't, that is, believe or feel or live in accordance with what the Bible teaches and thus are disqualified implicitly by the criterion of biblicism.

And now we're into it, for who, among evangelicals, gets to say the two (not one, but two) things entailed by such a response, namely (1) what the Bible says on any particular issue and (2) whether disagreement on such an issue is grounds for losing one's status as an evangelical? For let's recall that *of course evangelicals disagree about what the Bible says—and on lots of issues.* That's why evangelicals are (criterion 5) *transdenominational*: They already disagree on a host of issues, many of which are important—indeed, many of which were so important in church history as to break the Christian fellowship that evangelicals now are saying is possible even in the face of such disagreements. Modes and meanings of baptism and communion, forms of church government, styles of preaching and evangelism, priorities in mission, countless points of dogma—all these and more have been grounds for Christians to excommunicate each other (in one sense or another of that word), and yet evangelicals *as evangelicals* say, "Yes, those things matter enough that we're going to maintain denominational identities and distinctives—you're still wrong, by the way, about the sacraments—but we recognize you as an evangelical with whom we want to do kingdom business, so let's get going on that Bible school/rescue mission/evangelistic initiative...."

Therefore, since it is part of the very ethos of evangelicalism to recognize differences of opinion precisely about what the Bible does and doesn't say about a host of issues, many of them quite consequential, then when it comes to the present discussion, it now appears that none of us can properly say, "Well, anyone who holds to X can't be an evangelical, because the Bible clearly forbids X. And that's that."

Yet there is something troublingly odd about having to recognize a heretic as an evangelical. So where does that leave us? I will return to that question at the end, where I, at least, leave you. So let me first, as the editors request, set out my own position within evangelicalism.

## Defining John Stackhouse

I am, to coin a phrase, an evangelical of the evangelicals. Unlike my Baptist brothers in this volume, I was born into the true church, namely, the Plymouth Brethren. (I actually spent some of my boyhood in Plymouth, England, taking the Lord's Supper in one of the ur-churches of the movement.) I am a graduate of a Brethren Bible school on the Canadian prairies—where all the best Bible schools are, of course. And I continue to hold some of the Brethren's main teachings, such as a love for weekly communion, a high view of leadership but a low view of ordination, an expectation of substantial lay education in the Scriptures, and a conviction that everyone is called to engage in evangelism. I also, however, am a typical PB in that I have *left* the Brethren movement. (Patriarchalism was the driving concern, but generally poor preaching and a preoccupation with dispensational prophecy decoding were right up there also.)

I have since gone out into the big world to worship among whatever local congregation makes the most sense of my vocation—including, especially, those aspects of my vocation marked "husband" and "father." (Any parent knows that you go to church where the kids are best provided for, no?) So since that happy day when my wife and I married, we have belonged to a wide range of churches indeed, from Mennonite Brethren to Anglican, from independent to Christian Reformed, from the Christian and Missionary Alliance to the Reformed Church in America, and from Southern Baptist to, well, Canadian Baptist.

As for transdenominationalism, my résumé has it in abundance. A sampler on the Canadian side: president of Inter-Varsity Christian Fellowship chapters in high school and university, president of the Canadian Evangelical Theological Association, senior adviser to the Centre for Research on Canadian Evangelicalism, task force member of the Evangelical Fellowship of Canada and columnist for its magazine, guest lecturer at a wide range of Canadian evangelical schools, and currently a professor at another. Oh yes, and my PhD dissertation (and the only book so far that does this) gives a historical account of twentieth-century evangelicalism in that country.[10]

On the American side, I'm a graduate of, and former instructor at, Wheaton College Graduate School; I've written for and been on the masthead of *Christianity Today* and two of its sister publications; I have participated in a half dozen research projects with the Institute for the Study of American Evangelicals; and I've authored dozens of articles and book chapters in American evangelical publications, as well as authoring or editing a handful of books for American evangelical publishers. (The cherries on my American evangelical sundae? I've met Billy Graham, Carl Henry, and Francis Schaeffer.)

And in Britain, for good measure, I've written a large article in a theological guide for evangelicals edited by Alister McGrath; I've lectured at Tyndale House, Cambridge; and I've even managed to publish no fewer than three blatantly evangelical books with Oxford University Press.

Demographically, to be sure, I'm clearly toward the Left of North American evangelicalism. My politics skew sharply toward the center: I have voted for all three of Canada's major federal parties at different times and in the States would have to register as an independent. And major evangelical media figures such as James Dobson, Charles Colson, Franklin Graham, John Piper, and, yes, Al Mohler are on my right on any matter on which we disagree (although, to be sure, we agree on a great many things).

---

10. Stackhouse, *Canadian Evangelicalism*.

Yet I'm not on "the Left" per se. As I indicated, I am no cheerleader for the Democratic Party in the United States or the Liberal or New Democratic parties in Canada. I usually disagree with Jim Wallis's public pronouncements, too, and sometimes, although much less often, with Ron Sider. And, not incidentally, quite a few evangelical theologians are to my left. I'm not even all that fond of Karl Barth, who seems to me too liberal—which puts me decidedly toward the center, if not the right, of contemporary evangelical academic theology. Still, I can't say I'm in "the center," pleasant (and self-aggrandizing) as that would be, because the poll data all show that there are a lot more American, and even Canadian, evangelicals to my right than to my left on any spectrum I can think of.

So I will concede that my position, theologically and ethically, is not in the center. But I will yet maintain (concessionary feelings having now dissipated) that my position is, nonetheless, precisely in the "sweet spot" of evangelical positions. Thus it is right where Kevin and Al and Roger ought to be, and doubtless will be at the end of this project—as will, I trust, you, too, esteemed reader.

Kidding aside, *of course* I think I'm where I ought to be and you should be, too: that's what all of us think about our own positions, no? But let's proceed now to the bones of contention tossed into this pit of theological controversy by our bellicose editors and see how things look from my corner of the contest.

## Evangelical Cooperation

According to the definition of evangelicalism I set out above (again, with due honor given to my betters, David Bebbington and George Marsden), evangelicals don't just happen to cooperate: evangelicalism is *marked by* cooperation, by transdenominational partnerships to further the mission of God and the church in the world.

In this perspective, the Evangelicals and Catholics Together (ECT) initiative makes perfect sense. Let's note, first, that the evangelicals involved haven't been confused about whether their counterparts are evangelicals. They're not, and that's why they're called Catholics. Indeed, the Catholics show no interest in being called evangelicals and joining our club.

Instead, both sides show a genuine ecumenicity of concern: that the body of Christ be not needlessly divided (note that they are willing to keep it divided in a number of what they judge to be needful respects); that doctrinal confusion in particular be eliminated (and who can be against that?); that doctrinal agreement can be reached as far as possible (ditto); and that better Christian relations be enjoyed thereby, including possibly even joint projects in matters of common concern.

Indeed, the ECT movement shows theologians following three previous connections of Catholics and evangelicals, namely, the pro-life movement; the earlier fellowship in the charismatic movement that blossomed in the 1960s and 1970s; and the even earlier cooperation of certain Catholic leaders and churches with the evangelistic work of Billy Graham — cooperation that shocked many evangelicals in the 1950s and 1960s the way ECT shocked a number of evangelicals a full generation later. Since that time, many evangelicals have been grateful for books by Jean Vanier and Henri Nouwen, for songs by Taizé and John Michael Talbot, for theological stimulation from John Paul II and Benedict XVI, and for ethical and political provocation from Richard John Neuhaus and his compatriots at *First Things*.

So ECT is best seen, I think, as theologians finally joining a party already well under way. I confess that I don't know that much was accomplished in the ECT conversation in terms of doctrinal clarification per se. I think the matter of who has meant what by "justification" and "faith" and "works" and the like is still open for substantial debate. But ECT yet matters because of what it signifies: a willingness among evangelicals to undertake serious theological work with anyone who can help them do so, even as those evangelicals also hope to provide some benefit to their interlocutors. In this sense, ECT matters as a positive sign amid the many other negative indicators of an ongoing "scandal of the evangelical mind."[11]

The consequent initiative among evangelicals to assuage fears among those who were unhappy about ECT (I mean the Alliance of Confessing Evangelicals in particular and perhaps R. C. Sproul most particularly) strikes me as perhaps politically necessary. We need no further useless fractures among fractious American evangelicals, so if relationships got mended, I'm all for it. But it also seems to be me to be theologically insignificant. Indeed, the statement of agreement finally hammered out

---

11. Mark A. Noll, *The Scandal of the Evangelical Mind* (Grand Rapids: Eerdmans, 1994).

and presented with great fanfare in the pages of *Christianity Today* actually made some things worse as it might have made some things better.[12] However much the statement mollified the watchdogs of certain Protestant boundaries on the one side, it annoyed and alienated evangelicals of other stripes, particularly as it failed to include the crucial category of sanctification in any substantial way and as it ruled out inclusivism as an illegitimate option for evangelical thinking.[13]

An exercise in perhaps even less usefulness was the Manhattan Declaration (2009). The theological and ethical problems in this document—and there are several—deserve attention, but not here.[14] What does deserve mention here is the contrast behind the empty windiness of this sort of project—telling whoever will listen in the general public things they already know about the evangelicals involved and acting as if to do so is somehow both courageous and effective—versus the vast reaches of evangelical cooperation that are indeed both courageous and effective. From World Vision and similar relief and development agencies, often among the very first responders to "hot spots" of disaster and need; to the International Justice Mission wielding the force of law to rescue victims of slavery and the sex trade; to the World Evangelical Fellowship and the Lausanne Committee networking evangelists, missionaries, theologians, and many others to spread the gospel better and to protect Christians around the world from religious discrimination; to the copious educational enterprises of American evangelicalism, from preschools to graduate schools and including homeschooling on a large scale, which provide resources also for evangelical education in many other lands—all of these are examples of substantial evangelical cooperation that manifestly gets things done.

Theologically, however, it is remarkable that one cannot point to similar enterprises anywhere on anything like this scale. The Evan-

---

12. "The Gospel of Jesus Christ," *Christianity Today* (June 14, 1999), http://www.christianitytoday.com/ct/1999/june14/53.0.html.

13. Full disclosure: I initiated the letter to the editor that decried these aspects of the "Celebration" document. Cosigners of the letter included such substantial evangelical theologians as Nancey Murphy, Gerald McDermott, Alan Padgett, Jonathan Wilson, Cornelius Plantinga, and Nicholas Wolterstorff; see http://www.ctlibrary.com/ct/1999/october4/9tb006.html.

14. I was among many critics who blogged about this: "The Manhattan Declaration: A Waste of Everybody's Time?" (November 22, 2009), http://stackblog.wordpress.com/2009/11/22/the-manhattan-declaration-a-waste-of-everybodys-time/.

gelical Theological Society (ETS), meetings of the Alliance of Confessing Evangelicals, and similar groups perhaps keep certain flames alive (not least the bonfires of heresy hunting). But it is not obvious to me, at least, that *any* substantial theological progress has emerged from their many meetings. Instead, unlike cooperative organizations in most other realms of evangelical effort, they have been most effective in the negative mode of *policing*, making sure theology stays safe.[15] That is a valuable role to play, let me be sure to affirm. But that is the effect I see being almost exclusively the result of evangelical cooperative action in theology beyond the occasional conference that does issue in a volume of substantially helpful essays.[16]

Open theism is a fascinating case in point, so I shall turn to it now.

## Evangelical Theology and Open Theism

The phenomenon of open theism seems immediately to belie my last contention, since it was indeed hatched in evangelical institutions, including lengthy arguments in the ETS, and is nothing if not innovative — at least within the framework of North American evangelicalism. (Those familiar with process thought were not so surprised by open theist suggestions.) Still, no one would suspect the institutional homes of the leading lights of this movement of actually fostering such theology. Greg Boyd left his academic post at Bethel University while Huntington College removed John Sanders from his. The late Clark Pinnock

---

15. The Evangelical Theological Society and its journal in particular is where you go when you want to complain about another evangelical's theology and particularly if you want to establish certain boundaries of evangelical acceptability. So Robert Gundry comes up for trial in the mid-1980s; the open theists come up a decade later; and feminist evangelicals have come up more recently because they cannot possibly square their views with a proper understanding of the Trinity. (Actually, we can.) Again, I'm all for theological controversy if a genuine threat needs to be met. But even as I don't think any of these causes célèbres warranted the degree and kind of furor that attended them, my main point is this: what you *don't* find at the ETS or in its journal is theology that makes much *positive* difference. And, as far as I can see, the main figures in constructive evangelical theology generally have little or nothing to do with it or its counterparts (such as the Alliance of Confessing Evangelicals and the like).

To turn from criticism to creation, it would be well to convene a group of evangelical thought leaders and ask them what sort of cooperative structures would foster better evangelical theology, perhaps the way the Society of Christian Philosophers or the Institute for the Study of American Evangelicals has been so successful in their own disciplines.

16. I think, for example, of various summer institutes and other projects at Calvin College, the Wheaton Theology Conference, and our own short-lived but productive theology conference in the previous decade — out of which have come provocative books on Christology, apologetics, postliberalism, theology of religions, ecclesiology, and more.

likely would have been fired from many an American school but was likely too prominent to be dislodged from McMaster Divinity School in his native Canada—and, not incidentally, there has never been as strong and strict a tradition of orthodoxy enforcement among Canadian evangelicals as there has been in the United States.[17]

But does holding to open theism mean one is not an evangelical? Contrary to those who would answer monosyllabically on either side, I must say instead, "It depends."

Should an open theist eschew any of the convictions of evangelicalism I have outlined above, then by definition, no, he or she is no longer properly called an evangelical. And perhaps some open theists do. But I don't know of any who do, and particularly not among the theologians just named.

So I would say instead that open theists are, to my knowledge, genuine evangelicals. They are just *wrong* evangelicals. They have mistaken beliefs, in my view, about the nature of God and a number of related matters. So their views deserve respectful and vigorous engagement, in hopes that error will be reduced, truth will predominate, and everyone involved will be edified thereby. Indeed, since they are manifestly evangelicals (again, per the definition I have set out), then those of us who disagree with them as fellow evangelicals ought to be particularly careful to hear them out in case it is we, not they, who are mistaken on one point or many. But we engage them respectfully—even, dare I say, with familial affection—in the concern to help fellow evangelicals improve their theology if they have, in fact, gone astray on some theological matters. And this is how we ought to view them if we take seriously the definition of *evangelical* that I am using.

After all, I think my coauthors, Roger, Al, and Kevin, are wrong about some things, too, as they must think about me in return. And what I think one or more of them is wrong about is not inconsequential, whether in matters of gender, ecumenism, predestination, politics, or something else. But I don't doubt that they each meet the definition

---

17. I make this point at length in my *Canadian Evangelicalism*. Intriguingly, Pinnock taught at one of the schools at the heart of one of the few important fundamentalist battles in Canadian history. And the heirs of the victors in that battle—not their fundamentalist opponents—ran Pinnock's school. See the introduction, chapter 1, and the conclusion in Stackhouse, *Canadian Evangelicalism*.

of "evangelical"—nor do the publishers, hence our inclusion in this volume! And that is the interesting question I raised at the start of this essay: What definition of evangelical *will* include the four of us, without thereby reducing *evangelical* to something general, such as "observant Protestant Christian," so that we no longer need the term *evangelical* at all? I think we have such a definition at hand, and it would be both conceptually and practically useful to maintain it—against those in our number who would either narrow or expand it.

In this light, I proceed to the last of the editorially assigned topics of evangelical theological controversy: penal substitutionary atonement.

## Christian Theology and Penal Substitutionary Atonement

I give the game away immediately in this heading. Penal substitutionary atonement, far from being merely some sort of *evangelical* marker or bone of contention, is instead a vital and nonnegotiable part of *Christian* theology in general, without which any understanding of salvation is seriously deficient.

Evangelicals appreciate the many *subjective* benefits of the atonement. We are grateful for this display of Christ's love for us, his solidarity with us, and his example to us. Typically, however, evangelicals rejoice particularly in the *objective* benefits of the cross. Mysterious as it remains even to the wisest minds, the fundamental Christian affirmation is that the cross of Jesus doesn't just *show* us things, it *did* something once for all. That is why it was necessary: not merely as a symbol pointing to something else (the love and sympathy of God in the face of the enormity of human sin), but as a world-changing event that did indeed direct the love and sympathy of God to deal effectively with the enormity of human sin.

Two principal images have been used by Christians to explain what Jesus accomplished on the cross: Christ as Sacrifice, and Christ as Victor. The former harks back to the extensive symbolism of Israelite temple worship, in which animals were killed and offered to God as substitutes for the human sinners who gave them up. "Life for life" was the basic principle, because sin at its root is the repudiation of life. The Hebrew prophets themselves made clear that these rituals together formed an elaborate picture of both God's holiness (God views sin as mortally serious, and therefore the most graphic symbolism of life and death was necessary to portray its cost and its redemption) and God's mercy (God was willing to accept animal substitutes, although it makes no logical or moral sense to do so: how can the blood of bulls or goats possibly make up for human sin?). The ultimate payment for, the ultimate cost of, human sin had to be borne by human beings.

Evangelicals often recur to the language of financial transactions to make this point. I owe you a thousand dollars. I cannot pay you. You can take me to court and try to make me pay you, but let's say that I truly have no resources to do so. So in some legal systems you can press charges and have me put in prison to work off the debt. But there is no such provision of forced restitution in our legal system. My going to prison might quench your thirst for vengeance, but it doesn't deal with the debt.

Your other choice, however, is to forgive the loan. What this means, strictly speaking, is that you "pay yourself" the thousand dollars on my behalf. Of course, you will always have a net loss of a thousand dollars. What you have done, though, is removed my name from the list of debtors and taken the loss yourself.

In any situation of forgiveness, four elements are actually in play. Three are obvious: the offender, the offended, and their relationship. But a fourth must be borne in mind, else the cross makes no objective sense as sacrifice. Let's consider another example.

Little Trevor has been told many times by his mother not to touch her fine linen tablecloth. But Trevor loves to crawl up on one of the dining room chairs to gaze down at this vacant canvas. One day he succumbs to its allure and begins to improve it with his crayons.

An hour later, his horrified mother shrieks as she enters the dining room to see Trevor's ornamentation extending from one end to the other of the family heirloom.

Trevor, recognizing at once that he has disobeyed and upset his mother, whom he loves, bursts into tears and cries out, "I'm sorry, Mommy! I'm sorry! I'm sorry!" He runs toward her and buries his head in her legs, sobbing out his repentance.

Trevor's mother is an unusually good person and immediately drops to her knees to hug him. "That's okay, honey," she whispers. "I forgive you."

So the offender, Trevor, has repented. His mother, the offended, has forgiven him. And their relationship is mended in mutual love. But the fourth element, the tablecloth itself, remains ruined regardless of her forgiving him.

The Bible speaks of sin this way: not just as a rupture in a relationship, but as an objective state of affairs that requires reparation. There is a debt still to be paid, a ruined tablecloth still to be restored. Here is the ancient concept of guilt, a consequence of any action that strays from goodness, whether intentional evil or not. The Old Testament law provided a ritual to atone for actions that deviated from goodness even as the perpetrator of them had no intention of committing evil (Lev. 4). Figures in the Bible are depicted as transgressing God's rules and suffering for it even when they had no idea they were doing wrong (Gen. 20:9). We can't just clap each other on the back, shake hands, or hug and then walk away, as crucial as it is also to restore good relations between us.

Jesus repairs it. Jesus pays it. Jesus bears it. Jesus absorbs it. Jesus, somehow, and whatever "it" is, makes things right by his sacrifice of himself.

We can now see one important reason why the doctrine of the Trinity is vital to the Christian understanding of things. If God and Jesus are different beings, then Jesus on the cross looks like just one more scapegoat being punished for the sake of other humans' sins. Indeed, now we would have Christianity championing human sacrifice. And we would have the same conundrum we had before: how can punishing someone else possibly suffice for my offenses? Many liberal feminist theologians have gone even further to accuse this idea of sacrifice as sanctioning child abuse: God the Father victimizes his Son.

If the doctrine of the Trinity is stoutly affirmed, however, then it is *God* as Son who hangs on the cross, as *God* looks on as Father and Spirit in the added suffering of grief over the Beloved.

Evangelical theologians, therefore, must not jettison substitutionary atonement. Gustav Aulén's rejection of the "Latin" theory of sacrifice in favor of the *Christus victor* motif seems to rest on what he sees to be its emphasis on the human side of Jesus rendering something up to God, rather than seeing God involved in every dimension of the Atonement. And Aulén's latter-day evangelical champions share this same worry. But they need not worry, for a firm Trinitarianism prevents the idea of sacrifice from becoming anything other than God's self-giving on our behalf.

Penal substitutionary atonement, therefore, is essential to Christian theology and therefore to evangelical theology. As it has in every century in which it has been championed, it poses unpopular ideas that confront human hubris. We tend to think we're not all that bad. We just need a good model (*imitatio Christi*) and perhaps an external rescue (*Christus victor*) and a fresh start (recapitulation). But we are not so (hopelessly) bad that someone needs to *die* because of our sins.

But we *are* bad, and *this* bad. We cannot be saved simply by improving our role models or circumstances. And so the penal substitutionary idea that we sinners can, by the grace of God, be relocated forensically in(to) Christ is great good news!

To be sure, evangelicals, like all Christians, should preach and teach *more* than penal substitutionary atonement, as I affirmed at the start of this section and as I maintained earlier in regard to the regrettable limitations of the "Celebration" document.[18] Nonetheless, in my every encounter with it, current evangelical disquiet about penal substitutionary atonement seems to me to be unnecessary. Properly construed, in the light of Scripture's rich teaching (from the sacrifices commanded in the Torah to Jesus' teaching about his role as suffering servant in the Gospels, to the rich language of the Epistles, to the apocalyptic figure of the Lamb looking as if it were slain), substitutionary atonement is a nonnegotiable part of the Christian understanding of salvation, and evangelicals do well to keep teaching it clearly and enthusiastically.

But suppose somebody *doesn't* teach it? Does that make him or her not an evangelical? According to the definition I have been using, such a person might well still be an evangelical. Indeed, the discussion in this section takes for granted that some (genuine) evangelicals are uneasy about substitutionary atonement, and a few even hostile to that idea. But they remain evangelicals nonetheless: still putting Christ and the cross in the center, still drawing from Scripture and testing everything by it, still concerned for sound and thorough conversion, still active in working with God in his mission, and still cooperating with evangelicals of other stripes. Evangelicals who diminish or dismiss substitutionary atonement seem to me to be in the same camp as my evangelical broth-

---

18. I expand on this theme in my chapter "Jesus Christ" in *The Oxford Handbook of Evangelical Theology*, ed. Gerald McDermott (Oxford: Oxford University Press, 2010), 146–58.

ers and sisters who espouse open theism: truly evangelicals, and truly wrong about something important.

Again, however, I think that's true about one or more of the other authors in this volume on other topics of great seriousness as well. They are *wrong* evangelicals but *genuine* evangelicals. And I trust they will bless me with the same status. We'll see in the responses that follow!

## To Be Evangelical, to Be Christian

Let's return now to the question that troubled me, and perhaps you, at the beginning of this essay.

I have set out a definition of evangelicalism. Those who share that set (and that *entire* set) of convictions I am calling evangelicals. Yet what about those whose doctrines — or affections or practices — seem wrong? I have said that the open theists I know can yet be recognized as evangelicals. I think they are mistaken about this or that matter of doctrine, but I don't see that mistakenness as imperiling their status as evangelicals.

I also allowed, however, that they, or others in their movement, might not be. Why? Well, perhaps they do not hold to one of the five convictions of evangelicalism. If so, then they are not evangelicals, and that's that. But perhaps instead I judge that their beliefs deviate so far from orthodoxy that the question is not now whether they are evangelicals but whether they are (more basically) heretics and, we must further specify, *so* heretical that they cannot be judged to be fellow Christians.

Certain Mormons can and do share all five convictions of evangelicals, but they are not evangelicals, because their beliefs, affections, and practices show them to be *not Christians*. I am not presuming to pronounce on their state before God. I don't mean "not Christian" the way we sometimes mean it, namely, "unsaved." For the purposes of this discussion, we need not enter into the mysterious realm of sorting out who will enter the kingdom of heaven and who won't.

Instead, we can say more simply, Mormonism differs so markedly from orthodox Christianity that the vast majority of Christians and, until relatively recently, the vast majority of Mormons saw the two religious identities as not only different, but even competitive for the title of "true church of Jesus Christ."

I referred to John Wesley earlier as requiring that those with whom he would have Christian fellowship would be those who were *actually Christians*. And if they were, and wanted fellowship with him and particularly wanted to cooperate with him in the work of revival, then he extended his hand gladly.

Wesley sometimes withdrew his hand, however, from those he felt were compromising the work to which he was committed. His break with George Whitefield is the most famous case in point in terms of Wesley's Arminianism versus Whitefield's Calvinism. And there were other ruptures, including difficulties with his beloved brother Charles over Methodism's place within, or without, the Church of England.

Yet even here Wesley helps us. For he was not trying to establish and police boundaries of who was and who wasn't an evangelical, much less who was and who wasn't a Christian. His priority was preaching the "new birth" and drawing others into it and beyond it into full sanctification. Thus, if he judged Whitefield's or Charles's views to compromise this work, he would part from them in order to pursue the work better. I am not defending Wesley on the particulars here, and I don't doubt that Wesley had personality flaws, some of them serious and consequential. But in this crucial instance, I see him acting with the typical pragmatism of the evangelical. Can you partner with me in getting some good thing done? Then climb aboard. If not, then I'm going to keep moving without you.

This pragmatism explains why so many other prominent evangelicals have not maintained strict boundaries of "evangelicalism" in a wide range of important work, from Billy Graham partnering with nonevangelicals and (even) Roman Catholics in evangelism to Jerry Falwell extending his hand even further to welcome Jews, Mormons, and anyone else who would form a "moral majority" with him in the interest of certain political and cultural concerns. It explains why evangelicals at the time of this writing would partner with media figures such as Glenn Beck or politicians such as Sarah Palin, whose beliefs, affections, or practices many would say fail to meet minimal standards of authentic Christianity. For many evangelicals, the question of who is and who isn't an evangelical isn't particularly important. What matters is who can help us in a particular instance with a particular task we are undertaking in the work of the kingdom.

So I come to two conclusions. First, defining *evangelical* is centrally the task of defining an adjective modifying the noun *Christian* or *Christianity*. And I think that's pretty easy and clear, in fact, as I have tried to show in the definition I have rendered.

The question of who and what can properly be called "evangelical," however, depends on the more basic matter of Christianity. Thus, if a person or an institution is not Christian — in belief, affection, and practice — then he, she, or it cannot be called "evangelical." If open theism teaches what is not orthodox theology about God, then it cannot be called evangelical, since it won't (even) be Christian. The same goes for those who construe atonement without substitutionary atonement: they run the risk of simple heresy — forget whether they get to keep their "evangelical" credentials or not. (They don't.)

And ah, there's the rub. For who gets to say what is *too* heretical and what is orthodox *enough* among evangelicals — to work together on this or that project? (I trust the pragmatic theme I am sounding by now is quite clear.) Wesley broke off relations for a long while with Whitefield over beliefs. Charles Finney was excoriated by many of his fellow evangelicals, as he is to this day, over beliefs and practices. Dispensationalism was denounced among evangelicals as a radical error in the nineteenth century, while now in the twenty-first its doctrine of the rapture is virtually a synecdoche for evangelical belief. Billy Graham has been accused of fatal compromise in his practices even as his doctrine has been unimpeached. And Pentecostals have experienced an inconsistent and ambivalent welcome among mainstream evangelicalism. So even as evangelicals typically let secondary and tertiary matters "ride" in order to cooperate on projects of primary importance, the question remains of just what matters do matter so much that (a) we cannot cooperate or (b) we cannot recognize each other as evangelicals.

Historically, it has been the prior question that has occupied most evangelical interest, given evangelicals' pragmatic concern to get good things done by whatever means lie at hand. But the latter question has come to matter particularly in the United States, I suggest, as the post–World War II movement that took the label of evangelicalism has become institutionally distinct and powerful. No longer is evangelicalism in the United States merely a renewal movement within existing ecclesiastical structures, but it has become a multifarious quasi-ecclesiastical structure in its own right: what George Marsden termed "the evangelical denomination" some decades ago.[19] While a similar phenomenon is evident in other countries, in America in particular the question of evangelical identity looms large when what is at stake is membership on certain boards or admission to college or seminary faculties or eligibility for financial support or qualification for leadership posts. In this context, it matters a lot who meets the definition of *evangelical*. And that is doubtless why this volume is produced in America, rather than in some other country. The stakes are high here for a lot of people, while they aren't anywhere else. So the heresy hunting will continue, as I would frankly say it has to: so much is on the line. Boundaries will continue to be policed because the property being guarded is so valuable.

Let's be clear, however, that it is not the gospel that is in jeopardy, nor the spread of the kingdom of God. Not even the health of the church is in question. No, it is institutional evangelicalism over which we contend in such instances. That can be a worthy concern, to be sure. I myself have been blessed by many evangelical institutions, and I'm glad for them to be maintained in integrity. But it's good to keep in focus what is and what isn't involved in any particular dispute, and to govern our rhetoric accordingly.

May I also exhort my fellow evangelicals to be careful not to wall ourselves into a compound of fretful or, worse, chauvinistic conservatism such that we cannot learn anything from our neighbors — and even from our own theologians who have been cowed into mere correctness for fear of being tossed over said wall. The boundaries of who and what can be called "evangelical" have shifted over the centuries, in fact. Those once kept outside the camp are now composing our worship songs, teaching our students, writing our books, and leading our prayer retreats — to our great blessing. So let's be wary of building any walls that are too thick to alter, let alone move.

It would be well indeed to alter the metaphor. Let us instead see our priority as keeping vital things vital. The body can tolerate peripheral challenges and even benefit from dealing with external influences so long as the core remains sound. Let's be sure to recognize the creative

---

19. Marsden, "Introduction: The Evangelical Denomination," vii–xvi.

possibilities that exist on the edges as we encounter the rest of the world. Here are new stimuli and new resources by which God can give us yet new gifts.

To remain open to additional blessing doesn't mean we can be reckless on the boundaries, of course. Terrible problems can emerge on the frontier, and we must not be ingenuous, as too many evangelical theologians and church leaders are today, about welcoming heterogeneous ideas, affections, and beliefs. As frustrated and confined as we might feel within certain evangelical communities and institutions, we must not allow ourselves to perceive verdancy where it doesn't exist. Instead, we should add to our evangelicalism only what is truly consonant with our central convictions.[20]

In short, evangelicalism cannot be sharply characterized in its beliefs, affections, and practices beyond understanding it to be observant Protestant Christianity expressed in authentic, vital discipleship issuing forth in mission with similarly concerned Christians of various stripes. As such, the definition of evangelicalism is inherently contestable, as it has been since Wesley and Whitefield disagreed over it, only because the definition of *authentic and healthy Christianity* is inherently contestable.

Of course I don't mean that "mere Christianity" is contestable in every respect. I have noticed that even college textbooks on world religions share a kind of Vincentian canon as they describe the essentials of the Christian religion in much the same way. But I do mean, as I have tried to indicate in this essay, that quite important disputes of belief, affection, and practice have emerged among evangelicals, and that disputing simply can't be avoided, because evangelicals are Christians and Christians, it has been rather widely noted, do disagree from time to time on this or that. Sometimes evangelicals have been willing to put up with each other's differences — over matters that have divided others into separate congregations and denominations — in order to get certain things accomplished. At other times, evangelicals have judged the differences to be too large. Strikingly, however, the question of who belongs and who doesn't seems to me to be always a matter of what level of sameness of belief, affection, and practice must we share to get

---

20. John G. Stackhouse Jr., "Evangelical Theology Should Be Evangelical," in *Evangelical Futures: A Conversation on Theological Method*, ed. John G. Stackhouse Jr. (Grand Rapids: Baker; Vancouver: Regent College Publishing; Leicester: Inter-Varsity, 2000), 39–58.

this particular task accomplished? And only when there are evangelical institutions and desirable positions within those institutions at stake does it matter quite so much who can and who can't be granted an evangelical membership card. Most of the time, other levels of definition (Christian or not? Pro-life or not? Calvinist or not? Feminist or not?) matter more.

Therefore, we evangelical Christians, like all Christians everywhere, ought in each situation to strike a good balance between conservation and discovery, between critique and creativity. And evangelicalism will continue to be a vibrant and effective part of Christ's church precisely as it is neither bellicosely conservative nor blithely innovative, but faithful in both senses: to be loyal and to be effective. I trust that this will be true of my fellow writers, as I pray God it will be true of me.

# A FUNDAMENTALIST RESPONSE

## KEVIN T. BAUDER

In his presentation on "generic evangelicalism," John Stackhouse has produced an essay that is noteworthy for its charitable tone. It makes a number of useful contributions. To name one, I deeply appreciate his pointing out the distinction between orthodoxy, orthopraxy, and orthopathy. The Reformers and their heirs have often insisted that fundamentals (essentials of the gospel) could be practical as well as doctrinal, and fundamentalists have typically agreed. By introducing orthopathy into the conversation, John implies that ordinate affection is also at the core of Christianity. Though my discussion has been rather closely focused on doctrine, I agree that heteropathy is deadly to genuine Christianity. I would simply point out, however, that none of the three categories can stand in for either of the other two. All three are essential to the Christian faith, and all three must be cultivated and defended.

John's essay is also useful because of its unusual candor. One of the most telling sections occurs late in the discussion, where John suggests that the debate about evangelical identity is not so much about the gospel or the spread of the kingdom of God as it is about control of evangelical institutions. Given the condition of the human heart, I suppose he is at least partly right.

This is the aspect of John's essay on which I propose to focus. Perhaps at this point, a fundamentalist interlocutor might be useful. Since the 1940s, fundamentalists have traveled a different institutional road than the rest of evangelicalism. We have, so to speak, created a parallel universe with our own apparatus of denominations, schools, mission agencies, and publishers. While we occasionally sojourn in broader evangelicalism (to attend school, for example, or to publish for a non-fundamentalist readership), we tend to stay pretty close to home. Most fundamentalists have simply lost interest in the apparatus of mainstream evangelicalism. We are not trying to reclaim the National Association of Evangelicals (which was never ours to begin with) or to gain control of the Evangelical Theological Society (though some of us are still members).

Consequently, we fundamentalists are much less concerned with the question of who is *an Evangelical* (perhaps with a capital *E*?) than we are with the question of what it means to *be evangelical* (definitely with a small *e*). This distinction is highly relevant to the present discussion. From a fundamentalist perspective, people who are not evangelical have no license to call themselves Evangelicals.

This is where John's argument will resonate with most fundamentalists, for he affirms that in its broadest (fundamentalists would say, its *proper*) sense, to be genuinely evangelical is simply to be Christian. It is to receive and uphold the evangel—the gospel. No one should be called an evangelical who is not a Christian.

When I use the word *Christian*, I agree with John that we should not get into the business of deciding who is really saved. Because of the invisible nature of saving faith and because of the complications introduced by the human capacity for inconsistency, we have no infallible way of detecting who possesses true faith in the gospel. What we can do, however, is evaluate who professes faith in the true gospel. We cannot judge the truth (reality) of their faith, but we can—and must— judge the truth (veracity) of the gospel they profess. No one who denies the gospel should be called a Christian, and consequently no one who denies the gospel should be called an evangelical.

The foregoing understanding of *evangelical* permits Christians to recognize and cooperate with one another amid tremendous diversity. As John notes, evangelicals may and do differ over many areas of doctrine and practice. As long as those differences do not damage the gospel (I would say, as long as the differences do not pertain to fundamentals), then some degree of mutuality is possible. To what degree will depend on the nature of the differences and the requirements for any given level of mutuality.

John points to the legitimate diversity (he calls it *transdenominationalism*) of evangelicalism. This diversity seems obvious: evangelicals are Baptists, Presbyterians, and Wesleyans. They are Calvinists and

Arminians. They are covenant theologians and dispensationalists. They hold all of the standard eschatological theories. They differ in their philosophies of ministry, their appropriation of culture, and their use of female preachers. While these differences have put a strain on their relationships at some levels, they have not been judged so severe as to void Christian fellowship.

With respect to these differences, fundamentalism has paralleled the larger orbit of institutional evangelicalism in America. Consequently, one might ask where fundamentalism differs from — and is critical of — John's "generic evangelicalism." My answer to that question will take the form of a narrative, a sort of history of evangelicalism as fundamentalists remember it.

The progenitors of John's "generic evangelicalism" were the neo-evangelicals of the 1940s and 1950s. By today's evangelical standards, the original neo-evangelicals were surprisingly uniform and conservative in their theology. Between neo-evangelicals and fundamentalists, however, stood two significant differences.

The first difference was over the status of the Pentecostal and charismatic movement. Fundamentalism and Pentecostalism originally developed as separate phenomena. Where fundamentalism represented primarily a doctrinal and ecclesiastical reaction against the incursions of liberal theology in the mainline denominations, Pentecostals reacted more against the perceived worldliness and spiritual torpor of those denominations. The result was a fundamentalism that was doctrinally focused while sometimes affectively deficient, paralleled by an emotional Pentecostalism that was (as fundamentalists saw it) doctrinally deficient.

For the most part, fundamentalists did not see Pentecostals as apostates. They admitted that Pentecostals usually affirmed the gospel, but they still believed that Pentecostalism represented a very significant error. While fundamentalists generally recognized Pentecostals as brothers and sisters in Christ, they were wary of forming too close an alliance. That attitude persists to the present day. Fundamentalists are almost unanimously and firmly cessationist, and they do not look with favor on mutual endeavors with any of the three waves of the charismatic movement.

When the neo-evangelicals broke with fundamentalism during the 1940s, however, the new movement welcomed the participation of

Pentecostals. That openness has continued. Today, many evangelicals subscribe to at least some elements of charismatic theology, and many of those who do not affirm charismatic theology are at least open to it.

Nevertheless, the difference over Pentecostalism was the lesser of the disagreements between fundamentalism and the new evangelicalism. A greater difference involved the willingness of the neo-evangelicals to make common cause in Christ's name with church leaders who denied the gospel. This tactic was first employed with Protestant liberals then extended to Roman Catholicism and Eastern Orthodoxy.

Fundamentalists insisted that no distinctively Christian recognition or fellowship should be extended to people whose theology denied the gospel (as they thought liberalism and Catholicism did). For their part, neo-evangelicals were happy to recognize at least some liberals and Catholics as fellow-Christians. Part of their motivation was apologetic. Neo-evangelicals were enthusiastic apologists, and they believed that a credible, scholarly articulation of evangelical principles could bring hordes of liberals into the evangelical camp. Part of their motivation was cultural and ecclesiastical. After World War II, civilization seemed in imminent danger of collapse. Neo-evangelicals saw themselves as the saviors of the West. They wanted to use the structures of the mainline denominations to help achieve their goals. In short, they wanted back *in* where the fundamentalists had wanted *out*. To gain readmission, however, they had to distance themselves from the fundamentalist dictum that all liberals were apostates.

Part of their motivation was also evangelistic. Actually, this motivation was hardly distinguishable from the neo-evangelical desire to rescue the West (just listen to Billy Graham's sermons from the 1950s and early 1960s). Evangelistic effectiveness required big crowds. Liberals, and later Catholics, could deliver bigger crowds than fundamentalists could. So a deal was brokered, first with mainline liberals, then with Catholics and the Orthodox. In exchange for extending recognition as Christians, neo-evangelicals gained ecumenical support for evangelistic crusades.

Fundamentalists believed that this was quite literally a deal with the devil. They saw mainline liberals, not only as apostates, but as ecclesiastical pirates who had stolen denominations and other institutions from the Lord's people. From a fundamentalist perspective, liberals were enemies of Christ, pure and simple. To make common cause with them in the name of Christ—to extend Christian recognition to them—was akin to ecclesiastical treason.

Fundamentalists believed that they had left the denominations in order to uphold the gospel itself. They left in order to put an ecclesiastical chasm between themselves and apostasy. What the neo-evangelicals tried to do was to span this strait, to put a Mackinac Bridge between the evangelical world and the ecumenical world.

In fairness, it should be said that the neo-evangelicals hoped for a great mass of liberal theologians to cross over the bridge into evangelicalism. They were encouraged in this hope by the flow of theological history, for that was exactly the moment when old liberalism was being dismantled by neo-orthodoxy. Ecumenical theologians were once again talking about the reality of sin and about a supernatural Christ. To those steeped in the older liberal tradition, Barth sounded almost like a fundamentalist. These trends encouraged a sense of exhilaration on the part of new evangelicals.

So the bridge was built. Yet hordes did not rush across from liberalism into evangelicalism. True, a handful did eventually trickle across—a Thomas Oden here and an Eta Linnemann there. One wonders whether such people would have crossed even without a bridge—perhaps, like C. S. Lewis, being carried across the chasm by Mother Kirk. At any rate, never more than a sprinkling came from *there* to *here*.

There was a crossing over, however. Indeed, the bridge has been virtually mobbed ever since Daniel P. Fuller brought his ThD back from Basel. Evangelicalism has seen a mighty crossing from *here* to *there*. Evangelicals have tripped over one another in their rush to appropriate the putative insights of whatever theologies and methodologies were on the other side of the bridge. After all, the other side held all that was thought to be daring and insightful and authentic and provocative and—let's be frank—*fashionable*.

The problem is not that evangelicals interacted with liberals at the academic level or that they studied liberal theology—obscurantism is no answer. The problem is that by welcoming liberals into Christian fellowship, neo-evangelicalism abandoned the gospel as the boundary between Christianity and apostasy. Since it was now possible to assume that liberal categories were somehow compatible with Christian truth, evangelicals slowly amalgamated with much that was on the other side of the chasm. The result is that we now have people stationed all the way along the bridge, well over into what used to be liberal territory, all of whom nevertheless identify themselves as evangelicals. *That* is the heritage of John Stackhouse's "generic evangelicalism."

The original neo-evangelicalism was characterized by a bundle of goals. One important goal was to gain influence in those centers of ecclesiastical power that had been abandoned to liberals. This influence — this power — was necessary in order to further the neo-evangelical social and evangelistic agenda. A second key goal was to defend and maintain Christian orthodoxy by presenting a vigorous apologetic in the most credible and scholarly fashion. In the long run, these two goals could not be held together, and those who identified with the neo-evangelical movement had to choose between them. Either they had to surrender elements of orthodoxy, or else they had to surrender their pursuit of recognition and influence.

The precise moment when the new evangelicalism broke apart was when Harold Lindsell published *The Battle for the Bible*.[21] Both Lindsell and Harold John Ockenga, who wrote the foreword, were among the original neo-evangelicals. Lindsell was editor of the neo-evangelical flagship publication, *Christianity Today*. His book was not an attack by fundamentalists or other opponents. It was an alarm sounded by those at the center of the evangelical movement. Lindsell and Ockenga meant to hold orthodoxy at the cost of influence, and they also meant to expose those for whom influence was more important than orthodoxy.

Lindsell called for ejecting the evangelical Left from the evangelical movement, and he partly got his way. In the short term, opportunities and funding for left-leaning evangelicals became slim. In the long run, however, those on the left established new bases of support, from which they gained the liberty to express their views without fear of retaliation. The rest of evangelicalism might grouse about them, but little more could be done. In the long run, evangelicals who tended toward the left managed to gain more respectability, at least in the academy, than any other segment of the evangelical movement.

Today the Left draws the entire evangelical movement like a huge theological magnet. Views that would have been seen as heterodox in

---

21. Harold Lindsell, *The Battle for the Bible* (Grand Rapids: Zondervan, 1976).

1947 or as antievangelical in 1975 are regarded as mainstream in 2011. Theological derring-do has become the way to make one's name in the evangelical community—even at the expense of the clarity, and sometimes the integrity, of the gospel. The net result is terrible confusion, not merely over the definition of evangelicalism, but over the meaning of the gospel itself.

And that is the third and most important difference between fundamentalists and generic evangelicals. No fundamentalists advocate open theism or Word-Faith theology. No fundamentalists deny the inerrancy of Scripture or downplay the importance of penal substitution. No fundamentalists confuse the gospel with a social agenda, and no fundamentalists are advocating universalism, inclusivism, accessiblism, or postmortem evangelism. We are not ignorant of these theologies, however. We know and understand the arguments.

We reject them because the gospel does not allow them. They are incompatible with the evangel. Because they are incompatible with the evangel, they ought to be incompatible with evangelicalism.

Fundamentalists are evangelical. We believe, however, that the definition of evangelicalism is being debated only because the founders of "generic evangelicalism" made bad choices about the evangel itself. Denying the gospel its rightful position as the boundary of Christian recognition and fellowship is the very thing that had produced the increase of theological and ecclesiastical flabbiness. This is an error that, to some degree, generic evangelicalism continues to perpetuate.

### R. ALBERT MOHLER JR.

John Stackhouse is admirably ambitious in stating his purpose as reflected in his essay. He proposes to offer "a definition of evangelicalism that lets us all feel we are authentic evangelicals, without defining evangelicalism so broadly that it becomes useless as a descriptor of a particular kind of Christianity." In other words, he calls for a "generic evangelicalism" that includes a very wide swath of contemporary Protestantism but retains some distinctive character.

From the onset, John stakes his claim to move beyond the "binary" divisions that have been proposed by figures on both the left and the right of the contemporary spectrum. As far back as 1998, he called for a strategy that would avoid the "perils of left and right."[22]

In that article, cited early in his essay, John referred to typologies proposed by theologians Millard Erickson (resist postmodernism versus embrace it) and Roger Olson (traditionalists versus reformists). As he explained:

> The trouble with such typologies is that they presuppose a uniform conservative theology against which postconservatives can define themselves; a traditional theology that reformists want to alter; and an evangelical center or Right in comparison with which all of the theologians in question are definitely to the Left. It is this general assumption, as well as the questionable grouping of quite disparate theologians onto one side or the other of a divide, that mars such maps of contemporary evangelical thought.[23]

That statement certainly helps me to understand what John is doing in his essay. When he sets out his "Definition 1" and "Definition 2" on

---

22. John G. Stackhouse Jr., "The Perils of Left and Right," *Christianity Today* (August 10, 1998), http://www.christianitytoday.com/ct/1998/august10/8t9058.html.
23. Ibid.

the way to making his proposal, he is to some degree knocking away the particularities and preoccupations he sees as a hindrance to his big-tent definition of evangelicalism that will "let us all feel we are authentic evangelicals."

On the way to making his argument, John certainly covers a lot of territory. He offers a basic understanding of evangelicalism that centers in the evangel, the good news concerning Jesus Christ. So is *evangelicalism* just another word for Christianity? Yes and no, he says. The term is not, he asserts, on par with the denominations or broader traditions. Instead, it is a movement that calls for "fidelity in doctrine, fervency in piety, and faithfulness in mission."

Well, it is hard to imagine any movement that claims to be Christian that would not claim all three of those goals. But John then suggests that evangelicalism is, at heart, a renewal movement to correct deficiencies in the church's achievement of those three goals.

John's Definition 1 of *evangelical* draws upon the work of British historian David Bebbington, who suggested the criteria of crucicentrism, biblicism, conversionism, and activism. Each of these, he accepts, must be defined. Furthermore, he wants to add George Marsden's criterion of transdenominationalism to the mix.

That last criterion allows John to sideline the standoffish groups that may share theological commonalities with evangelicals but do not join in common efforts. That sets John's second model of evangelical definition.

His Definition 2 is more institutional, identifying evangelicals as those who belong to "a historical movement known as evangelicalism"—which he locates historically in the eighteenth-century revivals and awakenings.

I was both impressed and interested when John then proceeded to define as evangelical only those "who have not departed from the characteristic emphases of those revivals" or "who have since identified themselves with this evangelical tradition."

Those qualifications, and others John inserts along the way, are evidence of serious thinking and intellectual honesty. He understands that some would like to claim to be evangelicals who have departed from theological orthodoxy. At the same time, he accuses some evangelical organizations and movements of attempting to truncate the larger evangelical movement in order to privilege their own theological commitments on what John sees as nonessential matters.

So what are the essential matters? John finally lists five evangelical characteristics: crucicentric, biblicist, conversionist, missional, and transdenominational. In other words, John brings us back to where he began, with a lot of fruitful thought and analysis thrown in for good measure.

The reader has to get to the end of John's essay to see the picture in the frame, and at that point, John's understanding of evangelical definition comes into pretty clear focus. He really does believe that an evangelical is, in essence, a Protestant Christian who shares certain urgent hopes for the renewal of the church and a historic sense of belonging to the movement known as *evangelicalism*.

Ruled out, by his definition, are heretics (who are not actually Christians at all) and those who hold to theologies that are simply not recognizably Christian (like the Mormons). Ruled in are just about all who would claim the emphases of evangelicalism and would identify with the movement, but are not heretics or other non-Christians.

Thus, if you are not a heretic and you claim these commitments and identity with the movement, you are an evangelical, and no one, John asserts, should say that you are not, no matter how much we may differ theologically.

So if we are using the terminology of evangelicalism as a centered or a bounded set, John apparently believes that the movement should include all who affirm the center (thus a centered set) and none who are heretics or non-Christians (thus a bounded set).

Now, I know of no one else who has framed the argument in this way, and I think John has made a genuine intellectual contribution in this proposal. As a matter of fact, I think that his proposal would be extremely useful for the national media, observers of North American religion, and sociologists. I will go so far as to say that, if we bracket the theological concerns, John's proposal is head and shoulders above anything else I have seen.

But I do not think his proposal works so well in the theological arena, and that is my primary concern. I cannot bracket those concerns. The shortcomings of John's definition become clear to me when he deals with the extent to which evangelicals must accept divergences from the central commitments.

He signals this concern in a really powerful way when he asks, "Can one be an (authentic) evangelical and, say, hold that covenantal domestic and romantic partnerships between homosexuals should be recognized by the church as sanctioned by God?" His answer, quite apparently, is yes.

That is not all. He raises similar questions about prosperity theology (which I would identify as a heresy) and the Word-Faith movement (another heresy, in my book), and other theological movements, including open theism.

He does not identify with the open theists, yet he suggests that unless they are heretics (which he apparently does not believe), they are evangelicals. "They are just *wrong* evangelicals," he states. "They have mistaken beliefs, in my view, about the nature of God and a number of related matters."

So reason demands that we ask just how "wrong" an evangelical can be and remain an evangelical. As I read John's essay, it appears that he believes a person may be very wrong indeed on major doctrinal issues and remain an evangelical. Who is to say they are not? John asks.

At this point, as John anticipates, many of us will reach for the hammer to break the glass on the fire alarm. John knows that at least some of us participating in this project will disagree "on just how orthodox, orthopath, and orthoprax one must be to count as a genuine evangelical."

Count me in that number. To the credit of his rigorous analysis, John makes us think with extreme care. Be careful, he warns, not to state your case too strictly. After all, evangelicalism has been transdenominational from the beginning, and this covers a lot of really serious theological ground. You mean, he asks, that evangelicals can accept disagreement on matters as theologically consequential as baptism and church government, but not on matters such as same-sex marriage or open theism?

Well, that is a good question, but in the end, I believe that endorsing same-sex marriage or open theism places one outside the evangelical tent. Affirming biblicism (as cited by David Bebbington as well as by John Stackhouse) does not rule out disagreement on baptism (as church history has shown), but it does rule out denials of the revealed text. This kind of issue, in my view, points to the necessity of biblical inerrancy as a control doctrine to protect the integrity of what it means to affirm the Bible as the written Word of God.

John seems to struggle with this balance when he deals with the question of penal substitution. I was pleased and reassured to read John's hearty affirmation of the importance and centrality of penal substitution to the gospel and thus to evangelical identity. He goes so far as to argue that any theology that rejects penal substitution is "seriously deficient." And yet he ends that discussion by affirming that even those who deny penal substitution with hostility to the doctrine "remain evangelicals nonetheless." Here again, John finds those he calls *wrong* evangelicals but *genuine* evangelicals.

The bottom line is that John and I are locked in an honest disagreement over this fundamental question: just *how* wrong can you be and remain an evangelical? On this question I stand, clearly, in a different place than John. I do not think John's proposal identifies evangelicals in a way that ensures that all who bear that designation can be counted on to bear a true witness to the gospel of Jesus Christ.

Doctrines have implications, even as the gospel has implications. One of the most pressing challenges for today's generation of evangelicals is determining the acceptable range of doctrinal positions that will, nonetheless, produce a faithful witness to the gospel of Jesus Christ and to the central evangelical affirmation of the Scripture principle.

Speaking of those whom he identifies as "*wrong* evangelicals," John warns, "Those of us who disagree with them as fellow evangelicals ought to be particularly careful to hear them out in case it is we, not they, who are mistaken on one point or many."

That is a good statement of theological and intellectual charity. We do need to listen to each other with particular care. At the same time, our current moment calls for more than a dispassionate listening session. Charity cannot be used as an excuse for nourishing theological error.

John is right, of course, that there is no institutional mechanism that can determine these questions for the entire evangelical movement. There is no evangelical high court. In the end, this is one of the limitations of evangelicalism as a movement.

All this reminds me of how thankful I am that I am a Baptist before I am an evangelical. As a member of a Baptist church and as a professor within a Southern Baptist seminary, I am held accountable, with all of my fellow members and colleagues, to certain definite beliefs that are explicitly stated in confessional form. John may be right that there is no evangelical magisterium that can prevent anyone from claiming to be an evangelical, no matter how divergent his or her theology may be. But my church can and should impose its discipline, even as my denomination should protect its membership and my seminary must ensure the orthodoxy of its faculty.

In other words, John's essay helps me to affirm even more energetically my belief that the only way evangelicalism can be retained as a definable theological movement is by means of a glad and eager confessionalism. The largely parachurch character of evangelicalism ensures that this will be difficult. That is why, at the end of it all, John's fascinating essay reminds me that *evangelical*, no matter how well defined, is just not enough. The term is essential as it points to a movement, but that may well be the extent of its usefulness.

After all these things are considered, I am all the more thankful for the church. At the end of the day, the confessional church must do what the evangelical movement cannot — confess with specificity the faith once for all delivered to the saints.

## ROGER E. OLSON

Actually, in spite of John Stackhouse's expectation, I think my definition of evangelicalism fits him quite well. And I see myself reflected in his definition and description of evangelicalism. I think we are more or less on the same page. I don't know whether he will agree, but that is how I interpret our chapters.

Before I plunge into some specific responses to John's chapter, I'd like to elucidate a few matters that may not be as clear as I'd like in my own chapter. First, when I speak or write about evangelicalism, I always assume people know that I think all evangelicals are Christians; therefore, anyone who is not a Christian cannot be an evangelical. I tend to plunge into defining *evangelical* with that assumption without anticipating that some people may not fully understand. Let me be clear about something I *thought* all of us who set out to define and describe evangelicalism agree on: all evangelicals are Christians, but not all Christians are evangelicals.

What difference does that make? When I delineate the common, unifying features of evangelicalism, I may not make as clear as I should that there are *other* features shared by all evangelicals—those shared by all Christians! With John, I affirm that Christians are people who have a personal faith in Jesus Christ that transforms their lives and who normally believe certain things about God, Jesus Christ, humanity, and salvation.[24]

So if I haven't made it clear before, let me say unequivocally that an evangelical is always a person who, like every Christian, trusts in Jesus

---

24. I say "normally," because much depends on a person's ability to know and understand these matters; I wouldn't hold a child or new convert to the same standard as a mature Christian. I also say "normally," because I want to be open to different interpretations of doctrines; I'm often surprised to find that a person who I think *isn't* a Christian because of seemingly radically different beliefs *is* one because he or she is simply using words differently.

Christ in a personal, life-transforming way, and who, to the extent able, believes in the God revealed in the Bible and in Jesus Christ as God incarnate, and who believes human beings can be saved only through the atoning death of Jesus Christ on the cross and his bodily resurrection.

The second clarification I'd like to make is about an important distinction I sometimes assume everyone understands but often find they don't. That is the distinction between the *evangelical ethos* and the *evangelical movement*. I think a lot of confusion arises from ignoring that distinction, and I have been guilty sometimes of not making it clearly enough myself. Kevin, Al, and John all seem to confuse the two at some points. Let me explain.

The evangelical ethos is a Christian way of life marked by the four common hallmarks of evangelicalism set forth by Noll and Bebbington and mentioned by Al, John, and me. John and I think they are very helpful for defining evangelicalism. He adds one, and I add another one. I accept his fifth characteristic — transdenominationalism — as true of the *evangelical movement* but not of the *evangelical ethos*. In other words, a person or church may very well display an evangelical ethos but not be part of the evangelical movement stemming from the renewal movements of the seventeenth and eighteenth centuries (pietism, Puritanism, and revivalism) or of the post–World War II, postfundamentalist evangelicalism that has centered around Billy Graham, the National Association of Evangelicals, *Christianity Today*, and the like.

For example, many Christians in the Restorationist and Anabaptist movements and some Lutheran and Reformed Christians have not been "movement evangelicals" and show little to no interest in transdenominational cooperation. Many Christians in the Churches of Christ and the Independent Christian churches do not consider themselves or their churches part of Stackhouse's (and my) transdenominational, cooperative movement. The same can be said of many Christians in the Lutheran Church–Missouri Synod and the Southern Baptist Convention. *Some* in these denominations (and others) embody the evangelical ethos, but their churches do not identify with the evangelical movement.

Hopefully, all movement evangelicals *do* embody and live out the evangelical ethos. The evangelical movement, if it is anything, is a transdenominational (including some nondenominational churches, organizations, and individuals) movement to promote the evangelical ethos as a renewing power within Christianity and society. But it does not have a monopoly on the evangelical ethos. In fact, I would argue, some Roman Catholics (perhaps especially charismatic Catholics) show forth the evangelical ethos without belonging to the movement.

I'm a little unclear which meaning of *evangelical* John has in mind in his chapter. It seems he is focusing on movement evangelicalism. All I want to say about that is that *evangelical* can rightly be applied to people who don't belong to the movement. I think I could have made that clearer in my chapter with regard to the Churches of Christ and the Seventh-day Adventist denomination. So I'll say it here and now and hope this will shed some light on my chapter if not John's as well.

I find myself disagreeing with very little in John's chapter. I agree very heartily with him about open theism and the penal substitution model of the atonement. The former is, I judge, theologically mistaken without being so serious a departure from evangelical identity as to make it not an evangelical option. The latter is, I agree, normal for evangelical faith without being necessary, so that people who question it are automatically thereby excluded from either the evangelical ethos or the movement. (John does seem to contradict himself when he says, on the one hand, "Penal substitutionary atonement ... is essential to Christian theology and therefore to evangelical theology," and, on the other hand, that evangelicals who diminish or dismiss it are truly evangelicals.)

I especially agree with John's point that in these matters and others there is no evangelical authority who decides who's "in" and who's "out" of the movement (to say nothing of the ethos!). He rightly asks the heresy-hunting evangelicals, "Who gets to say what is *too* heretical and what is orthodox *enough* among evangelicals...?" And he is right that this task of sorting out who really belongs and who does not really belong to institutional evangelicalism is worth discussing but ultimately cannot be settled. Just as "authentic and healthy Christianity" is an inherently contestable concept, so is "authentic evangelicalism," whether we are talking about the ethos or the movement. That does not mean evangelicalism is compatible with anything and everything, as some fear, but only that defining it precisely and deciding who's "in" and who's "out" is part of its uncertain and unsettled nature. For making our tentative decisions, we have no alternative but to turn to history without allowing history to make evangelicalism something static.

So why is my account of evangelicalism called "postconservative" and John's "generic"? In most ways they are very much alike. The only substantial difference I can see is one of degree, not kind. John says, "Let's be sure to recognize the creative possibilities that exist on the edges [of the evangelical movement] as we encounter the rest of the world." That is precisely what I mean by postconservative—a cautious openness to new, creative possibilities of evangelical thinking *insofar* as they are rooted in fresh and faithful interpretation of Scripture. "Postconservative" simply means *not* privileging "the received evangelical tradition" so much that nothing new or different can ever appear. It means greeting new theological proposals *arising among evangelicals on the basis of fresh and faithful biblical interpretation* with cautious openness and not rejecting them in knee-jerk fashion just because they are new and different.

Some critics have assumed that *postconservative* means unfettered theological experimentation, what John calls being "reckless on the boundaries." (I prefer his term "frontiers" over "boundaries," as a movement can have the former but can't have the latter.) The problem is, of course, that some guardians of evangelical tradition, perhaps suffering from a disease I call "hardening of the categories," greet *every* new proposal as if it were reckless. How do I know they do this? Because I have seen that reaction "close up," as it were. It is clearly recognizable when critics do not wait to make sure they have correctly understood a new proposal before jumping to condemn it as "beyond the boundaries." I have yet to read or talk to any critic of open theism, for example, who clearly understands it. If they do understand it, their ways of describing it fail to reveal that.[25]

I suspect, although I could be wrong, that John is more cautious about new theological proposals than I tend to be. For me, as for most or all postconservatives, questioning tradition in the light of Scripture is a good thing as long as it does not amount to antitraditionalism. It is one thing to question and test and something else to reject. A

---

25. For example, almost every outspoken evangelical critic of open theism who wants to exclude it from evangelicalism says it is denial of omniscience and/or is simply a new form of process theology. Both assertions are patently false. It is, to be sure, a denial of most *traditional* notions of omniscience, but that's different. And its differences from process theology are greater than its similarities.

postconservative evangelical can and should respect the great tradition of Christian orthodoxy and the received evangelical tradition while at the same time testing them by the litmus test of biblical faithfulness. I regard what N. T. Wright is doing with his "new perspective on Paul" a prime example of this, which doesn't mean that I agree with it. It means that I regard his practice of *sola* (or *prima*) *Scriptura* as more truly evangelical than any static, rigid traditionalism that shuts down every new theological project just because it threatens time-honored doctrinal formulas. I have no idea how John regards Wright's project, but I suspect he approaches such new ways of thinking with greater caution and perhaps even a more negative bias than I do. However, he is clearly not a neo-fundamentalist who attacks people who dare to think in fresh but biblically committed ways as nonevangelical. I think he and I are close, just looking in different directions.

# POSTCONSERVATIVE EVANGELICALISM

### ROGER E. OLSON

Most of us who identify ourselves as evangelicals and are interested in preserving that label have had frustrating and confusing experiences with it.[1] I was invited to serve on an ecumenical panel of religious leaders to discuss the Gulf War. A Lutheran bishop sat next to me and asked whom I was there to represent. When I replied, "I guess the evangelical community," he bristled and announced, "Evangelical? We're the evangelicals!" (He was a bishop of the Evangelical Lutheran Church in America.) I didn't have time to explain that we were probably using the label in different senses.

Surfing channels, I happened to land on a well-known and widely viewed prime-time talk show. The host was interviewing a seminary dean about the evangelical view of controversial social issues. I didn't feel that the dean represented me or millions of other evangelicals like me. But his presence on that talk show implied to millions of viewers that he spoke for all evangelicals.

A well-known conservative Christian historian of American religion chided me for referring to his friend, a well-known conservative theologian, as an evangelical. "Why do you call him an evangelical when he doesn't want to be part of your evangelical movement?" The

---

1. Editor's note: Roger Olson's other writings on evangelicalism include *How to Be Evangelical without Being Conservative* (Grand Rapids: Zondervan, 2008); *Pocket History of Evangelical Theology* (Downers Grove, Ill.: InterVarsity, 2007); *Reformed and Always Reforming: The Postconservative Approach to Evangelical Theology*, Acadia Studies in Bible and Theology (Grand Rapids: Baker, 2007); and "Postconservative Evangelical Theology and the Theological Pilgrimage of Clark Pinnock," in *Semper Reformandum: Studies in Honour of Clark H. Pinnock*, ed. Stanley E. Porter and Anthony R. Cross (Carlisle: Paternoster, 2003), 16–37.

problem was that his friend, whom I also count as a friend, was then director of a group with the word evangelical in its name.

I invited a knowledgeable and articulate professor of theology from a nearby fundamentalist seminary to speak to my church history class at an evangelical liberal arts college about fundamentalism. He wore the fundamentalist label proudly and spoke passionately about how fundamentalists are not evangelicals (in the sense of the modern evangelical movement that he referred to as "neo-evangelical"). As I walked him to his car afterward, I thanked him and offered to return the favor by speaking to a class at his seminary. He said without any acrimony or disdain, "We won't be inviting you."

A recruiter for a college and seminary known for promoting itself as fundamentalist set up a table at my college. I mentioned that I would probably not refer my students to his seminary. "Oh, why?" he asked. I talked about the difference between fundamentalists and evangelicals and how my students were probably more open and progressive than his seminary would allow. He responded, "Oh, you've got us wrong; we're changing." I asked, "If Billy Graham offered to speak in your chapel free of charge, would your president invite him?" He replied, "We're moving in that direction."

At the end of a protracted and sometimes heated professional society meeting where a panel of experts was discussing the meaning of evangelicalism, a nonevangelical theologian from a mainline Protestant denomination stood up and said, "I think an evangelical is anyone who loves Billy Graham." The two hundred or so scholars in the room all broke out in applause.

As these true anecdotes reveal, the problem with identifying who is authentically evangelical is that "evangelical" and "evangelicalism" are essentially contested concepts. Ever since 1976 when *Newsweek* published a cover story titled "the year of the evangelical," a veritable industry has developed around attempting to define these terms and identify their boundaries. My thesis is that this is an interesting but ultimately futile project. And yet it is one we scholars of evangelicalism cannot seem to give up on.

## Evangelicalism Has No Definable Boundaries

The reason that evangelical and evangelicalism are essentially contested concepts is that, unlike the Roman Catholic Church and some other religious organizations, the evangelical movement has no headquarters or authoritative magisterium. If a person wants to know who is a Roman Catholic, he or she can at least look to the Vatican for help. The Roman Catholic Church is a worldwide organization and not merely a spiritual movement. Unlike evangelicalism, it has a headquarters and a magisterium.

Evangelicalism is like the charismatic movement or the new thought movement or the New Age movement in that they are all religious-spiritual networks and coalitions without any membership. The people who associate with them are extremely diverse but have some common interests; they lack any single spokesperson even if each one has celebrities who aspire to being its pope. Each one includes organizations, but none is an organization.

All that is to say that evangelicalism has no definable boundaries and cannot have them. An organization has boundaries; a movement does not. And without boundaries it is simply impossible to say with certainty who is and who is not an evangelical; all one can do is accept anyone's claim to being an evangelical insofar as he or she shares certain common commitments identified by historians of the movement. Those common commitments, which I will explicate later, form a center of the evangelical movement that has no boundaries. Every movement may be said to have a center; the adherents of the movement gather around that center and allow it to define at least a part of their lives.

## Centered Set vs. Bounded Set

Thus, evangelicalism is a "centered set" as opposed to a "bounded set." A common response to my claim that evangelicalism is a centered and not a bounded set (and the claim that it is both reduces to the claim that it is a bounded set) is that "there cannot be a center without a circumference." (Here "circumference" is synonymous with boundaries.) This is simply false. There are many sets of entities with centers but no boundaries or circumferences. I will offer examples after explaining the phenomenon more fully.

I borrow the concepts "bounded set" and "centered set" from evangelical missiologist Paul Hiebert (1932–2007), who described them in detail in his groundbreaking 1978 article,[2] but others have used them

---

2. Paul Hiebert, "Conversion, Culture and Cognitive Categories," *Gospel in Context* 1, no. 4 (October 1978): 24–29.

as well. A centered set is a group of entities (persons, numbers, objects) that have something in common but also differ in significant ways. Most important for our purposes here, the centered set has something in common that unifies its members in spite of their differences. That something may be a gravitational or magnetic force, or it may be an experience or interest. The reason these entities do not compose a bounded set is that nobody can identify the precise boundaries around them, and therefore, at least in some cases, it is impossible to say with certainty exactly which entities belong to the set and which do not.

A bounded set is composed of entities whose precise membership is at least in principle identifiable. Such a set may have a center, but relationship to it is not the only or even the best way to identify membership in the set if that is what someone is trying to do. One can look outward from the center and "see" definite boundaries within which all members in some sense exist. Entities outside those identifiable boundaries do not belong to the set even if they are close to it and claim to be in it.

Let's return to the reality of centers without circumferences. Mathematicians deal with what they call "fuzzy sets" of numbers as well as definite sets of numbers. Astronomers deal with cosmological sets of stars, planets, and other objects, some of which are identifiable by a center but have no definite boundaries. An example is the Milky Way. Even our solar system may seem to be a bounded set of entities, but the debate over whether Pluto is a planet indicates otherwise. Also, there may be comets or other objects that have not yet been identified that belong to the solar system. A centered set, then, like a fuzzy set in mathematics, is one that admits of degrees of membership where absolute limits of membership elude identification.

## Movement vs. Organization

Most important to my point here is the difference between movements and organizations. Almost by definition, a social movement is a centered set unless and until it becomes an organization, which is when it becomes a bounded set. But then it is no longer a movement. I argue (and would like to hear someone argue convincingly otherwise) that a social movement cannot have boundaries. That is what makes it a movement and not an organization. The moment a movement gets organized and has boundaries (e.g., by establishing definite membership), it is no longer a movement. (People may still call it a movement, but that is a misnomer.)

Evangelicalism has no definite membership because it is a movement and not an organization. The Evangelical Theological Society, on the other hand, is an organization and thus has definite, identifiable membership. A person might be voted out of the ETS, and nobody would then claim he or she is "part of the ETS." Somewhere there exists a definitive list of members of the ETS and an authority that decides who belongs and who does not. Thus, the ETS, like all true organizations, is a bounded set.

The same is not true, and cannot be true, of evangelicalism, which includes the ETS but is not identical with or limited to it. For example, the National Association of Evangelicals, founded in 1942 (before the ETS) and composed of about fifty denominations and thousands of churches and organizations, has a statement of faith that does not include biblical inerrancy. The ETS requires its members to affirm that belief. Because the ETS is not evangelicalism itself, inerrancy cannot be regarded as necessary to being authentically evangelical. It is what theologians call *adiaphora*—a nonessential belief.

Does all this mean that evangelicalism is a chimera—a fantasy or illusion? Certainly not. It does exist—as a movement. And we have to settle for that. Attempts to put boundaries around it appear silly if not disingenuous. As a movement it has certain features, and the main one—the one that identifies it as a movement—is a common center or core. Exactly what that center or core is may be debatable. But if there were none, it would not be a movement. Everyone knows, however, that it is a movement.

### Sociology vs. Theology?

Some critics will say (as they have said to me before) that I am talking about sociology whereas they are talking about theology when they assert that evangelical boundaries exist. They might agree with me that the evangelical movement, as a sociological phenomenon, cannot have definite boundaries. But they argue that there can and must be theological boundaries to the concept "evangelical" or else it is meaningless. But I ask them how to separate theology from sociology in this case. What is "evangelical theology" but theology done by evangelicals?

Well, perhaps history can help. What are the theological roots of the evangelical movement? That is helpful for identifying the center, but it hardly helps identify boundaries. As anyone who has studied evangelicals of the past knows, they have always been a diverse bunch. Who is to say which theologians and confessional statements were historically normative for all evangelicals? Anyone who attempted to do that would invite an argument from heirs of other evangelical theologians, revivalists, and leaders who adhered to other confessional statements.

Evangelical historian and theologian Donald W. Dayton has delineated two evangelical histories: the Puritan-Presbyterian one and the pietist-Pentecostal one. (I am taking some liberties with his terminology, but I am confident he won't mind since we have discussed these matters a lot.) In fact, much of the trouble of defining evangelicalism today stems from the fact that our evangelical ancestors belonged to two quite distinct traditions that really came together only because of revivals such as the Great Awakenings and the early antiliberal fundamentalist movement (which before 1925 was actually just resurgent conservative Protestantism).

I think that contemporary evangelicalism is an unstable compound composed of two incompatible traditions. These joined together in uneasy coalition to fight liberal theology's takeover of Protestant institutions and to provide a conservative ecumenical alternative to the National Council of Churches. One tradition is rooted in Protestant orthodoxy and reveres the Westminster Confession of Faith (or something similar such as the Congregational Savoy Declaration). It is heavily doctrinal and suspicious of experiential spirituality. The other tradition is rooted in pietism and revivalism and thrives on experiences such as conversion and sanctification (as a second definite "blessing" subsequent to conversion). Sometimes heirs of this tradition are wary of too much doctrinal precision and especially anything that smacks of "dead orthodoxy."

Both traditions value something of the other's ethos, but each tends to emphasize its own ethos as more important for defining authentic Christianity and, by extension, evangelicalism. These two evangelical Protestant traditions joined in an uneasy alliance in 1942 with the founding of the National Association of Evangelicals. Of course, evangelicalism did not begin with that event, but it was a turning point in evangelical history. Much of what people call evangelicalism today harks back to that event and its aftermath, including the founding of *Christianity Today*, Fuller Theological Seminary, and the Billy Graham Evangelistic Association. None of these are directly related to the NAE, but they were made possible, I would argue, by the founding of the NAE and its unique uniting of disparate evangelical bodies and traditions.

Because it is an organization, even if one that uniquely represents a movement, the NAE adopted a doctrinal statement that all members must affirm. It is relatively brief, so as to include as many evangelicals as possible while at the same time clearly affirming the essentials of Protestant Christian faith. The old motto "In essentials unity, in nonessentials liberty, in all things charity" has often been used to describe the ethos of the NAE and its faith statement, which does not include biblical inerrancy. Within the NAE one finds cooperating together denominations as diverse as the Adventists (the Advent Christian Church), Pentecostals (who numerically probably make up the majority of NAE members), Presbyterians and Reformed, Holiness (Nazarenes and Wesleyans), and even the Worldwide Church of God—the denomination founded by Herbert W. Armstrong that later rejected his aberrant teachings and embraced evangelical faith.

There can be no doubt that the NAE, since its founding, has been a "big tent" organization striving to include as many self-identified evangelicals as possible. While the NAE is not the evangelical movement, its inclusive ethos marked the movement for decades. The only evangelicals who would not join were and are the Southern Baptist Convention (some Southern Baptists reject the label "evangelical," and its leadership claims it is not really a denomination and therefore should not join such ecumenical bodies) and various self-identified fundamentalist groups, many of which consider the NAE too inclusive and not sufficiently separated from the liberalism of the mainline churches. They have their own parallel umbrella organization called the American Council of Christian Churches (ACCC), which was founded a year before the NAE. It refused to join the NAE because it allowed Pentecostals to join. From its founding, however, the NAE has been open to fundamentalist denominations and churches insofar as they can affirm its statement of faith (which most, if not all, could do).

Evangelical theologian Donald Bloesch expressed well the relationship between contemporary evangelicalism (since 1942) and fundamentalism:

> Evangelicalism unashamedly stands for the fundamentals of the historic [Christian] faith, but as a movement it transcends and corrects the defensive, sectarian mentality commonly associated with Fundamentalism. Though many, perhaps most, fundamentalists are evangelicals, evangelical Christianity is wider and deeper than Fundamentalism, which is basically a movement of reaction in the churches in this period of history. Evangelicalism in the classical sense fulfills the basic goals and aspirations of Fundamentalism but rejects the ways in which these goals are realized.[3]

In spite of their differences of style, I believe "evangelicalism" includes both ACCC-type and NAE-type evangelicals. It also includes most, if not all, Southern Baptists. And, of course, it also includes many churches and individuals in the so-called mainline Protestant denominations who want to revive and renew them.

So, returning to the main question, how does one separate or even distinguish between "evangelical theology" and the sociological phenomenon of evangelicalism? It would be possible to do that only if there existed an evangelical magisterium. But the preceding paragraphs demonstrate there is no such thing. Neither the ACCC, nor the NAE, nor *Christianity Today*, nor even Billy Graham speaks for all evangelicals; none of these or anyone else has the authority to identify "theological boundaries" around evangelicalism. I suspect some within the Evangelical Theological Society would like to do that, but who gives them that authority?

## Evangelicalism's Center Is Definable Historically

I once spoke to a gathering of thirteen evangelical liberal arts college presidents. They were leaders of the Christian College Consortium made up of the leading evangelical colleges in America. After I spoke, I listened as they debated the nature of evangelicalism and evangelical theology. Their diversity of opinions led to some heated discussions. The president of a conservative, nondenominational college argued that evangelical identity depends on adherence to the orthodox creeds of

---

3. Donald G. Bloesch, *The Future of Evangelical Christianity* (Garden City, N.Y.: Doubleday, 1983), 22.

Christendom (presumably the Apostles' Creed and the Nicene Creed if not also the Athanasian Creed). The president of an evangelical Friends (Quaker) college rejected that claim. The president of a college rooted in the Anabaptist and pietist traditions also rejected that claim and chided the president who made it for attempting to enforce doctrinal uniformity on everyone else.

The presidential debate well illustrates the difficulty of identifying evangelical theological boundaries; surely those men (they were all men!) held some doctrinal commitments in common, but their disagreement demonstrated that no absolute boundary lines exist.

So how, then, can we keep the concept "evangelical" from becoming compatible with anything and everything? I understand the anxiety felt by some conservative evangelicals even if I do not feel it as acutely as they do. They fear a slippery slope of evangelical doctrinal drift and downgrade. Some of us with roots in the pietist-Pentecostal paradigm of evangelicalism are more afraid of dead orthodoxy among evangelicals. Some of those of the Puritan-Presbyterian paradigm don't seem to share that concern.

I do not see any other recourse for solving this problem of evangelical identity (both theological and sociological) than turning to history. Fortunately, several noted historians have worked on this for decades and have identified four (and I will add a fifth) hallmarks that together form the center of the evangelical "set." Some are experiential and some are theological; for these historians, evangelicalism is a combination of both.

A leading evangelical publisher, InterVarsity Press, is producing a set of volumes by influential evangelical historians tracing the history of the contemporary evangelical movement back to its earliest roots. The series' editors are highly regarded evangelical historians Mark Noll and David Bebbington, and its general title is *A History of Evangelicalism: People, Movements and Ideas in the English-Speaking World*. These volumes offer detailed descriptions and examinations of evangelical revivals and leaders going back to the Great Awakenings of the sixteenth century in Great Britain and America. The first volume focuses on the three grandfathers of the contemporary evangelical movement — revivalists John Wesley, Jonathan Edwards, and George Whitefield.[4]

---

4. Mark A. Noll, *The Rise of Evangelicalism: The Age of Edwards, Whitefield and the Wesleys* (2003); John Wolfe, *The Expansion of Evangelicalism: The Age of Wilberforce, More, Chalmers*

So what do Noll and Bebbington identify as the hallmarks of authentic evangelical faith as displayed by the various individuals and groups that have historically been called evangelical and have been regarded by almost all evangelicals as their progenitors? What common features and family resemblances unite this otherwise blooming, buzzing confusion? According to Noll and Bebbington, authentic evangelicalism today, in continuity with its historical roots and antecedents, always displays four features or hallmarks: conversionism, biblicism, crucicentrism, and activism.[5]

## Conversionism

By "conversionism" Noll and Bebbington mean belief in and experience of a spiritual conversion to Christ by faith that is not reducible to a ritual of initiation into a church or merely "turning over a new leaf." For evangelicals, conversion must be personal (which does not necessarily imply individualism) and always involves decision if not emotion. In other words, evangelicals believe that authentic Christian faith always involves being twice born (to borrow a phrase from William James); a real Christian cannot be only once born (i.e., natural birth). The "new birth," variously called regeneration or being "born again," is a work of God either antecedent to (as in Calvinist theology) or immediately subsequent to (as in Arminian theology) a personal acquisition and expression of faith in Jesus Christ that also involves repentance for sins.[6]

Anyone who studies evangelical movements as revivals of authentic Christian faith and renewals of the church within Protestantism has to recognize this as their most common feature. It can be expressed in

---

*and Finney* (2007); and David W. Bebbington, *The Dominance of Evangelicalism: The Age of Spurgeon and Moody* (2005).

5. Mark A. Noll, David W. Bebbington, George A. Rawlyk, eds., *Evangelicalism: Comparative Studies in Popular Protestantism in North America, the British Isles, and Beyond, 1700–1990* (Oxford and New York: Oxford University Press, 1994).

6. Calvinism is that type of Protestant theology, common among evangelicals, that emphasizes God's sovereignty and human depravity to the extent that the new birth, regeneration, must logically (not necessarily chronologically) precede conversion because humans are too sinful by themselves to choose to repent and trust in Jesus Christ alone for salvation. They must be reborn, "made alive," by the Holy Spirit *first* so that they can and will respond to the gospel call with faith. Arminianism is that type of Protestant theology, also common among evangelicals, that believes conversion, as personal repentance and faith, must precede regeneration (the new birth). The details of these two types of evangelical theology are spelled out in my book *Arminian Theology: Myths and Realities* (Downers Grove, Ill.: InterVarsity, 2006).

various ways and has no definite formula or outward expression, but it always involves the appeal to personal decision to live a new life for Jesus Christ through inward transformation by the Holy Spirit in response to repentance and faith.[7]

In other words, as a popular saying among evangelicals goes, "God has no grandchildren." The idea that anyone can simply "grow up saved" or be saved by means of a ritual such as baptism apart from personally exercising faith and experiencing conversion is antithetical to true evangelical faith. This does not mean that evangelical faith requires what the German pietists of the eighteenth and early nineteenth centuries called *Busskampf*—the struggle of repentance accompanied by tears and emotion. That has often been a feature of evangelical revivals of religion, but Noll and Bebbington and virtually all evangelical theologians and historians rightly see it as normal but not normative. In many cases, true evangelical conversion is quiet and inward, but it must be a definite turning point in one's life even if a person cannot later recall its precise time or setting.

Conversionism of the evangelical type assumes some surrounding doctrinal beliefs. The leaders of past evangelical revivals of religion and of fundamentalism and of modern and contemporary evangelicalism have always agreed that true salvation, beginning with authentic conversion to Jesus Christ, presupposes belief in Jesus Christ as Lord, Savior, and God even if the person being converted does not yet fully understand this. It also presupposes that only the Holy Spirit, who is also God, can bring it about; it is not the same as "turning over a new leaf" or achieving some enlightened spiritual state through self-help.

Thus, historically speaking, evangelical faith has always included at least implicit belief in the Trinity even as there are within evangelicalism different ways of understanding the details of that historic Christian doctrine. It has also always included understanding on some level that real conversion to Christ and inward transformation by the Holy Spirit (regeneration) is solely "by grace through faith" and not an autonomous achievement of the person.

---

7. Theologically, Calvinist evangelicals explain that the transformation logically comes before the decision, but they nevertheless always emphasize a connection between the inward work of transformation by the Holy Spirit and the outward decision and expression of repentance and faith.

An astute reader may wonder if I am now beginning to describe boundaries of evangelicalism. Doesn't "conversionism" as above described amount to a boundary? Not at all. Rather, this hallmark, together with the following ones, forms part of the gravitational center of evangelicalism; evangelicals are people who are drawn to these experiences and beliefs in a more than academic way. Evangelicals are people who experience these beliefs and believe these experiences. But it is not always possible to tell with absolute assurance who is "in" and who is "out" of the evangelical camp; some people are nearer the center than others, and some people are far away but moving steadily toward it.

The boundary edges of evangelicalism are fuzzy; the center is not. For example, a person might believe in baptismal regeneration but experience the new birth of conversion and promote it as normative. That was the case with John Wesley, the founder of Methodism and one of the first true evangelicals in the modern sense. The issue is ambiguity; these four hallmarks (together with the fifth that I will add and explain below) of evangelical faith are not litmus tests but common features of a diverse movement within which people experience and believe these things "more or less."

## Biblicism

The second historical and theological hallmark of authentic evangelical faith and therefore of authentic evangelicalism is *biblicism*. Noll and Bebbington define it as commitment to the authority of the Bible in all matters of faith and practice together with a special love for the Bible as God's Word containing everything necessary for Christian faith and life. Evangelicals display an especially high regard for the Bible and not only a "high view of Scripture" (which all conservative Christians hold). For evangelicals the Bible is the source and norm of everything spiritual; there is no higher court of appeal in matters of faith. But just as importantly, they love and obey the Bible. As one theologian has put it, for evangelicals "the Bible absorbs the world." Evangelicals do not bring the Bible to the secular world for verification; they view the whole world through the lens of the biblical narrative and worldview.

Commentators have expended a great deal of energy trying to identify the proper evangelical belief about the Bible. One issue that has plagued the evangelical movement for most of its existence is whether the

Bible is historically and scientifically accurate. Some evangelicals have insisted on its strict inerrancy in the original autographs; others have claimed that it is sufficient to regard the Bible as infallible in all matters of faith and practice while leaving open the possibility that the Bible may contain inaccuracies in matters not directly related to its main purpose, which is to identify God for us and show us the way to salvation.

Two precursors of the post–WWII, postfundamentalist evangelical movement were Princeton theologian Benjamin Breckinridge Warfield (1851–1921) and Scottish theologian James Orr (1844–1913). They joined hands across the ocean during the great controversy over liberal theology and destructive biblical criticism during the late nineteenth and early twentieth centuries. They were friends and embraced each other as equally evangelical in spite of the fact that Orr did not believe in the inerrancy of the Bible while Warfield did. Orr authored the very first chapter in the 1910 series of booklets called The Fundamentals, which probably gave the fundamentalist movement its name; Warfield authored the second one.

Although Carl Henry (1913–2003), often regarded as the "dean of evangelical theologians," affirmed biblical inerrancy, he did not consider it necessary for authentic evangelical faith. In 1976 evangelical theologian Harold Lindsell (1913–98) published *The Battle for the Bible*, which fell like a bombshell on the playground of evangelical theologians and leaders, because he claimed that strict biblical inerrancy is essential to evangelical faith.[8] Henry responded negatively. Well-known and highly regarded evangelical theologians Bernard Ramm and Donald Bloesch both denied biblical inerrancy. The issue has never been settled, and those who claim one must affirm inerrancy to be considered truly evangelical are trying to draw boundaries around the movement that have never existed and are out of step with Carl Henry, one of the fathers of the contemporary movement.

## Crucicentrism

According to Noll and Bebbington, the third hallmark of evangelical faith is *crucicentrism*, which means piety centered on the cross of Jesus Christ and his atoning death. Historically, evangelical revivals and renewals have begun by rediscovering and powerfully preaching

---

8. Harold Lindsell, *The Battle for the Bible* (Grand Rapids: Zondervan, 1976).

the gospel of Christ's atoning death on the cross. Evangelical hymnody and worship have traditionally focused on the "blood of Jesus," whether or not they highlight that exact phrase. What it means is not the literal "chemistry of the blood" (as one fundamentalist author claimed) but Christ's death as the way to reconciliation between God and the world.

Again, Donald Bloesch provides a helpful, if somewhat limited, definition of *evangelical* that focuses on this particular hallmark:

> Evangelical' can therefore be said to indicate a particular thrust or emphasis within the church[es], namely, that which upholds the gospel of free grace as we see this in Jesus Christ. An evangelical will consequently be Christocentric and not merely theocentric (as are the deists and a great many mystics). Yet it is not the teachings of Jesus Christ that are considered of paramount importance but his sacrificial life and death on the cross of Calvary. The evangel is none other than the meaning of the cross.[9]

Lest anyone misunderstand Bloesch, or my reason for quoting him here, he does not consider crucicentrism the be-all and end-all of authentic evangelical faith, but he does apparently (and rightly, I judge) consider a particular focus on the cross and the atonement as crucial to authentic evangelicalism. Together with him, I believe it is this thrust or emphasis that is most threatened within the evangelical movement as self-proclaimed evangelicals often soften the emphasis on Christ's death in favor of a seeker-sensitive or postmodern focus on Jesus as friend and example. The offense of the cross stands at the center of historic evangelical faith, and those who move away from that offense are, in my judgment and Bloesch's, moving away from authentic evangelicalism even if they are still part of the movement. Again, it is not a matter of someone being "in" or "out" but of degrees and direction.

Controversy has always existed among evangelicals over the issue of the scope of Christ's atonement and its exact nature. Did Christ die for all people or only for the elect as Calvinists claim? Arminian evangelicals, including Wesley, affirmed universal atonement without universal salvation. His counterpart in the British Great Awakening, who was also instrumental in the American Great Awakening, was George Whitefield, who affirmed limited atonement — that Christ's death was

---

9. Bloesch, *Future of Evangelical Christianity*, 15.

a sacrifice only for those God had from eternity chosen to be saved. The issue threatened to divide the evangelical movement in Great Britain in the 1740s, but Wesley and Whitefield reconciled, and for the most part their descendants in evangelicalism have agreed to disagree about this.

Recently a new controversy has broken out among evangelicals about the so-called penal substitution theory of how Christ's death reconciles God to the world and the world to God. Most evangelicals have affirmed that Christ suffered the punishment sinners deserve—God's wrath was poured out on him in our place as medieval theologian Anselm of Canterbury and Reformation theologian John Calvin affirmed. John Wesley also held this view of the atonement. However, throughout the history of evangelical awakenings and within the contemporary movement, there has always been some diversity of opinion. What all evangelicals agree about is that Christ's death was more than a moral example—it was the sacrifice for sins needed to make sinners acceptable to God.

### Activism

Noll and Bebbington's fourth and final hallmark of evangelical faith is *activism*, by which they mean evangelism and social transformation. This is what evangelicals are especially noted for publicly. Evangelicals preach the gospel and give witness of God's transforming power; they seek the transformation of society into something more like the kingdom of God (than it has been or is already) even if they do not think the kingdom of God is going to dawn through their efforts.

As with the other hallmarks, diversity exists within and around this one among evangelicals. Some are more actively involved in proclamation and witness, while others are more involved in social action. Some even eschew social action in any organized fashion aimed at "Christianizing the social order." All, however, consider some kind of action in the world for the cause of Christ essential to authentic Christianity.

# Respect for Historic, Christian Orthodoxy

So these are Noll and Bebbington's four essential hallmarks of authentic evangelicalism, and I concur with them while wishing to note, as they do, that tremendous diversity exists in their actual interpretation and application. They are not boundary markers but landmarks, not sides of a box but foci of attention and action.

Some critics have suggested that something is missing from these four hallmarks: a solid doctrinal content that gives cognitive shape to evangelical worship and norms its various personal and institutional expressions. Millard Erickson (b. 1932), a noted and influential conservative evangelical theologian, argues in his systematic theology that the enduring essence of evangelical faith (as of authentic Christian faith in general) is doctrine.[10] On the other hand, evangelical theologian Stanley J. Grenz (1950–2005) argues that evangelicalism's essence is a certain spirituality called "convertive piety" or (as I prefer to say it) "conversional piety."[11] Neither Erickson nor Grenz deny the importance of doctrine or spirituality; they simply place the emphasis differently.

To satisfy critics such as evangelical theologian David Wells, whose 1993 volume *No Place for Truth* laments evangelical doctrinal decline and drift,[12] I add a fifth hallmark of the evangelical movement to Noll and Bebbington's four: "respect for historic Christian orthodoxy." I realize that many conservative evangelicals will want this fifth hallmark to be stated more strongly; they will probably say it should be something like "firm adherence to historic Christian orthodoxy." Many evangelicals, however, have been and are noncreedal; their motto is "no creed but the Bible." That is true for many Baptists and independent Christians (e.g., Restorationists). However, I cannot conceive of genuine evangelical faith in a total doctrinal vacuum or in a context of radical rejection of the hard-won doctrinal orthodoxy of the early church fathers and sixteenth-century Reformers.

Here is where the debate over evangelical boundaries usually becomes most acrimonious and often even destructive. Some conservative evangelical theologians and leaders want to require hearty affirmation without mental reservation to doctrines such as the Trinity, the two natures of Jesus Christ, justification by faith alone, the virginal conception of Jesus, his bodily resurrection, and his second coming in glory. A problem arises, however, with the exact interpretations of these doctrinal beliefs. Notoriously, the Trinity is open to several interpreta-

---

10. Millard J. Erickson, *Christian Theology*, 2nd ed. (Grand Rapids: Baker, 1998), 110–11.

11. Stanley J. Grenz, *Revisioning Evangelical Theology* (Downers Grove, Ill.: InterVarsity, 1993).

12. David F. Wells, *No Place for Truth: or, Whatever Happened to Evangelical Theology?* (Grand Rapids: Eerdmans, 1993).

tions as is the incarnation. For example, is belief in the "kenotic theory" of the humanity and deity of Christ compatible with evangelical faith? (It affirms that the Son of God relinquished use of his attributes of glory to live a truly human life.)

Respect for, if not slavish adherence to, the great milestones of Christian doctrine is what some have called "generous orthodoxy," and I consider it a hallmark of genuine evangelicalism. I reserve the right, however, to consider someone evangelical even if he or she raises some questions about some of the historic doctrinal formulations. For example, Ronald Leigh wrote an article in the evangelical journal *Christian Scholar's Review* called "Jesus: The One-Natured God-Man."[13] From within the evangelical movement, he questions the biblical and logical validity of the classical Christology of Chalcedon: the "hypostatic union" doctrine that Christ has two distinct natures, one human and one divine. He affirms Jesus' full and true deity and humanity but argues for a more cogent expression of that belief than the one declared by the bishops at the Council of Chalcedon in AD 451.

Does that mean Leigh was not an evangelical when he wrote that article? I don't think so. Those who wish to set up firm doctrinal boundaries around evangelicalism (which is really impossible since it is not an organization!) often want to exclude revisionists such as Leigh even though they argue from Scripture and affirm the absolute lordship of Jesus Christ as God and Savior. (Leigh has told me that the editor of a well-known and widely read evangelical theological journal declined to publish his article on the grounds that it departed from the creedal status of the Chalcedonian definition of the two natures of Jesus Christ.)

Similar self-appointed gatekeepers of evangelicalism led a movement during the late 1990s and early 2000s to exclude some evangelical theologians from the Evangelical Theological Society for denying the traditional formulation of God's attribute of omniscience even though they affirmed their own version of omniscience and argued that it is more biblical than the traditional one. The open theists, who believe God knows the future insofar as it is already settled but not insofar as it is not yet settled, survived the attack on the authenticity of their

---

13. Ronald W. Leigh, "Jesus: The One-Natured God-Man," *Christian Scholar's Review* 11, no. 2 (1982): 124–37.

evangelicalism largely because the majority of members of the ETS adhere to generous rather than rigid orthodoxy.

# Evangelicalism Has Unity but Not Uniformity

All the foregoing is to say that in spite of the fact that evangelicalism is an essentially contested concept and in spite of the reality of evangelical diversity and in spite of the movement having no boundaries, evangelical unity does exist. What does not exist is evangelical uniformity. The vast majority of contemporary evangelicals heartily adhere to and affirm the five hallmarks explained above. Some raise questions about some of them or at least about some of the ways in which they have been traditionally stated and practiced. Sometimes it is not possible to say with absolute certainty whether a person or a church or an organization is authentically evangelical or whether they even lay claim to that identity.

## Case Study: The NAE and Oneness Pentecostalism

Let me offer a case study of this unity in diversity of contemporary (i.e., post–World War II, postfundamentalist) evangelicalism. When I taught theology at a well-known evangelical college and seminary, the state affiliate of the National Association of Evangelicals, which represents many but certainly not all evangelicals in the United States, sought my advice. The state organization was deciding whether to admit a certain applicant church to its ranks. The problem was, however, that the church was not solidly Trinitarian; its roots were in a non-Trinitarian form of Pentecostalism called Oneness Pentecostalism, whose doctrine of the Godhead is too close to the ancient heresy of modalism (that God is one person with three manifestations) for many evangelicals' comfort. However, this particular church was evangelical in every other respect and, so I was told, was moving gradually toward a more robust Trinitarian affirmation.

My counsel was to admit the church to membership as long as it was clearly moving in the right direction and thereby help it keep moving in that direction. I don't know what the state organization finally decided.

When I offered this case study to the group of evangelical college presidents meeting in their annual conference, one of them took my president aside and told him to fire me because I gave that advice to the evangelical organization. To him, you see, it is not enough to be fully

Trinitarian, as I am; an evangelical must also be firmly opposed to anyone who isn't already solidly Trinitarian. To me this smacked of the old fundamentalist doctrine and practice of "secondary separation": refusing fellowship with anyone who has fellowship with heretics.

## Broad Tent vs. In or Out

The difference between my vision of evangelical identity and that college president's has to do with boundaries. He thinks of evangelicalism as a bounded set; he would refuse to acknowledge a person or church as evangelical if it did not pass a litmus test of orthodoxy. To him, apparently, a person or church is absolutely either "in" or "out" of evangelicalism. I, on the other hand, regard evangelicalism as a "broad tent" that includes a great variety of people all facing toward the center. It is difficult to tell exactly who or how many are under that tent; the sides are open and permeable. But I identify people as "at the tent meeting" by virtue of which direction they are facing and moving. There is no definite membership; there are many attendees. But if someone under the tent is a mocker or stalking away in anger or disgust or sitting in a car in the parking lot watching but in no sense participating, I have no hesitation saying that person is not "at" this revival meeting—even if physically present. It is not as if anything goes.

## The Ambiguity of Evangelical Diversity

I realize this proposal for identifying evangelicalism will not satisfy many critics; they will want litmus tests and something akin to card-carrying membership even if the "card" is invisible and exists only as the score given to a doctrinal test. What many of them have not come to terms with is the ambiguity of evangelical diversity. Who will write the doctrinal test that determines who is and who is not really evangelical? Who will interpret it? Who will draw the boundaries and patrol them? These critics have yet to come to terms with the nature of evangelicalism as a movement without a magisterium. One sometimes has to wonder if some of them see themselves as a magisterium and hope to exercise that kind of authority and power by means of a rhetoric of exclusion—convincing evangelical leaders to look to them rather than to anyone else when they have to decide whom to hire or publish.

On the other hand, some evangelicals seem even to me to regard the concept as too broad and inclusive; they come close to emptying it of all content. With the conservatives of the movement, I consider *evangelical* meaningless if it is compatible with anything and everything.

## Case Study: Seventh-day Adventists and the Churches of Christ

One effort that disappointed me was the volume *The Variety of American Evangelicalism*, edited by two highly respected evangelical scholars.[14] Its editors, Donald Dayton and Robert Johnston, are erudite historians of the evangelical movement and stand solidly within its ranks. Dayton has taught at several leading evangelical institutions, and Johnston has served as professor of theology at Fuller Theological Seminary for many years. Together they led a series of professional society meetings of historians and theologians examining the concepts *evangelical* and *evangelicalism*. The attempt was worthwhile, and the meetings and the book that grew out of them shed much light. But in the end, it appeared as if Dayton might be correct to suggest that the term *evangelical* has lost meaning.

Under Dayton and Johnston's broad tent of evangelicalism gather not only Pentecostals and Mennonites (two groups I consider generally, with some exceptions, evangelical) but also Seventh-day Adventists and the Churches of Christ. The latter are more questionable. That is not to say individual Adventists and Church of Christ ministers and members cannot be evangelical; it is only to say that both groups have historical and theological distinctives that seem to conflict with core commitments of evangelical faith. Evangelicals have traditionally regarded both groups with some suspicion, and those groups have returned that sentiment.

In my opinion, it is always worth considering that we may have been wrong about another faith tradition, and I am willing to do that in these cases. Perhaps that is all Dayton and Johnston were attempting to do by including them in their book. However, until and unless the leaderships of the Adventist churches[15] and the Churches of Christ reconsider

---

14. Donald W. Dayton and Robert K. Johnston, eds., *The Variety of American Evangelicalism* (Downers Grove, Ill.: InterVarsity, 1991).

15. I wish to note here that some Adventist churches are fully evangelical. An example is the Advent Christian General Conference that is a full member denomination of the National

their traditional views, I am reluctant to stretch the evangelical tent to include them.[16]

At least from the point of view of most evangelicals (and many others), Adventists traditionally believe in and practice a Sabbatarianism—observance of Saturday as the day of the Lord—that borders on legalism and works righteousness. Their teachings about the atonement and the "investigative judgment" stand in some tension with traditional evangelical commitments about salvation. The tradition of the Churches of Christ is to consider believer's baptism by immersion "for the remission of sins" an essential aspect of salvation. To most evangelicals this smacks of salvation by works (or a work). Also, to a great extent, both Adventism and the Churches of Christ tend to reject other churches as less than fully Christian, and they have tended to shun fellowship with them. Of course, it is possible that much of that results from evangelicals' suspicious attitudes toward them.

Nevertheless, it seems to me to stretch the meaning of evangelicalism to include groups such as Seventh-day Adventism and Churches of Christ.[17] If evangelicalism is viewed historically, theologically, and sociologically, it does not seem comfortably to include these or many other groups on the fringes of American religious life.

At the conclusion of Dayton and Johnston's volume about evangelical diversity, Dayton expresses some reservations about the very value of the concept *evangelical*. That is understandable given the wide latitude granted various faith traditions in relation to being evangelical. With many conservative evangelicals (I prefer to call myself

---

Association of Evangelicals. The questions I raise in this context have specifically to do with the status of the Seventh-day Adventist Churches. It is interesting to note that the Advent Christian General Conference affirms two doctrines widely considered heresy by fundamentalists and conservative evangelicals: soul sleep and annihilationism. However, these doctrines have not kept these churches out of the NAE. This is a perfect example of generous orthodoxy. These are nonessential areas of doctrine where beliefs other than these have been normal but are not normative for evangelical identity. I argue that when one looks closely at the NAE, for example, one finds tremendous diversity such as this. My fear is that some conservative evangelicals, perhaps of a fundamentalist mind-set and spirit, would like to turn nonessentials into essentials and exclude theologians and perhaps even churches that do not adhere to their particular interpretations of the "received evangelical tradition"—even if those theologians and churches are solidly within the evangelical camp historically and sociologically.

16. Individual Adventist churches and Churches of Christ may be out of step with their denomination's traditional beliefs and practices, and in that case I have no problem considering them fully evangelical.

17. I want to make clear that this is by no means a judgment about salvation.

"postconservative"), I wish to maintain a greater sense of evangelical unity than Dayton and Johnston's treatment seems to allow without embracing uniformity—something I fear many conservative evangelicals look for.

### Defining Evangelical and Evangelicalism

So, how, then, do I define *evangelical* and *evangelicalism*? I'm tempted to say, paraphrasing a Supreme Court justice, that while I can't define who is an evangelical, I know one when I meet one. If I have to define them, I do so by referring to a large and diverse mostly Protestant Christian renewal movement generally characterized by Noll and Bebbington's four hallmarks plus my fifth one. Sociologically, I identify evangelicalism by referring to leaders such as Billy Graham, publications such as *Christianity Today*, and organizations such as the National Association of Evangelicals; in other words, I view it as a religious-spiritual-theological network characterized by certain common commitments embodied especially in these persons and organizations. Historically, I refer to a religious-spiritual-theological tradition within Protestant Christianity stemming from the pietists and Puritans with special flavoring from the great American revivals and fundamentalist opposition to liberal theology in the "mainline" Protestant denominations. But I refuse to talk about evangelical boundaries or about anything approaching an evangelical magisterium. I value its movement character and its diversity as well as its unity.

# Issues Threatening to Divide Evangelicalism Today

In the final paragraphs, I would like to address a few controversial issues threatening to divide evangelicalism today. These can serve as case studies of my thesis that evangelicalism is theologically (to say nothing of sociologically) diverse in spite of a shared history and common core of commitments.

### Inerrancy

I have already discussed the inerrancy issue; those who argue that inerrancy is a boundary of evangelical identity have simply not learned their history and, in my opinion, are attempting to impose their own shibboleth on everyone else. For one thing, defining the concept is notoriously difficult. Defenders of inerrancy cannot agree among themselves what it means, and the Chicago Statement on Biblical Inerrancy (1978) kills the concept with the death of a thousand qualifications. If inerrancy (whatever that means) is essential to authentic evangelicalism, why is it not explicitly stated in the NAE statement of faith?[18]And why have so many noted evangelicals over the years rejected it (Presbyterian Orr, Nazarene H. Orton Wiley, Baptist Bernard Ramm, United Church of Christ Bloesch, Baptist Clark Pinnock, and many others)? Are these luminaries of evangelical theology not really evangelicals? That would be difficult for anyone to prove. All they could do is assert it and hope others believe them.

## Penal Substitution

A second controversial issue every author in this book is addressing is the atonement of Christ. I have already alluded to it and suggested that there is no single evangelical theory of the atonement. While the penal substitution theory (that Christ bore the punishment for sins in the place of sinners) may be normal, it could hardly be said to be normative. Many evangelicals in the Holiness movement (Nazarenes, Wesleyans, Free Methodists, and others) prefer the governmental theory (that Christ bore an equivalent punishment to that deserved by a sinner). Many Anabaptists prefer to think of Christ's death as a martyrdom that unmasks the powers, and some evangelicals emphasize the *Christus victor* theory going back to some early church fathers and Luther. Who is going to say with any authority that the penal substitution theory is normative for all evangelicals? Evangelicals have always emphasized the objective side of the atonement and shunned a purely subjective theory (e.g., that Christ's death was merely a great object lesson of God's love). But no one objective theory has ever been uniformly affirmed by all evangelicals. Again, all the NAE statement of faith says is that Christ's death is "vicarious" and "atoning." That falls far short of affirming a full-blooded penal substitution theory.

---

18. It does affirm that Scripture is "infallible," but many evangelicals would distinguish that from inerrancy as I do.

## Common Ground with Roman Catholics

Third, some evangelicals have engaged in vigorous and constructive dialogue with Roman Catholics, much to the dismay of other evangelicals, which led to a 1994 document titled *Evangelicals and Catholics Together* that was amended in 2002. The evangelical and Catholic signatories affirmed that there is no substantial disagreement on the basic doctrine of salvation and that evangelicals and Catholics should not attempt to evangelize one another. At least that is how many interpreted the document. Some conservative evangelicals were dismayed at this and called on their signing evangelical brothers and sisters to disassociate themselves from the document if not the dialogue.

I do not think dialogue between Christians is ever a bad thing; it's probably a good thing between Christians and adherents of major world religions as well. And it seems to me obvious that at least some Catholics are Christians. I do think, however, that the signatories of the document were too optimistic about agreement between evangelicalism and Roman Catholicism on the doctrine of salvation. That is, I think they jumped the gun. However, unlike fundamentalists and conservative evangelicals who condemned the project, I do not see the signatories' efforts as a betrayal of evangelical faith. I think their intentions were good even if some of their conclusions were flawed. Specifically, it seems to me that the Catholic Church needs to repudiate the language of "merit" in association with human acquisition of salvation before real theological agreement can be reached.

I am not saying, however, that *Evangelicals and Catholics Together* transgressed some evangelical theological boundary. It simply stands as something extraordinary (outside of what is normal) for evangelicals. That is intriguing and perhaps a little troubling but is hardly grounds for condemnation or even demands to recant.

## Open Theism

Finally, the evangelical theological world was rocked between approximately 1995 and 2005 by controversy over so-called open theism. Evangelicals Clark Pinnock, John Sanders, Greg Boyd, and others suggested that the traditional theological idea of God's foreknowledge is wrong and that the God of the Bible does not know the future exhaustively and infallibly except insofar as he knows all the possible futures. I was very much involved in this controversy in that I defended the open theists as not heretical; and just for doing that I was criticized by fundamentalists and some conservative evangelicals. One threatened to get me fired from my teaching position merely because I would not take a stand with him against open theism.

It seems to me that this controversy was overwrought; it was accompanied by a great deal of unwarranted hysteria. One leading evangelical author publicly denounced Clark Pinnock as not a Christian and announced that he would not have fellowship with him. To me this smacked of the worst example of fundamentalist separatism, and yet that evangelical leader would not consider himself a fundamentalist (except in the sense of affirming the core fundamentals of the faith). Some critics denounced open theism as process theology in spite of the fact that all the open theists affirm God's omnipotence and creation *ex nihilo* — two doctrines that process theology rejects.

In my opinion, this whole emotional brouhaha over open theism was fueled by a pent-up desire by fundamentalists calling themselves conservative evangelicals to test evangelical theological boundaries (which, as I have made clear, do not even exist). Ultimately, they failed. The ETS did not expel any open theists. *Christianity Today* called for continuing dialogue and debate over the issue rather than premature closure to it. One troubling aspect of the controversy was that, so far as I could tell, few of the critics of open theism even understood it. I had the advantage of knowing the leading open theists personally, so I could ask them questions about what they wrote and inform myself as to their exact intentions. Many critics did not even try to enter into dialogue with their open theist brothers; they simply rejected their thesis out of hand while failing to understand it adequately.

Occasionally, well-known evangelical leaders even misrepresented open theism in order to stir up controversy. One wrote that a leading open theist had endorsed process theology when, in fact, all the open theist said was that he sympathized with the "relational ontology" of Charles Hartshorne, a leading process theologian, while making clear he did not agree with process theology's denials of omnipotence, the Trinity, creation *ex nihilo*, and a host of other doctrines. Another critic of open theism wrote that a leading open theist admitted dependence on process theology, but the page he cited in the open theist's book clearly said otherwise. It stated only that open theism and process theology share a few common ideas but denied that open theism depends on process thought.

This controversy was the most dismaying and disillusioning thing I have experienced in my fifty-some years of being an evangelical. Never before have I known of evangelical leaders and scholars of repute factually misrepresenting fellow evangelicals' views in order to marginalize, if not exclude, them. I concluded that something of the old (perceived) fundamentalist spirit of narrowness and divisiveness that led to the founding of the NAE as separate from the ACCC had crept back into postfundamentalist evangelicalism. Or, to put it another way, I perceived segments of the postfundamentalist evangelical movement slipping back into the old fundamentalism out of which it grew in the 1940s.

## Conclusion

In sum, I view evangelicalism as a broad and inclusive movement of people, churches, and organizations commonly committed to certain experiences and beliefs in varying degrees. As a movement, it is unified without uniformity. Its unity is found in certain historical and theological family resemblances; its diversity is found in interpretations of the core, unifying beliefs and experiences. The core or center of the movement is composed of five discernible commitments: conversionism, biblicism, crucicentrism, activism, and respect for the great tradition of Christian orthodoxy. Evangelicalism as we know it today grew out of revivalism and fundamentalism and has tried to take the best from both traditions while leaving their worst excesses behind. When it coalesced in the 1940s, it drew into itself two broad streams that live uncomfortably together and sometimes fall into conflict with each other: (1) experiential Christianity stemming from continental pietism and the Great Awakenings in Britain and (2) America and Protestant orthodoxy shaped largely by the Puritans and the nineteenth-century theologians of the old Princeton school of theology (mostly Presbyterians).

This evangelical movement can have no boundaries because it is a movement, but it is defined by its center composed of the five common commitments mentioned above. Unfortunately, the movement's unity is gradually dissolving due to increasing tensions between the historical streams drawn into it in the 1940s. Evangelicals concerned with defending maximal conservatism are replicating fundamentalist narrowness and exclusivity of the past while maintaining their ties to the movement dubbed "neo-evangelical" by fundamentalists in the 1940s. They are easily identified by their obsession with "evangelical boundaries." Evangelicals concerned with renewal and relevance are perceived by their more conservative counterparts as walking if not rushing down the path forged by Protestant liberalism in the nineteenth century. However, as long as they hold on to evangelicalism's core commitments, they remain evangelicals whatever critics say, because the critics are no evangelical magisterium.

# A FUNDAMENTALIST RESPONSE

## KEVIN T. BAUDER

In this volume, Roger Olson and I represent opposite extremes on the evangelical spectrum. Evidently, neither of us is entirely convinced that the other belongs on the spectrum at all! Nevertheless, I relish the opportunity to interact with Roger. I have two reasons. First, Roger is a gracious and charitable man who, in spite of our differences, has taken the trouble to encourage me personally in the theological task. Second, Roger is a theologian who says what he means.

Roger wishes to distance himself from any notion that evangelicalism has any definable boundaries. Instead, he argues instead for a centered evangelicalism that is held together, not by a checklist of doctrinal or practical requirements, but by a number of family resemblances. For Roger, the attempt to define a boundary around evangelicalism appears "silly if not disingenuous."

Such candor is commendable. Furthermore, Roger backs up his argument with important evidence. He notes that contemporary evangelicalism lacks consensus on a number of rather significant issues, and he demonstrates that this lack of consensus is not a recent phenomenon. The empirical diversity of self-identified evangelicals—past and present—certainly lends weight to Roger's thesis.

This diversity is persuasive, however, only for those who are attempting to define evangelicalism inductively, that is, by examining particular evangelicals. Roger is driven to such an inductive treatment by his unwillingness to allow anyone to have the authority to define evangelicalism a priori. He rightly recognizes that commitment to an a priori definition entails the imposition of static boundaries. He fears that those who recognize such boundaries constitute an evangelical magisterium.

Roger appeals to the four hallmarks of authentic evangelical faith that were articulated by Mark Noll and David Bebbington (John and Al both also mention these) rather than to any binding definition of evangelicalism. These marks include conversionism, biblicism, crucicentrism, and activism. To these, Roger adds a fifth hallmark: respect for historic, Christian orthodoxy. He specifies, however, that this respect must be a "generous orthodoxy," and he reserves the right to recognize some people as evangelicals even if they question historic doctrinal formulations.

As examples of his generous orthodoxy, Roger cites several possibilities. He allows that in some instances neither monophysitism nor Sabellianism should bar one from the evangelical fold. Nevertheless, his generosity does have limits. He is uncomfortable with recognizing either Seventh-day Adventist or of Stone-Campbell (Church of Christ) theology as genuinely evangelical. Even here, though, he admits that individuals within those traditions may be evangelical.

In sum, Roger's concerns are really two in number. First, he views evangelicalism primarily as a movement, and he insists that movements by definition cannot have boundaries. Second, he repeatedly expresses concern that those who attempt to impose boundaries on the movement are acting in the role of an evangelical magisterium.

But what if we do not begin by defining evangelicalism as a movement? What if we begin by defining evangelicalism as an idea? I suggest that such an approach yields a far more fruitful understanding of evangelicalism, and one that requires considerably less guesswork than Roger's.

Supposing we wanted an empirical description of evangelicals, we would have to begin with the idea. How could we even know whom to examine unless we first had some idea of what an evangelical is? Surely self-identification is not the key. One would not seek to define innocence by examining the careers of imprisoned convicts who protested that they were innocent. By the same token, we cannot define evangelicalism by interviewing the usual suspects who identify themselves as evangelical.

For example, we cannot define *evangelical* by inspecting (let's say) the doctrinal statement of the National Association of Evangelicals (to which, incidentally, many fundamentalists such as John R. Rice and Bob Jones lent initial support). Nor is it relevant that the NAE statement refers to infallibility rather than inerrancy. Most evangelicals of the 1940s simply did not distinguish these concepts.

Furthermore, the debate is not really over centered versus edge-bounded definitions. Even an edge-bounded definition may allow for the existence of borderline cases (more on this in a moment). On the other hand, a centered definition works like a rubber band. The further one gets from the center, the more the family resemblances have to be stretched. At some point, the rubber band snaps, and at that point, one is no longer attached to the center at all.

Whether the idea of evangelicalism is defined by its center or its boundary, then, matters less than whether we can articulate the idea in the first place. I believe that we can, and we can do it without having to appoint some sort of magisterium. The place that we need to begin is with the label *evangelical* itself.

The heart of the name *evangelical* is, of course, the word *evangel*. What is the evangel? It is simply the gospel. An evangelical, then, is someone who adopts a particular attitude or stance toward the gospel. Needless to say, that attitude or stance is (at minimum) one of approbation and appropriation.

Evangelicals do not deny the gospel. Evangelicals do not tamper with the gospel. Evangelicals do not question the gospel. The moment one detaches oneself from the gospel, whether in principle or in practice, one is no longer entitled to be called an evangelical.

At first blush, it may appear that we have simply moved the problem of definition back one step. We may define *evangelical* in terms of adherence to the evangel, but do we then not have an obligation to define the evangel? Furthermore, does not this definition also require an evangelical magisterium?

The answer should be obvious to any evangelical. It is not up to us to define the gospel. We are responsible to recognize and receive the gospel. We are further responsible to uphold and defend the gospel. Never are we given the responsibility or even the opportunity to define the gospel.

The definition of the gospel comes from Christ himself. It is revealed in Scripture, the same Scripture that pronounces anathema against those who make up their own gospels. Either the gospel is clear or it is not. If it is not, then we are of all men most miserable. Let us eat and drink, for tomorrow we die.

If, on the other hand, the gospel is clear, then we can immediately tidy up a good bit of quibbling about what it means to be an evangelical.

We can set the evangelical house in order—and we can do it without impaneling a Protestant magisterium. We need not appeal to theologians or institutional executives. We need to appeal only to the gospel itself—and if either theologians or institutional presidents have trouble understanding the gospel, then so much the worse for them.

No one who denies the evangel can be reckoned as an evangelical. It does not matter whether the denial comes in practice or in principle. It does not matter whether it is explicit or implicit. The gospel stands as the touchstone of any legitimate evangelicalism.

What this means is that the fundamentals of the gospel are also the fundamentals of evangelical identity. Someone who denies fundamentals of the gospel is implicitly denying the evangel itself. Such a person has no title to the name *evangelical*.

At this point, we need to return to Roger's evidence that evangelicalism lacks a consensus on several important issues. What matters is not whether the usual suspects can agree about these issues, but whether they are essential to the biblical gospel. Does the gospel depend on the doctrine of the Trinity? Then an anti-Trinitarian cannot be an evangelical. Does the gospel depend on a Christ who is one person in two natures? Then a monophysite cannot be an evangelical.

Please understand that I am not arguing over the eternal destiny of such people. Sometimes people deny in their speculative systems the very things on which they depend in their hearts. A person may be intellectually committed to a denial of the gospel while inconsistently but nevertheless really trusting the gospel. Our role is not to determine who is or is not going to be in heaven. That determination requires a knowledge of hearts that goes beyond anything we possess.

We have all met or read someone who was committed to an idea that implicitly damaged the gospel, but who nevertheless gave evidence of genuine trust in Christ and devotion to God. Some of Roger's historical examples fit this category—for instance, when he cites James Orr as an evangelical who did not believe in the inerrancy of Scripture. What do we make of these examples?

This kind of question is not unique to evangelicalism or even to theology. For example, suppose we begin with an understanding of *dog* that involves the concept *quadruped*. Subsequently, we encounter a dog limping about on three legs, wearing only a stump where the fourth would have been. Then, walking through a freak show, we see a five-legged dog on display. Finally, at a circus we observe a dog walking on its hind legs. Do any of these episodes really count against the notion that a dog is a quadruped?

A three-legged dog is a mutilated quadruped. A five-legged dog is a malformed quadruped. And a dog that walks on its hind legs is a curiosity, but it is still a quadruped. None of these phenomena leads us to reexamine our definition of *dog* or to deny that a dog is a quadruped.

We can say the same of Roger's approach. If we adopted it, we would be forced to impute normative status to mutilations and monstrosities. We would then have a hard time (as Roger actually does) saying what is an evangelical. It is better to suggest that, even if some monophysites, Sabellians, open theists, or anti-inerrantists might be personally evangelical, they are nevertheless like dogs walking on their hind legs. Much as that trick might provoke us to wonder, we certainly do not permit it to redefine the categories.

At this point in the discussion, we hardly have to imagine Roger's incredulity. He expresses it as he puts forward a number of names as test cases. These cases are of different kinds, but three are of particular interest: Bernard Ramm, Donald Bloesch, and Clark Pinnock. Of these he asks, "Are these luminaries of evangelical theology not really evangelicals? That would be difficult for anyone to prove. All they could do is assert it and hope others believe them."

*Au contraire.* Evangelicalism is defined by the evangel. No one who denies the evangel—in principle or in practice, explicitly or implicitly—ought to be reckoned as an evangelical. Because of what people like Ramm, Bloesch, and Pinnock have denied, many evangelicals have absolutely no trouble seeing in them the very kind of threat from which a faithful shepherd must guard the flock. They have stretched the rubber band beyond the breaking point.

And these three are old news. More than a few theologians and churchmen, still wearing the tag *evangelical*, have moved even further from the center. Roger himself expresses his discomfort with some who are being recognized as evangelicals today. Given the current condition of evangelical theology, however, and given Roger's commitment to "broad tent evangelicalism," one wonders whether anyone at all can be excluded.

Viewed from a merely empirical point of view, the contemporary evangelical movement certainly is a broad tent. It is not, however, a revival tent. It is more akin to a circus tent, or perhaps a menagerie of ecclesiastical oddities and curiosities. As amusing as some occupants of this tent may be, it is not to be confounded with the household of God, which is the church of the living God, the pillar and ground of the truth.

Roger pleads for a generous orthodoxy. After all, who could possibly object to generosity? The problem is that we are permitted to be generous only with things that belong to us. Suppose I generously give away Roger's money. As long as it is his money that I am giving away, then I am not really being generous. I am simply a thief.

The same is true of orthodoxy. The evangel is committed to us as a trust. It does not belong to us, but to the one who shed his blood on the cross and who arose from the dead. While we proclaim salvation freely in his name, we are not permitted to jettison or downplay any aspect of the gospel. If we muddy the gospel, then we are not being generous. We are dooming souls to hell (the reality and eternality of which, incidentally, are essential to the gospel).

Evangelicalism is about the evangel. The evangel is not hidden or obscure. Title to the name *evangelical* must rest on loyalty to the evangel. If we look closely at those who profess to be evangelicals while calling the evangel into question, we may just discover sharp teeth under their woolen overcoats.

# A CONFESSIONAL EVANGELICAL RESPONSE

## R. ALBERT MOHLER JR.

Roger E. Olson tells us that those, like himself, who have an interest in preserving the label *evangelical* "have had frustrating and confusing experiences with it." One can hardly argue with that statement, and the confusion and frustration can be exasperating at times. And yet here we are, having this discussion once again.

In all probability, future generations of evangelicals will find themselves in the same confusing and frustrating position, if simply because the total set of those who claim this label seem to have no means of defining it consensually and definitively.

Roger is a gifted writer, and his recollection of past experiences that demonstrate a considerable semantic range for the use of evangelical will be familiar to all who have a stake in this discussion, even if our own account would differ in personal respects.

As a matter of fact, this confusion is as old as the postwar evangelical movement in America, when theological conservatives such as Harold J. Ockenga and Carl F. H. Henry sought to use the term as a means of indicating a theological trajectory that was fully orthodox but not fundamentalist. Seeking to distinguish themselves simultaneously from the intellectual defensiveness they perceived in fundamentalism and from the theological aberrations of theological liberalism, they variously attempted to brand their new movement as evangelical, or even as the New Evangelicalism.

And yet, even some among the "card carrying" community of theological liberals attempted to claim the term (such as Harry Emerson Fosdick). No one said it was going to be easy.

To his credit, Roger gets right to his argument. He affirms the claim previously made by others that evangelical and evangelicalism are "essentially contested concepts." Thus, an attempt to define what it means to be an evangelical — at least with boundaries — is "an interesting but ultimately futile project."

Yet he cannot resist the urge to dive into the debate. As a matter of fact, few individuals have given as much attention to these questions as Roger has in recent years. As he says, he cannot give up on the question.

Nor can I. The issues are just too important, and the term is just too essential to our times. Roger's essay was productive for my own thinking, and I am thankful for that. As a matter of fact, even as I will disagree with Roger on the most central question to this debate, I will end up on the question of evangelical definition in at least partial agreement with him.

That central question, at least by my reckoning, is the question of whether evangelicalism has both a center and recognizable boundaries. In reality, no other issue really matters much until that question is settled. Once it is, that answer will largely determine everything else.

On this question, Roger is bracingly clear. "Evangelicalism has no definable boundaries and cannot have them." Well, no one can argue that he is evasive. He even raises the stakes by arguing, "It is simply impossible to say with certainty who is and who is not an evangelical; all one can do is accept anyone's claim to being an evangelical insofar as he or she shares certain common commitments identified by historians of the movement."

Is it "impossible to say with certainty who is and who is not an evangelical"? Do we have to accept anyone's claim so long as they accept "certain common commitments"? As his essay makes clear, he not only believes these things to be true, but he also is ready to defend his argument from all comers.

And here I come. I respect his argument enough to counter it with my own. Yet my own argument will from henceforth and forevermore be informed by Roger's vigorous defense of his thesis. That is what makes an exchange like this so valuable.

Years ago, when I was a young Southern Baptist looking for theological friends and theological self-definition, I first encountered the issue of evangelical identity. I read Paul Hiebert's article, cited by Roger, when I saw it cited in an earlier exchange on evangelical identity. Hiebert's use of set theory was extremely helpful, I thought. And from that reading onward, I was convinced that, in order to be coherent, evangelicalism must be seen as both a centered and a bounded set.

Roger sees evangelicalism as exclusively centered (though Roger might not like any association with exclusivism). Evangelicalism is a movement, he insists. Organizations have boundaries, but movements do not and cannot. Efforts to establish boundaries "appear silly if not disingenuous."

So, how do we recognize an evangelical? He or she affirms certain core commitments. Tellingly, without any opportunity for collaboration, Roger, John, and I all turn to British historian David Bebbington for his articulation of evangelicalism's core commitments: conversionism, biblicism, crucicentrism, and activism. If nothing else, it appears that Bebbington's list is a good place to start.

For Roger, these hallmarks are not boundary markers at all, but landmarks. Evangelicalism is marked by unity, not uniformity, he says. As a movement, evangelicalism is evident as "a great variety of people all facing toward the center." It is a "tent meeting" where those within the movement are seen facing and moving in the same direction.

There is no boundary on the outside of the movement; the box has no walls. Efforts to establish evangelicalism as a bounded set, he at least implies, is evidence of a neo-fundamentalist agenda that he will fight with vigor.

At the same time, he acknowledges that the term is meaningless "if it is compatible with anything and everything."

So here is my fundamental assessment of Roger's thesis: he really means it, except when he doesn't.

This is by no means a charge of hypocrisy. To the contrary, Roger is an amazingly candid and expressive partner in this exchange. I think the essential problem is that he cannot really hold, as much as he wants to, to the logic of his argument.

The key problem for his center-but-no-boundary argument is that the center has to be defined. Even the generalized definitions we might borrow from David Bebbington imply boundaries. Roger might counter that this just betrays my own habit of mind, but I think he betrays the same.

When he writes of conversionism, he states that this central affirmation "assumes some surrounding doctrinal beliefs." He then defines some of those surrounding beliefs, including some affirmation of the Trinity and of salvation by grace through faith.

Seeing himself do that, he quickly defends himself against the charge that he has just done what he argues could not and must not be done — define a doctrinal boundary. "Not at all," he claims. Instead, he was, he says, just defining the "gravitational pull" of evangelicalism's theological center.

I am unconvinced. I understand what Roger is arguing, but I think he shifts his argument significantly in a crucial respect. When he considers Seventh-day Adventism and the Churches of Christ, he asserts, rightly I think, that "until and unless the leaderships of the Adventist churches and the Churches of Christ reconsider their traditional views, I am reluctant to stretch the evangelical tent to include them."

These two groups see themselves as facing and moving in the same direction as evangelicals, but Roger correctly sees their affirmations of the central evangelical commitments as essentially compromised by other publicly stated beliefs.

Now, I will take Roger at his word that he does not believe we can set any theological boundaries around evangelicalism, but I think he just did that very thing. He had to, of course, for otherwise the central affirmations would devolve into meaninglessness, which he does not want.

I think the real question is where those boundaries are to be drawn. Roger calls for a "generous orthodoxy" and a big evangelical tent. One of the great strengths of his argument is his emphasis on the movement's lack of a magisterium or central authority. Reading his essay will convince most readers that evangelicalism, as a movement, is institutionally unstable in this respect — incompetent in performing any adequate boundary-making task.

I acknowledge this historical incompetence, but I differ with Roger in hoping that such a competence can be developed. Indeed, I believe that this is one of the central questions now facing the evangelical movement. Lacking an evangelical magisterium, we are left with the challenge of developing a vigorous and substantial evangelical consensus by means of persuasion and argumentation. The emergence of a wholesome evangelical consensus fidelium will assist evangelicals to maintain theological fidelity through the hard work and discipline of both public and private argumentation and discussion without the structure of a magisterium.

I believe that Roger, despite his best and most honest efforts, does see the need for some boundaries. Yet he does not want to devote much attention to these boundaries, and—even more urgently—he fears that the boundaries, if ever established clearly, would potentially exclude many he sincerely wants to include, including himself.

At this point, another of Roger's arguments comes into play. Early in his essay he describes evangelicalism as "an unstable compound composed of two incompatible traditions." The terms "unstable" and "incompatible" gain our attention immediately. Roger argues that the evangelical movement brought together one tradition rooted in Protestant orthodoxy and another tradition rooted in pietism and revivalism.

Later in his essay he laments what he sees as the dissolving of this historic unity "due to increasing tensions between the historical streams drawn into it in the 1940s." Elsewhere, Roger has suggested that there are now really two evangelical movements, "fundamentalists and neo-fundamentalists, on the one hand, and moderate to progressive evangelicals on the other hand." He concludes, "It's just a matter now of dividing the property."[19]

When Roger addresses issues like biblical inerrancy and the concept of penal substitution, he sees (in the case of inerrancy) a shibboleth and (in the case of penal substitution) a belief that is normal but not normative. He sees the controversy over open theism as "overwrought" and evidence of "unwarranted hysteria."

These observations underline where Roger and I differ on the most basic issues of evangelical identity and the future of the evangelical movement. I believe that affirming the Bible's inerrancy and the propositional nature of divine revelation is essential to the integrity of evangelicalism and the future vitality of the movement. Similarly, I believe that denying penal substitution as the central biblical concept for our understanding of the atonement is, in the end, fatal to our witness to the gospel. I see open theism as a fundamental revision of the doctrine of God. Open theism denies the total omniscience of God and thus contradicts not only the Reformed tradition but also classical Arminianism. Furthermore, I am convinced that embracing antireal-

---

19. Roger E. Olson, "The Promised Response to Bell's Love Wins," http://rogereolson. com/2011/03/25/the-promised-response-to-bells-love-wins/.

ism and denying propositional truth produces theological and doctrinal disaster.

Evangelicalism must be both a centered and a bounded set. The real question is where those boundaries should lie. Roger wants to forge a postconservative vision of evangelical theology. I believe that this vision undermines the very center of evangelical conviction and commitment.

We are largely in agreement on the genealogy of the movement and its current bifurcation into two parties, or even two rival movements. We just stand on different sides of the arguments over evangelical identity and the future direction the evangelical movement must take.

Roger concludes his essay by suggesting that evangelicals "concerned with defending maximal conservatism are replicating the fundamentalist narrowness and exclusivity of the past." Those he defines as "concerned with renewal and relevance" are, he knows, seen by others as "walking if not rushing down the path forged by Protestant liberalism in the nineteenth century."

Yes, this is how the two groups see each other. As a parting shot to the conservatives, Roger speaks on behalf of the postconservatives: "However, as long as they hold to evangelicalism's core commitments, they remain evangelicals whatever their critics say, because the critics are no evangelical magisterium."

He is right, of course, that there is no evangelical magisterium. Instead, we are left with the power of persuasion and witness. Roger is a powerful advocate for his vision of evangelical identity, and my own arguments are strengthened and sharpened by my experience of wrestling with his. We both write in the hope of persuading others to our position. That is what makes an exchange like this so important, if lamentably rare.

## JOHN G. STACKHOUSE JR.

Key to Roger Olson's essay are his anecdotes. Every theologian is a human being first, and each of us writes theology out of our particular context, including our individual experiences. His anecdotes show us at least two facts: he has been wounded by those to his right, and he has tried hard to protect and support people he sees to be victimized as he was. This laudable empathy, however, has sometimes led Roger to a more expansive understanding of evangelical identity than would square with most definitions of evangelicalism, including mine—and perhaps also including his.

Brother Roger claims that evangelicalism cannot be described with any strong confidence because "the evangelical movement has no headquarters or authoritative magisterium." We social scientists and historians, however, face the problem of defining movements all the time, and we don't feel ourselves necessarily at sea just because there is no central authority to ask. Indeed, a whole generation of evangelical historians has worked pretty hard to define evangelicalism, and I think we have done a pretty good job of it. We now can indeed know "with certainty who is and who is not an evangelical"—except for those on the fringes. Does anyone seriously doubt that Billy Graham is an evangelical? Or John Wesley? And so on.

But probably Brother Roger would agree with me on this point, and his emphasis is not on the easy cases but on the hard ones, on those whose distance from the center or whose adoption of doctrinal views at the secondary or tertiary levels bother their fellow evangelicals enough that the latter wonder about the authentic evangelical identity of the former. Let's see about that—about those in the "boundary lands," as I'm calling them.

I don't follow Brother Roger's logic when he says that because the National Association of Evangelicals has a statement of faith "that does not include biblical inerrancy" then "inerrancy cannot be regarded as necessary to being authentically evangelical." Maybe the NAE is wrong. Maybe the NAE simply *assumes* inerrancy. Indeed, I think Roger makes far too much of the NAE. He cites "the founding of *Christianity Today*, Fuller Theological Seminary, and the Billy Graham Evangelistic Association" as if "they were made possible ... by the founding of the NAE." Many of us historians would argue the reverse: it was the career of Billy Graham and his network of contacts, supporters, colleagues, and friends that formed the main matrix out of which this new evangelicalism emerged. Thus, to look to the NAE, as Brother Roger does, for a definitive example of evangelicalism is problematic.

It is perhaps significant that nowhere in Brother Roger's essay does he mention the Missouri Synod Lutherans, who were courted by the founders of the NAE and who were the other large group conspicuously not joining up with the NAE besides the Southern Baptists. But the Lutherans don't fit the "two tradition" genealogy of Brother Roger and Donald Dayton, so they just don't show up. If they did show up, we would see that defining evangelicalism is more complex than the balancing of—or struggle between—two competing traditions.

In Canada, furthermore, the Mennonite tradition has been quite important in twentieth- and twenty-first-century evangelicalism. And Anabaptist ideas have been affecting a wide swath of American evangelicals for more than a generation, thanks largely to John Howard Yoder and Ronald Sider. So, again, to see contemporary evangelicalism as "an unstable compound composed of two incompatible traditions" strikes me as simplistic.

It is the more simplistic when the "Puritan-Presbyterian" tradition is characterized as being "heavily doctrinal and suspicious of experiential spirituality." To be sure, the history of Puritan and Reformed piety does feature episodes, movements, and individuals of this sort. But it also features many instances of strong experiential spirituality, notably the Great Awakening itself, originating as it did in the American colonies among Congregationalists and Presbyterians. And does Brother Roger really want to suggest what critics of the pietist and revivalist movements suggest, namely, that it is not to be taken seriously as an intellectual tradition?

Here again we see Brother Roger employing a "two-party" paradigm, a paradigm much too common in maps of American society, in which many of us do not recognize ourselves in either party and plead for a more complex mapping of the situation rather than lining everything up on one side or another of a great gulf fixed: reason versus experience, tradition versus innovation, dogma versus piety, authority versus freedom, Calvinist versus Arminian, (Red versus Blue?), and so on.

What's particularly strange about Brother Roger's penchant for dichotomizing is his repeated call for a "generous orthodoxy." I'm all for that, too, but I wonder if the desire to be generous is really advanced by dividing evangelicals into two kinds of people — a move that might make mutual recognition and embrace more difficult.

We do need to draw a line, but I draw it between evangelicals and nonevangelicals, not between evangelicals. Brother Roger clearly hates insistence on doctrinal statements and refers to them as litmus tests — as if litmus tests are always bad things. But the litmus test was developed to give us useful information, and for someone to fail to pass the litmus test of adherence to the Nicene Creed or to the confession that the Bible is the supreme written authority for faith and practice tells us useful information. Among other things, it tells us this person is not an evangelical. Brother Roger speaks of the "hallmarks" of evangelical faith and says that they "are not litmus tests but common features of a diverse movement within which people experience and believe these things more or less." But I respectfully disagree. How "less" could you believe in the deity of Christ or the authority of Scripture or the necessity for conversion and still be called an evangelical? At an important basic level, you either believe in the full deity and humanity of Jesus Christ or you don't, in the Scripture as the Word of God written or you don't, in the necessity of the new birth or you don't. We might well argue about what all of these claims mean at the next level of theological specification, but if you disagree at the first level, you're just not an evangelical.

Therefore, to say that evangelicalism is a "big tent" that includes anyone who is "facing toward the center" is to use too vague a metaphor. We certainly have left behind the centered set metaphor. Every element in a centered set has to embrace all of what constitutes the center. Not "face toward it," but embrace it.

In this regard, Brother Roger is quite correct as he adds his "fifth hallmark" to his definition of evangelicalism, namely, "respect for historic Christian orthodoxy." (Strange, though, how someone as obviously concerned as he is with piety and mission doesn't talk about orthopathy or orthopraxy much in his essay.) He writes, "I cannot conceive of genuine evangelical faith in a total doctrinal vacuum or the context of radical rejection of the hard-won doctrinal orthodoxy of the early church fathers and sixteenth-century Reformers."

I daresay these affirmations, however, are not as robust as would suit Brother Kevin or Brother Al. Roger says, in fact, "I reserve the right ... to consider someone evangelical even if he or she raises some questions about some of the historic doctrinal formulations." So what about orthodoxy as a test for evangelicalism? Are evangelicals bound to believe what our forebears believed, plain and simple?

It seems to me that for an evangelical Christian, the creeds are always subject to Scripture. If one can find something wrong with a creed in the light of Scripture, one should say so, we should all think about that, and then we ought to revise the creed if necessary. In any given case, it seems to me that the issue is whether the alternative to a particular creedal formulation squares better with the defining convictions of evangelical Christian faith. If Ronald Leigh helps us improve our language about the nature of the incarnation, then how could we object?

Brother Roger thus presses the rest of us evangelicals to take seriously our common profession of the supreme authority of Scripture as written revelation. We all value the hard work our forebears have done in formulating theology. We all believe that the Holy Spirit helped our forebears do that work. We also, however, distinguish between the quality of guidance the Holy Spirit gave to the authors of Holy Scripture and the quality of the guidance the Spirit gave to the authors of even the most widely accepted creeds. Thus we must believe that the Scripture can always critique the creeds, and not vice versa.

I see no danger here, however. True, if we construe the task of theology as reconciling various authoritative texts, then the prospect of some of these texts disagreeing with each other is fearsome indeed. But if instead we view theology as the result of a particular group of Christians articulating what they have heard from God's revelation to them in their context, then we will expect that any particular doctrinal formulation will be, not timelessly true, but more or less accurate and helpful for other communities in other times—including the particular doctrinal formulations we recognize as the great creeds.

The great creeds have proven themselves across the centuries, across cultural and geographical lines, and across a wide range of confessional differences to provide statements with which the vast majority of Christians agree. It thus would be highly unlikely for someone now to find serious fault with one of them. Nonetheless, it is theoretically possible that one or another formulation could enjoy improvement, especially in the light of the gospel coming to quite new cultural contexts—such as sub-Saharan Africa, China, Korea, India, and so on.[20]

So we stand in the Great Tradition, yes, but always under the supreme authority of Scripture that is itself an instrument in the hands of its divine Author, who continues to teach us from it in the context of all the other things God is teaching us through all the other media with which God has blessed the world: science, literature, art, mystical experience, family life, and so much more. We are not people of the Book, but disciples of Jesus who, through the Holy Spirit, continues to teach the church not only what must be passed along as tradition but also what is fresh and new for our time—and for our time to add to that tradition as previous Christians have done.

Having said all that, I confess that I found quite startling Brother Roger's advocacy of Oneness Pentecostalism as an affiliate of the National Association of Evangelicals. It seems to me simply obvious that that tradition cannot be admitted since its talk of God varies greatly from orthodox Trinitarianism. To observe that "this particular church was evangelical in every other respect and ... was moving gradually toward a more robust Trinitarian affirmation" is encouraging but hardly sufficient. If he had claimed that their theology was biblically superior to orthodoxy, then at least we're talking about the right sort of claim, but he doesn't. Instead, I see Roger's generous empathy for those at the receiving end of doctrinal restrictiveness overwhelming his own definitional convictions.

---

20. Of course, I am aware that Christianity came to those parts of the world many centuries ago; I am referring to the new upwelling of the Holy Spirit in these parts of the world such that these communities are poised to contribute to the global theological conversation as they have not been for some time.

Indeed, I sincerely affirm Brother Roger's attempts to extend fellowship as far as one possibly can. I hope that in such a generous spirit he will be generous also to those who cannot reach, and do not want to reach, as far as he does. Much of the language of his essay indicates the pain he has suffered from being pounded by those on his right, and having endured a little of that pounding myself, I sympathize. Still, Roger describes the controversy over open theism generally in extreme terms, rather than allowing that open theism does have its difficulties and that some of its opponents were indeed well-informed, careful, courteous, and perhaps even correct. Indeed, I dare to say that I am one of those opponents, but even I share Brother Roger's distaste for the sort of polemics that characterized so much of the controversy in the Evangelical Theological Society.

Yes, a "generous orthodoxy" needs to be generous to both those on one's right as well as on one's left. And it needs to be orthodox, too, as I believe Roger's theology to be, even if his generosity occasionally prompts him to stretch the domain of evangelicalism rather too far.

# CONCLUSION

ANDREW DAVID NASELLI

Evangelicalism is divided, deeply divided. And it will not be helpful or truthful for anyone to deny this.

— Francis A. Schaeffer[1]

The religious terrain is full of the graves of good words which have died from lack of care — they stand as close in it as do the graves today in the flats of Flanders or among the hills of northern France. And these good words are still dying all around us. There is that good word "Evangelical." It is certainly moribund, if not already dead. Nobody any longer seems to know what it means.

–B. B. Warfield[2]

**W**e are certainly not the first ones to address the complex and important issue of evangelicalism. But we are not aware of another book that debates several major views like this one does.

## Background

This book compares and contrasts four positions on the current evangelical spectrum in light of the history of North American evangelicalism: fundamentalism, confessional evangelicalism, generic evangelicalism, and postconservative evangelicalism. I originally proposed this exchange because two of these positions, fundamentalism and confessional evangelicalism, have significantly influenced my Christian pilgrimage.[3] I grew up

---

1. Francis A. Schaeffer, *The Great Evangelical Disaster* (Wheaton: Crossway, 1984), 46.

2. Benjamin B. Warfield, *Biblical Doctrines*, The Works of Benjamin B. Warfield, vol. 2 (New York: Oxford University Press, 1932), 395. This is from Warfield's opening address delivered in Miller Chapel, Princeton Theological Seminary, September 17, 1915 (first published in 1916).

3. All fundamentalists are evangelicals, but not all evangelicals are fundamentalists. When I contrast fundamentalists with evangelicals, the latter refer to nonfundamentalist evangelicals.

in fundamentalism, and I have been exposed to evangelicalism, especially what Mohler calls confessional evangelicalism. The tiny fundamentalist Baptist Bible college I attended considered Bob Jones University too worldly on issues such as music and dress, and Bob Jones University is where I ended up earning an MA in Bible and PhD in theology while teaching Greek. Bob Jones University separates from "new evangelical" schools like Trinity Evangelical Divinity School, which is where I completed a PhD in New Testament exegesis and theology while serving as part-time faculty, teaching assistant to Robert Yarbrough, and research assistant to D. A. Carson, my doctoral mentor.

I mention this to share my vantage point on the spectrum of evangelicalism. I have many evangelical friends (mostly fundamentalists, confessional evangelicals, and generic evangelicals), and fundamentalists frequently discuss how they compare and contrast with evangelicals.

Two actions have repeatedly grieved me as I have observed fundamentalists and evangelicals from all over the spectrum interact. First, they often lob verbal grenades at one another as if they are opponents. Intramural debates have morphed into something much worse. People tend to assume that they have another person or group figured out and then write them off as palpably errant. Once that occurs, it is very easy to develop the mind-set that such "errant" groups are the enemy. Often distinct groups that are similar in many ways become so preoccupied with distinguishing themselves from each other that they lose perspective and have less energy and resources for more significant issues.

Second, fundamentalists and evangelicals often paint each other with a broad brush that lacks sufficient nuance. People have a tendency to stereotype and caricature groups of which they are not a part because they fail to see distinctions from a distance. Movements are complex, and pockets of people within a particular movement are often frustrated when others critique their movement without acknowledging its complexity or diversity. For example, many fundamentalists are understandably frustrated when evangelicals automatically lump them together with, say, the King James Only movement, anti-intellectualism, or legalism. People commonly misperceive or stereotype another's position and wrongly assume motives.

Misunderstandings abound at all levels in both the church and academy, and these misunderstandings foster unhealthy disunity. Collin

Hansen and I designed this book to help correct misperceptions and foster a better understanding of the spectrum of evangelicalism. Accurately clarifying similarities and differences is a step forward that results in less caricature and more productive dialogue and relationships.

## Summary

This summary of the book compares and contrasts how the four views define evangelicalism, defend their positions, and address three contemporary issues.

### Defining Evangelicalism

What exactly is evangelicalism? Defining it depends largely on one's approach, and there are at least two basic approaches: (1) sociology—a *descriptive* approach that most historians adopt, and (2) theology—a *prescriptive* approach that some theologians adopt.

Bauder and Mohler argue for theological definitions (informed by sociology) since, as Mohler says, "a merely descriptive definition of evangelical identity cannot provide an adequate foundation for evangelical coherence or credibility" (p. 74). Bauder argues, "No one who denies the evangel can be reckoned as an evangelical," regardless if one self-identifies as an evangelical, because "the fundamentals of the gospel are also the fundamentals of evangelical identity" (191). Mohler concludes:

> Evangelicalism refers to that movement of Christian believers who seek a conscious convictional continuity with the theological formulas of the Protestant Reformation.... Evangelicalism is a movement of confessional believers who are determined by God's grace to conserve this faith in the face of its reduction or corruption, even as they gladly take this gospel to the ends of the earth in order to see the nations exult in the name of Jesus Christ. (74–75)

Mohler, Stackhouse, and Olson each discuss David Bebbington's quadrilateral that describes evangelicalism sociologically: conversionism, activism, biblicism, and crucicentrism.[4] Mohler concludes, "These

---

4. Cf. Michael A. G. Haykin and Kenneth J. Stewart, eds., *The Advent of Evangelicalism: Exploring Historical Continuities* (Nashville: Broadman & Holman, 2008), which reflects on the reception of Bebbington's influential 1989 book.

criteria are so vague as to be fairly useless in determining the limits of evangelical definition" (73). Stackhouse and Olson, on the other hand, affirm Bebbington's quadrilateral and tweak it with additional points: Stackhouse adds (1) transdenominationalism and (2) the combination of orthodoxy, orthopathy, and orthopraxy; Olson adds respect for (not necessarily "firm adherence to") historic, Christian orthodoxy, namely, "what some have called 'generous orthodoxy'" (177).

## Defending Their Positions on the Spectrum of Evangelicalism
### Fundamentalism

Bauder defends the idea of fundamentalism, not the variety of fundamentalist movements — particularly not "hyper-fundamentalism" or the influence of populist revivalism. The idea he defends is that there are different levels of Christian fellowship within two poles on a spectrum:

1. Minimal Christian fellowship is based on the fundamentals, namely, "those explanations, presuppositions, and implications on which the gospel depends.... The gospel draws the boundary of Christian fellowship. Those who are outside the boundary must not be recognized as Christians" (29, 33).

2. Maximal Christian fellowship occurs when Christians are "united by the entire system of faith and practice, the whole counsel of God" (34). While Christians can fellowship with all Christians on a minimal level, they must "limit their cooperation" on other levels and separate "from Christian leaders who will not separate from apostates" (37, 40).

### Confessional Evangelicalism

Mohler describes his view with two metaphors.

1. A center-bounded set: "Evangelicalism is coherent as a movement only if it is also known for what it is not. Attention to the boundaries is as requisite as devotion to the center.... Our task is to be clear about what the gospel is and is not" (95, 96).

2. Theological triage: "We must develop the skill of discerning different levels of theological issues in order that we not divide over the wrong issues and betray the gospel. But when the issues are of the first order, we must be clear and determined lest we lose the gospel" (96).

## Generic Evangelicalism

Stackhouse argues: "Evangelicalism cannot be sharply characterized in its beliefs, affections, and practices beyond understanding it to be observant Protestant Christianity expressed in authentic, vital discipleship issuing forth in mission with similarly concerned Christians of various stripes. As such, the definition of evangelicalism is inherently contestable … only because the definition of *authentic and healthy Christianity* is inherently contestable" (141).

## Postconservative Evangelicalism

Olson argues that it "is an interesting but ultimately futile project" to attempt to define *evangelical* and *evangelicalism* and "identify their boundaries" (162). Organizations are bounded sets, but movements—like evangelicalism—are centered sets. "Evangelicalism has no definable boundaries and cannot have them…. And without boundaries it is simply impossible to say with certainty who is and who is not an evangelical" (163). Fundamentalists and conservative evangelicals are obsessed with narrow "evangelical boundaries."

## *Issue 1: Evangelicals and Catholics Together*

### Fundamentalism

Roman Catholicism "denies the gospel" (31). Evangelicals who approve of Evangelicals and Catholics Together (ECT) are mistaken, because "Christians cannot rightly extend Christian recognition or fellowship to those who endorse and proclaim the Roman Catholic gospel" (32).

### Confessional Evangelicalism

The Roman Catholic Church is not "a true church" (85), and contra ECT, Protestantism is not compatible with Catholicism on first-level doctrines such as justification by faith alone.

### Generic Evangelicalism

The ECT "initiative makes perfect sense" and is "a positive sign" (129).

### Postconservative Evangelicalism

"Unlike fundamentalists and conservative evangelicals who condemned the project, I do not see the signatories' efforts as a betrayal of evangelical faith." ECT "is hardly grounds for condemnation or even demands to recant" (184).

## Issue 2: Open Theism

### Fundamentalism

"The open theist understanding of foreknowledge implies a denial of the gospel" (30).

### Confessional Evangelicalism

"Biblical theism requires that we affirm that God is 'infinite in all his perfections,' as the creedal consensus has affirmed. This is a first-order theological issue" (93).

### Generic Evangelicalism

"Open theists are, to my knowledge, genuine evangelicals. They are just *wrong* evangelicals" (132).

### Postconservative Evangelicalism

Open theists are wrong but not heretical. The "whole emotional brouhaha over open theism was fueled by a pent-up desire by fundamentalists calling themselves conservative evangelicals to test evangelical theological boundaries (which, as I have made clear, do not even exist)" (185).

## Issue 3: Penal Substitutionary Atonement

### Fundamentalism

Penal substitution is essential to the gospel.

### Confessional Evangelicalism

"The doctrine of substitutionary atonement lies at the heart of the gospel, and the gospel is a first-order issue" (94). Rejecting penal substitution is evangelical revisionism that is merely a new form of Protestant liberalism.

### Generic Evangelicalism

Penal substitution "is essential to Christian theology and therefore to evangelical theology," but "evangelicals who diminish or dismiss substitutionary atonement seem to me to be in the same camp as my evangelical brothers and sisters who espouse open theism: truly evangelicals, and truly wrong about something important" (136).

## Postconservative Evangelicalism

While penal substitution "may be normal, it could hardly be said to be normative.... No one objective theory has ever been uniformly affirmed by all evangelicals" (183).

### Three Contemporary Issues

| View | Evangelicals and Catholics Together | Open Theism | Penal Substitutionary Atonement |
|---|---|---|---|
| Fundamentalism | Betrays the gospel | Denies the gospel | Essential to the gospel |
| Confessional Evangelicalism | Betrays the gospel | Denies the gospel | Essential to the gospel |
| Generic Evangelicalism | Does not betray the gospel | Wrong but does not deny the gospel | Essential to the gospel, but evangelicals may deny it |
| Postconservative Evangelicalism | Does not betray the gospel | Wrong but does not deny the gospel | Normal but not essential for evangelicals |

# Observations

1. Not all evangelicals will identify with one of the four views in this book. It seems impossible to classify evangelicalism in a way that satisfies all evangelicals, especially when some claim that evangelicalism doesn't exist![5] This book's title may give the impression that it presents *the* four views on evangelicalism, but the four views are merely four *major* views, not the only views. The spectrum could easily add other views, such as a more conservative fundamentalism—what Bauder calls

---

5. E.g., Carl R. Trueman, *The Real Scandal of the Evangelical Mind* (Chicago: Moody, 2011).

"hyper-fundamentalism" — to the right of historic fundamentalism. The evangelical spectrum is so complex and diverse, however, that no matter how you slice it, some people will feel marginalized.

2. Sometimes we aren't talking about the same thing when we talk about evangelicalism. So defining it is crucial to productive dialogue. Otherwise, we may disagree with others and talk past each other while assuming that we all define evangelicalism the same way.

3. Some evangelicals who do identify with one of the four views in this book will quibble with the way this book presents their view. For example, some fundamentalists may question whether the idea of fundamentalism that Bauder defends actually exists today in any substantial movement, and some postconservatives may not state the implications of their view so forthrightly.

4. In a broad sense, this book presents two views on evangelicalism rather than four. Views 1 and 2 (fundamentalism and confessional evangelicalism) are close to each other as are views 3 and 4 (generic and postconservative evangelicalism), and the distance between views 1–2 and 3–4 is significantly greater than between views 1 and 2 or 3 and 4. Bauder and Mohler agree on the most substantive issues, and their views are virtually identical on the three contemporary issues each contributor addresses.[6] Mohler agrees with Olson's assessment that evangelicalism is currently bifurcated "into two parties, or even two rival movements" (199) — what Olson describes as "fundamentalists and neo-fundamentalists, on the one hand, and moderate to progressive evangelicals on the other hand" (156). And Olson writes of Stackhouse, "I think we're more or less on the same page.... I find myself disagreeing with very little in John's chapter.... So why is my account of evangelicalism called 'postconservative' and John's 'generic'? In most ways they are very much alike. The only substantial difference I can see is one of degree, not kind" (158, 159).

---

6. They may disagree, however, on the timing of when to transition from separating from an institution by "purging out" to separating by "coming out." Fundamentalists are generally inclined to "come out" sooner than confessional evangelicals. For example, Bob Jones University published a book in the 1980s that confidently described the Southern Baptist Convention as hopelessly declining on a theologically liberal trajectory: David O. Beale, *S.B.C.: House on the Sand? Critical Issues for Southern Baptists* (Greenville, S.C.: Unusual Publications, 1985). Bauder admits, "Frankly, I doubt that any of us in fundamentalism believed that conservatives could ever gain control of the convention and its institutions. Nevertheless, Al and his allies in the SBC have largely reclaimed these assets for biblical Christianity."

5. Some people may come in contact with just a subset of one of these four views and assume that sample sufficiently represents the entire view. Confusion and caricature persist when such people critique a view they don't sufficiently understand. When critiquing another view, our aim should be to describe the view of another so well that they would say, "Yes, that's my view. You said it better than I could myself."

6. All four views agree that some people and groups who identify with their position may be poor examples and/or propagators of it. Some adherents are more winsome than others.

7. Judgmentalism is not exclusive to any particular view. It is easy to criticize people for their judgmentalism, especially those to the right of you, but everyone can be guilty of it. We might think of judgmental people as those with "stricter" views, but people with "looser" views can be judgmental too. Whatever our views may be on disputed issues, we can be guilty of judgmentalism.[7]

8. Few people consider themselves extreme. People commonly frame issues in a reductionistic way slanted in favor of their argument: (1) there are twits on the left and (2) wackos on the right, but (3) unlike those extremes, there's my reasonable middle way. Lyrics from a 1973 Stealers Wheel song come to mind: "Clowns to the left of me, jokers to the right, here I am, stuck in the middle with you." And when defending your view on the spectrum of evangelicalism, there will always be someone to both the left and right of you.

## Conclusion

If fundamentalism is right, then

- confessional evangelicalism risks making the gospel less central to its associations than it has to its message;
- generic evangelicalism betrays the gospel when it fails to recognize the gospel as the boundary of Christian fellowship;
- postconservative evangelicalism denies the gospel when it alters essential elements of the gospel itself.

---

7. Cf. Jerry Bridges, *Respectable Sins: Confronting the Sins We Tolerate* (Colorado Springs: NavPress, 2007), 141–48.

If confessional evangelicalism is right, then

- fundamentalism needs to be far more confessional on the fundamentals and needs to join the larger evangelical conversation rather than sit it out as a standoffish bystander;
- generic evangelicalism will become either less generic or profoundly nonevangelical;
- postconservative evangelicalism is not only postconservative but postevangelical.

If generic evangelicalism is right, then

- fundamentalism is narrower and nastier than it should be;
- confessional evangelicalism is simply a rebranded fundamentalism that oversimplifies and needlessly polarizes evangelicalism;
- postconservative evangelicalism is unbalanced because it underplays elements of evangelicalism that it thinks fundamentalism overplays.

If postconservative evangelicalism is right, then

- fundamentalism is (as E. J. Carnell said) "orthodoxy gone cultic";
- confessional evangelicalism is fundamentalism with manners;
- generic evangelicalism is postconservative evangelicalism in denial.

Regardless of your view on evangelicalism, we hope this book serves you well as you analyze evangelicalism's diverse spectrum. This debate is not trivial, nor is it merely academic. One day we will stand before God and give an account for how we respond to the *evangel*, and that includes how we relate to fellow evangelicals. "Conduct yourselves in a manner worthy of the gospel of Christ" (Phil. 1:27).

# SCRIPTURE INDEX

# GENERAL INDEX